Portraits
of
Grace

Stories of Salvation
from Wesleyan World Missions

Portraits of Grace

Stories of Salvation
from Wesleyan World Missions

John and Margie Connor, Editors

Copyright © 1999 by Wesleyan Publishing House
All Rights Reserved
Published by Wesleyan Publishing House
Indianapolis, Indiana 46250
Printed in the United States of America
ISBN   0-89827-201-7

Contents

Africa

Asia

Europe

South America

Pacific

Preface

The best portrait artist in New Guinea is David Willis; he has the ability to make people come alive on canvas. As our family was leaving Papua New Guinea, we asked David to paint a Mt. Hagen man. His portrait is one of our treasured possessions.

The aim of this book is to provide portraits of God's saving grace within the lives of people across the world. These stories of salvation reveal the power of the gospel. They show Jesus Christ redeeming and delivering people without regard to their national, racial or cultural background. The power of these testimonies is partly understood by how unique each person is and how uniquely Jesus Christ worked to bring them to salvation.

As you read the stories, written almost entirely by local believers, you may encounter issues difficult to understand or deal with—especially when local customs or religious practices are described. The editors, John and Margie Connor, have made a few explanatory notes, but by and large the stories stand as told. Our prayer is that your world will be enlarged and enriched by entering into the richness of other cultures. To catch the dramatic impact of some stories, we invite you to put yourself in the storytellers' place by reflecting on how you would feel if you had to stand alone for the sake of your faith in Jesus Christ.

The global Wesleyan family thanks John and Margie Connor who accepted the vision for this book and brought it to reality. They invited global Wesleyans to submit their stories, then deciphered handwriting and international English in order that we might celebrate changed lives. Thanks also to Laura Peterson of the Wesleyan Publishing House whose editorial skill and effective management brought the project to publication.

Most of all we are grateful to the Lord of the Harvest whose Spirit has been faithfully drawing the people from every tribe, language and culture to a relationship with the Lord Jesus Christ. We celebrate the hundreds of missionaries and thousands of national pastors who faithfully proclaim the message of salvation. Together we give glory to God.

Don Bray
General Director

Introduction

oreign missions is not about missionaries in foreign lands, buildings in foreign places, or philanthropic endeavors for foreign social needs. It is about the Great Commission and the command to "make disciples of all nations." This book is the real story of foreign missions and of the men and women who have been saved by faith through grace. There are missionaries, buildings, and philanthropy in these stories of grace, but the real story is the salvation of individual lives.

When I was a teenager, my parents were missionaries in Papua New Guinea. In those days our pastors could not read and, even if they could have, there was no Bible in their language. The pastors would come to the mission once a week to learn a Bible story which would then become their sermon for the coming Sunday.

My friends were Papuan boys my age who were attending the mission school. One week four or five of us decided to go to a friend's village for the weekend. This was an excellent experience, so the next week we went to another friend's village. On one of these trips we were in the local church on Sunday, which was our habit, and it came time for the pastor to preach.

He looked out at the congregation, abruptly stopped and then addressed me directly. "Johnny, can you read?" I answered that I could. Then he asked if I had a Bible. I did. He got very excited and asked if I would come and read the Bible and tell them directly what it said. I figured, "Why not?" So I did. I read what it said and told them what I thought it meant. It was simple; I didn't know any big theological words, Hebrew, Greek, homiletics, hermeneutics, or doctrinal technicalities. I just knew what it said and what it seemed to mean to me—that was all.

This became a rather popular thing and my friends and I found ourselves going to at least two churches each Sunday to read and explain. It was fun and they treated us nicely. I didn't think of this as "ministry." I was just a kid doing what kids do. One week the reading was about salvation by faith. When I finished, I realized that maybe somebody needed to be saved. I had no idea how to give an altar call, so I just stopped abruptly and asked, "Does anybody here want to get saved?"

A typical New Guinea man was sitting in the back. He was wearing the highlands wig which looks like an elongated hat with a couple of bones pushed up beside each ear. He had no shirt, shoes, or pants—just the usual loincloth in front and leaves behind. His body was smeared with pig grease. He raised his hand, then stood up and said, "I think I need this." I told him to come forward, kneel down and we would pray with him. He did; the Christians gathered around and began to pray, but I noticed he didn't pray. I stopped everyone and said something like "Hey, guy, you gotta pray." He looked at me blankly and then said he didn't know how; he'd never prayed before.

I told him to repeat the words I would say and prayed a very simple prayer of repentance. Much to my surprise, the Lord saved him! As I continued the circuit to the village churches over the next year or so, I always looked for this man. The next time I came to his village, this man who didn't know how to pray was called upon to lead the congregation in prayer. Before long he was leading the song service. He looked and acted differently and was growing in the grace of God. The last time I saw him, he was teaching a Sunday school class out under a large tree near the little village church. Not only was he a disciple, he was discipling others.

This is how I came to realize the power of the Word and the meaning of making disciples. I knew for sure that the power wasn't in the preacher. The power was in the Word. People learned all they could and then taught what they knew to others. Within the stories of this book you will see that pattern repeated time after time. The power of the Holy Spirit flows through His people, but is not limited to their efforts; He enhances their efforts. The simple becomes profound when God is at work.

Everyone who should be acknowledged in these articles has not been, especially the translators, often because we don't know for sure who they are.

We know some of them are missionaries like Orai Lehman (Mozambique), Jeff Fussner (Indonesia), and Ed Parman (Mexico). Some are national leaders like Lal Pulamte (India), Fely Pablo (Philippines), Cedric Rodrigo (Sri Lanka), and James Coleman (Liberia). To these essential people we give a big "Thank you." Without you this book would not be possible.

This book is the brainchild of Dr. Donald Bray, the general director of Wesleyan World Missions. He has heard many of these stories as he traveled the church and wanted you to hear them too. The area directors, mission directors, regional and national superintendents of the various mission units have also been very influential in getting these stories of grace together. I would especially like to mention Fely Pablo, the wife of the general superintendent (Dr. Alfonso Pablo) of the Philippine General Conference of The Wesleyan Church. She has worked tirelessly to collect, translate, type and send by e-mail or "snail mail" stories from the Philippines. Finally, I thank my wife, Marge, for typing, editing and encouraging until the task was completed.

Our prayer is that these stories of God's grace will touch your hearts and give you a renewed vision of what Wesleyan missions is all about—making disciples.

John Connor
Editor

Africa

Liberia

There are cultural aspects to every story in this book, too many to make note of or to explain. However, we will endeavor to make some cultural, historical and anthropological explanations section by section.

The following three stories are from war-torn Liberia. The struggle is between the ECOMOG, the East African peacekeeping force, and either "rebel" or "freedom fighters," depending on your perspective. In the first story, Annie speaks almost "offhandedly" and may seem calloused when speaking of the death of children or relatives. Child mortality is very high in Africa and most families would expect to lose some children under normal circumstances. When the circumstances are abnormal, the children are the first to suffer.

In the second story, while child sacrifice is abhorrent in any society, it is fairly common in many African cultures. In many cases the witch doctor will require certain organs from a child under a particular age in order to make his magic. The person who takes the child's life considers himself to be doing the whole family a favor. The thinking is that one child, who might die anyway, is an insignificant sacrifice when many will be enriched. A person who takes a stand against such a practice puts himself at risk with the powerful witch doctor, and at odds with what appears to be the best interests of the family.

In the last story in this section, Kona Brown breaks ties with Islam. This is a significant step that often entails total ostracism from family and community. Kona's decision to be a Christian is a total life change resolution. As with the stories in the section on Indonesia, the impact on a person who leaves Islam to be a Christian can scarcely be understood from a pluralistic and open society like that which exists in North America.

War Torn

• •

Annie Fatu Kamara
(told by James Coleman and Annie Kamara)

Annie Fatu Kamara was born December 31, 1956, to George and Makai Kamara of the Kpelle tribe. Because her parents raised her in the traditional way, she did not complete her high school education. She married and had three children. Her husband left her fifteen years ago and went to the United States to seek a better life. Disappointed with life, Annie went to live with her father in Bomi Hills and ran a small business to support herself and her family.

Annie's parents had an African religious background similar to that of the Muslims. When they migrated to Bomi Hills, Annie and her children got involved with Christian activities because many missionaries were working there at that time. Even though she attended the church, she did not have a personal relationship with the Lord Jesus Christ and never appreciated nor experienced the divine work of salvation. It was during the civil conflict that she was able to experience the work of the saving grace of our Lord Jesus Christ.

"My disappointment when my husband left me was not enough to draw me to Christ, but later the Liberian civil war brought shame and disgrace to us and the society of Liberia, and drew me nearer to the saving knowledge of Christ.

"It all happened when God delivered me from three dangerous situations. The first deliverance by an act of God was during 1992. My family and other relatives walked from Bomi Hills to Monrovia through the brush, as the roads were not safe. At that time it was not easy to lead sixty-seven people, including a four-month-old baby and several children. There was lots of suffering along the road to Monrovia. There was no food for four days. My mother was sick and I had to carry her on my back while holding one of the babies on my shoulders.

"The soldiers were raping women that they came across. But as God would have it, we were always requested to cook for them, so they did not rape us. Even though they killed one of my brothers, and two of the babies died from sickness, God delivered us from their hands and from those flying bullets until we got to safety—scratched, bruised and with swollen feet.

"The second deliverance was when the ECOMOG (the West African peacekeeping force) soldiers came to our rescue. When we arrived in Monrovia, one of my uncles took us to Gardnersville, where he gave us two rooms in his house to stay. After three weeks the rebel fighters spread around the outskirts of Monrovia, especially Gardnersville, where we were staying. It was another changing experience for me. When the NPFL (a paramilitary unit) fighters came to take over Gardnersville, they met stiff resistance from the Senegalese ECOMOG contingent. It was just the same as any terrible war around the world. On the morning of the arrival of the NPFL fighters, people began to move from one area to another with any belongings they could manage to carry with them.

"When news reached the ECOMOG that the fighters were in Gardnersville, they launched an offensive in our direction. This activated the fighters and they began to kill people indiscriminately. As a result we had to flee from Gardnersville. When my children and I came near the Stockton Creek Bridge, linking Gardnersville area to Free Port and Central Monrovia, it was terrible to cross because the ECOMOG and the NPFL fighters were exchanging fire and using all kinds of weapons. So we went into the swamp where we hid from 7 a.m. to 3 p.m.

"After the battle ended, the children and I left the swamp and crossed the bridge for Logan Town to my older sister's house. Actually, I was not myself when we left the swamp. I had become disoriented and crazy with worry. My body was covered with mission ants. The little baby (my sister's son) died and the other children were unconscious. We all were taken to the hospital for treatment. Praise be to God that we all got well.

"After the battle experience I went to visit my uncle, Philip Moore. My father was staying with him since he was displaced from Bomi Hills. At that time my father had been invited to Stockton Creek Wesleyan Church by his brother. There he was converted and is now a full member of that church. (Presently he is serving as chairman of the board of trustees, both the Wesleyan elementary and junior high school, and the local board of administration.)

"When I went to visit him at his house, he and my uncle invited me to worship with them along with my other sisters and brothers who had fled

Monrovia. My father told me that this was a special invitation and he urged me not to turn the invitation down. I believed it was the Lord who put this in the heart of my father, and so I invited all my brothers and sisters, especially the ones from Gbarnga. As God would have it, nine of us who had fled Monrovia attended church that Sunday. Rev. James N. Coleman spoke on the theme, "God delivers grace in the midst of danger," from 2 Kings 7:1-15.

"That day my heart moved within me and my mind began to urge me to go to the altar, which I did. When the pastor asked us to visit again, I was moved and I visited the next Sunday. Rev. Coleman preached on the sermon, "Come and see the Man, the giver of salvation," from John 4:28-30. After the message I decided to accept Jesus Christ and to know Him personally. After that I applied for membership along with my younger daughter. We went through the membership and baptism classes, after which we were baptized and received by Rev. Coleman into the Stockton Creek Wesleyan Church in 1994.

"The third experience was on April 6, 1996. Now that I had a new life in the Lord, I was not disturbed by the situation that occurred during that day

even though it was terrible.

"When the heat of the battle slowed down in Monrovia that day, Bomi Hills was cut off from Monrovia. This incident at Bomi Hills caused more than 100,000 human lives to be destroyed. All of my children were in Bomi Hills because we had just gone back to resettle. I had come down to Monrovia to look for food when the news reached me about the road leading to Bomi Hills being cut off from Monrovia. There it was, the battlefield between five factions—namely NPFL, ULIMO-J, ULIMO-K, Lofa Defense Force and the Congo Defense Force. One of my daughters died from hunger in this incident, but praise be to God that the rest of my children were saved."

Presently Annie Kamara is faithfully working with the Stockton Creek Wesleyan Church as the choir director, a member of the usher board, and as a teller. She also works with the local women in organizing the Micro-Business Revolving Funds of the Stockton Creek Wesleyan Church.

Annie operates a small business to support her family and pays her tithe faithfully. "Thanks be to God that I know Him now for my salvation and He is all to me of what I need," she said. "I know that my success of knowing Christ was not of my own strength, but rather it was the prayers of many that I have not seen, but who cared for my spiritual life.

"I want to express my thanks and appreciation to all those who prayed with me for my salvation, not leaving out the Wesleyan family abroad and in Liberia. Besides my conversion, Wesleyan World Missions was instrumental in delivering me and my family from death by starvation through The Wesleyan Church of Liberia. Rev. James N. Coleman and the church members gave us half a bag of rice and other items during the April 6, 1996 conflict and said it was from Wesleyan World Missions. Again, thank you for your prayers and physical care for someone like me that you have not seen, yet care for. I know that in Christ there is no division, east or west. Amen."

Abandoned but not Forgotten

Felicia Kaebeh Askie
(told by James Coleman and Felicia Askie)

Felicia Askie was born to Mr. and Mrs. Arthur N. Askie on April 16, 1969, in Montserrado County. She went to Catholic mission schools and was baptized in an Episcopal church in 1981, but she did not really experience the salvation of our Lord Jesus Christ. Her parents were not devoted Christians and she did not get along well with them. Her Christian life was not the way it ought to have been and she decided to seek for the true meaning of salvation, to know Christ for herself.

"My children's father approached me to sacrifice our two children. Already I had made the mistake of bearing two children by him without marriage. So, when he approached me to sacrifice our two kids simply because of the difficulties we found ourselves in, I told him there would be no condition that would cause me to engage in such an act. I looked in his face and said, "No, that is the work of the devil." You cannot imagine. He spit and slapped me in the face, threw me to the ground and kicked me in the stomach, which caused me to start bleeding from my nose. After that he walked out of the house and I never saw him for ten months. He left me with the children and with all the responsibilities. My parents never wanted to see me in that time of my misfortune. It was at this time in my frustration that a friend named Rebecca Johnson came to visit me. After talking and praying with me, she invited me to her church, Stockton Creek Wesleyan Church.

"During my first visit, the pastor preached on the theme, "Come ye that are weary and heavy laden" from Matthew 11:28. After the sermon I went forward for the altar call. From that day I started attending Wesleyan Bible studies and prayer meetings. Through counseling, I received the Lord Jesus Christ and now I am trusting in His grace for my life. I met real friends and we can share things in common such as testimonies, ideas, and I am now at ease with my problems. Presently I am a full member of the church. I am teaching one of the primary classes of the Wesleyan elementary and junior high school.

"I thank God for his saving grace through Jesus Christ that has made me to be among the saints. It is my prayer that He will keep me in His service and not let me return to Egypt (the world) and that I will grow in grace and His knowledge.

"I am also grateful to the Wesleyan family of America who were able to help us with relief items during our difficult times, for I was one of the beneficiaries of food and clothing from Wesleyan World Missions."

From Majority to Minority

• •

Kona Brown
(told by James Coleman)

I thank God through Jesus Christ for sending the true light. This is a woman who was born in the Muslim faith but crossed over when she saw the true light. She is now married to a Christian husband with whom she lives a happy life in the Lord Jesus Christ. This is how Kona received the Christian faith.

Kona Brown was born March 3, 1955, in Bong County. She is from a Muslim background and became active in the Muslim religion at the age of eighteen. Her deliverance process began during the heart of the seven-year Liberian civil war.

In the heat of the civil war, her father and mother died of sickness. Her husband was away from home when the attack came and thus able to escape

the rebel assault of the town. At that time it was not easy for the Madingoes (her tribe) because they were seen to be an enemy to the NPFL (a paramilitary unit) at the beginning of the Liberian civil war in 1990. The Madingoes, who were mostly Muslims, were considered to be collaborating with the late Samuel Kayan Doe and the Liberian Armed Forces that fought the NPFL. Movement was restricted. Kona decided to pray to God for safety. While going through those moments of fear, the NPFL killed her two brothers and one sister by cutting off their heads with a machete. She was in a state of shock and did not know what to do nor where to go.

Her husband's return brought little relief to her mind. God moved on his heart to build up hope by counseling her to trust in Jesus Christ. He told her how the Lord Jesus Christ had been with him throughout the civil crisis, and that the God he was serving was alive and able to carry them through only if they believed.

It was not easy to embrace a different religion when 96% of the citizens in their village of Godolee were Muslims. It was not easy to win her over to the Lord. But through prayers, fasting and counseling, she was able to change her mind and accept the Lord Jesus Christ. When she made up her mind in 1996, she looked her husband in the face and tears began to flow from her eyes. Then she said to him, "As of this date, I have decided to be a Christian."

Truly, Kona was converted, became a Christian and decided to live for Christ. She has gone through the membership and baptism classes at the Godolee Wesleyan Church, conducted by Assistant Pastor Zayzay Kollie. She was baptized by Rev. James N. Coleman and was received as a full member, along with eleven other persons, on Palm Sunday. Presently she is playing an active role within the Godolee Wesleyan Church's women's department. Her husband, Jehu Brown, is the president of the men's department.

Mozambique

M any of these stories take place at a time when Mozambique was under communist rule and at odds with the apartheid government in South Africa. However, the South African government needed the cheap labor force that came out of Mozambique, and Mozambique needed the cash that this arrangement brought into their country. Therefore, many people from Mozambique were recruited to work in South Africa. While there, Wesleyan missionaries evangelized this vast number of men who went back home behind the communist curtain when their contracts were finished.

Within this set of stories there are a couple of things to note. First is the paranormal aspects of a number of the stories. There are dreams, visions, and prophecies which God uses to accomplish His purpose. God works through culture, not necessarily against culture. Second, look for the importance of relationships, especially with respected or older people who can give wisdom and from whom wisdom is expected.

Spirit Possessed
●●●●●●●●●●●●●●●●●●●●●●●●
Amelia Matavele

My parents lived in the Mussengi area of the Manjacaze District in Mozambique, where they were Christian believers and members of the Njakazane Wesleyan Church pastored by Israel Malate. I was born in 1944 and have five sisters and one brother. As a child I used to enjoy going with my sisters and my mother to cultivate the fields where we grew corn, beans, peanuts and cassava plants. My brother spent much of his time looking after the cattle and goats.

Father stopped going to church and died in his backslidden state when I was about ten years old. My mother continued to serve the Lord and later became a pastor of the Chopal Wesleyan Church in one of the suburbs of Maputo.

When I was twenty years old, I moved to Maputo where my two older sisters were already living with their husbands and families. The demon spirits caused me to be ill and I went to a witch doctor for help. I was told that I needed to go through the ritual of being possessed by the spirits of my ancestors. When these spirits gained control of my life, I began to practice as a witch doctor or spirit medium, but I was not happy. I did know that God existed and I remembered the songs that I used to sing in the church when I was young person. I used to pray this prayer within my heart, "Lord, you know me and see that I am in darkness here under the sky."

Then one day, a Monday morning in March 1995, I was walking along and I saw a great light. I did not understand what the meaning of this experience was, but I suddenly had a desire for God's Word and I began reading the Bible. For the first time I began to hear and to understand clearly what the Bible was saying. My mother found me reading the Bible and she asked me to read with her. For several weeks we read the Bible together. I no longer felt any desire to enter into the house of the gods where I used to go to practice my witchcraft. For a period of two weeks when I would sit down to meditate, I had a vision of fire burning in the west. God revealed to me that I should burn the house of the gods with all the things that I used for witchcraft. I went to my younger sister to tell her about the vision that I was to burn the house of the gods. She advised me to go to our mother and tell her, so that she and the church people could set fire to the hut and pray for my deliverance.

The next morning my sister went to Mama to tell her what I had told her. At the same time I heard a voice saying, "Go now to the pastor and kneel," but I did not take it seriously. I went to the Central Market where I worked.

When I arrived there, I could not do anything since I was feeling so bad. I decided to go to the pastor, who was my mother, as my sister and the voice that I heard had told me to do. When I arrived, she prayed for me. Right there I was saved from darkness and delivered from the power of the evil spirits which we believed were the spirits of the ancestors. The house of the gods and all of its contents were burned as a demonstration of my faith in Christ.

Now I feel joy and peace inside my heart and I realize that Jesus has taken away my burden. I used to be filled with anger and bitterness and I was not ashamed of sin, but all this has passed away, thanks to Jesus. My prayer is that the Lord may save my family, including my sons-in-law. I have five children—three daughters and two sons. I wish that all paths may be led by the Lord and His will may be done in my life. I want to be His faithful disciple so that when I present His truths found in the Bible, no one may disapprove. I want to learn the teachings of Christ in detail.

Fearful Shepherd Becomes Fearless Shepherd

●●●●●●●●●●●●●●●●●●●●●●●●●
Daniel Machate Cossa

, Daniel Cossa, was born on the 12th of March, 1948. Our home was in the Xai Xai (pronounced "shy-shy") area of the Gaza Province of Mozambique. My parents worshiped the spirits of the ancestors. In the midst of our family homestead, which consisted of a cluster of small huts, there was a tree called the place of worship. We lived in constant fear that some day we might be bewitched by some enemies. We had no peace at all. When illness came, the witch doctor was hastily sought.

Since my father died when I was very young, my mother raised me. I do not have any memory of my father. When I was twelve years old, I was given the responsibility of herding the family goats and sheep which belonged to my grandfather. We were told that the very old men and women are often guilty of bewitching people in the community. One day I saw a very old person coming in my direction and I became so terrified that I ran away and hid. When I looked back to see what had become of the flocks I had been attending, I was surprised to see that they too had run away.

At the age of fourteen, I was enrolled in school at Xai Xai Beach Primary School. At that time I used to go to Sunday school at the Macambacueni Wesleyan Church, where Rev. Macambaco was the Pastor. This was where I first began to hear the Word of God and came in contact with the Lehman missionary family. Then in the year 1968, I left Xai Xai and moved to Maputo to look for work. During the day I worked, and at night I attended classes at the secondary school, where I completed my sixth-grade studies. On Sundays I used to go to the Mafalala Wesleyan Church where Pita Muianga was the pastor. During a revival service in 1971, I felt God's conviction in my heart. Pastor Pita Muianga was preaching from the Gospel of John 3:3: "Unless a man is born again, he cannot see the kingdom of God." That was when I gave myself to the Lord by confessing my sins to Him and asking for His forgiveness. Then I received Jesus into my heart as my Lord and Savior. From that time I felt a deep peace and joy in my life and there was a real difference between my old life and this new life. After a while I was baptized and became a member of the church.

In 1972, I married a lovely Christian girl named Lidia. The Lord has blessed our marriage with six children—two boys and four girls. We worked for the Lord in the various activities of the local church and felt the Lord guiding us in our lives and helping us to grow in Him. In 1975, I was appointed as a local preacher working under the leadership of my pastor in the local church. In 1978, I was granted a district minister's license; in 1980, I was elected as the district secretary. Then in 1982 I felt the call of God upon my life, leading me to work for God in a full-time capacity.

In January 1985, I took my whole family and moved to Swaziland, where Lidia and I enrolled at Emmanuel Wesleyan Bible College (EWBC). This was during the time of the civil war in Mozambique. There were times that we encountered vehicles that had been hit by mortar and machine gun fire from the guerrilla forces. In some cases, the occupants had been killed and the cars were still burning as we came on the scene. These were very frightening times, but the Lord protected us from this danger. While we were at EWBC, I was appointed as the pastor of the Joy Mission Church. Although we were of the Shangaan tribe, the Lord helped me to minister to the Swazi people and they responded to the love of God through our ministry. We graduated from EWBC in November 1997 and returned to Mozambique. We were later appointed to pastor the Mafalala Wesleyan Church in Maputo, the capital city of Mozambique.

After becoming a Christian, I began praying for my family and witnessing to them. Whenever I was at home and my family had a ceremony in which they would consult the spirits of our dead ancestors, I did not participate. Instead, I would go and sit in a separate place some distance away. When they asked me why I did not join them in the ceremony, I explained that I had committed my life to God, the Creator of the heavens and the earth; I trusted

Him for all my needs and I no longer lived in fear of death or of being bewitched. Now all of my brothers and sisters have become Christians because of the consistent testimony that they have seen in the life that Lidia and I have lived before them.

The fear and hopelessness that we once knew have all gone away. Now things have become new in the Cossa family. Our whole trust is in our Lord Jesus Christ.

Two years after my graduation from Bible college, I was ordained as a minister at the 1989 District Conference. Then at the 1991 Conference I was elected to serve the Church in Mozambique as national superintendent. My whole purpose is to bring glory to my Lord and Savior, Jesus Christ. Praise His Name. Amen.

Layman Church Planter
Ernesto Massango

M y name is Ernesto Massango. I was born in 1928 in the area near to Manjakaze in Gaza Province, Mozambique. Although my parents were not believers in Christ, I was converted in 1935. I do not know the exact date but it was the year of the great famine in Mozambique. We were out in the fields harvesting peanuts and we were sitting down for a rest under the shade of a tree. Mother said, "Do you see that white man coming towards us?" We all jumped up in fear and were about to run for our lives, but Mother said, "Do not be afraid, he is coming with Kosini Matsombe." He was a man of our community whom we all knew and trusted.

When they came to where we were, Mother greeted them and exchanged news about our health and about recent events in the community. Then the white man asked her, "Are you worshipers of the true and living God?" We did not understand his words, which were spoken in the Zulu language, until they were translated by Matsombe into our Shangaan language. Mother said, "I would like to worship God, but I am possessed by demons." The missionary said, "That is what I wanted to hear you say. If you will pray and put your faith in God, He will deliver you from the demons and they will leave you." Mother said, "That is what I will do. I will pray and believe in God." Missionary Isaac Lehman then asked, "Will you allow your children to come to the church?" Mother said, "You can ask them if they would like to come."

He asked us through Matsombe's interpretation and we agreed to come. Then he said, "Let us pray." He led in a prayer and when he had finished he asked if we knew where the church was. Mother said that she knew where it was and that it was not far from our home. They said good-bye to Mother and went on their way.

That evening after we arrived at home, we heard the church bell ringing. We said, "Mother, do you hear the bell?" She said, "You may go." So off went the three of us, my two older brothers and me. When we got there, many people of our community had gathered together to hear the missionary preach as Matsombe translated for him. When the meeting ended, Matsombe told us that we were welcome to keep coming to his home to meet together with his family to worship God. So after Missionary Isaac Lehman had finished his work and moved on, we stayed and continued to meet together. When the evening services did not end until late at night, Pastor Matsombe would loan us blankets so that we could sleep at his home and not have to go home in the dark. This was how I got into the habit of going to church, and I have continued in my faith since then.

In 1944, I left home and came to the big city (Maputo) to look for work. For about a year I did not go to church. Then in 1945, "Grandpa" Zakariya Makuluve asked me, "Why do you not go to church?" I said, "I don't know where it is." He said, "Come to my house on Sunday and we will go together." He showed me the place in Dlangaleni where they worshiped in the home of Pastor Nhlongo, even before the streets had been built in that area. Then in 1950 I left and went to work in the gold mines of South Africa and worshiped at the City Deep Church, which was built by Rev. Lehman. In the years that followed, I lived and worked in various places and attended church wherever I could find Christian fellowship.

In 1962 when I returned to Maputo, I was received into the fellowship there by Pastor Makuluve. I was married in 1965 by Rev. Titos Novela and one year later I moved to the suburb of Bemfica. After visiting a number of churches in the area and not feeling satisfied, I went to Pastor Pita Langa and sought his advice. He encouraged me to start a Wesleyan church in my home in Bemfica and he promised to pray for me and to visit me with encouragement.

Within one week God had given me one family who began worshiping with us. By the end of the month we had three families; Pastor Langa was very happy to hear about it. At our request, he sent Alberto Mandlati to be our pastor. The Lord gave us more families and helped us to build our church, which was dedicated in 1981. I just want to continue to live in the Lord until the day I leave this earth. Then I want to go to see Him and the two pastors, Lehman and Matsombe, who rescued me from my sinful life when I was a young person.

African Girl Becomes Pastor
● ●
Lidia Cossa

The family into which I was born in 1953 was a heathen family that had no knowledge of the love of Christ. We believed in and trusted in the spirits of our dead ancestors to protect us and give us good health and fortune. We did not have any peace or harmony in our home. My father died when I was very young and I do not remember him at all. I was raised by my mother.

Throughout my childhood years, I used to go to church and Sunday school at the Macambacwini Wesleyan Church, where I was taught about God and His love for me. When I was sixteen years old, I was in church one day when the Word of God was being preached and I felt a deep conviction in my heart. I went to the altar and I yielded myself to the Lord. I confessed to Him that I was a sinner and asked the Lord Jesus Christ to forgive my sins. From that time onward there was peace and joy that I felt deep within my heart. During my teenage years and ever since, I have found great joy in singing the songs of the church and praising my Lord.

It has been a joy to see my mother become a Christian through the testimony I have given to her about Christ. She is now serving the Lord.

My husband Daniel and I were married in 1972. Our home is a happy home that has been blessed by God. We have four daughters and two sons. It was quite a challenge for us to move to Swaziland with the whole family in January 1985, so that we could attend Emmanuel Wesleyan Bible College, but God was with us. At the end of 1987, Daniel and I both graduated from the three-year certificate course and returned shortly afterwards to resume pastoring in Maputo. We recently celebrated our 25th wedding anniversary with a full ceremony in which we restated our marriage vows.

In 1993, the Lord saw fit to give me the responsibility of pastoral leadership over the Mafalala Wesleyan Church. My husband had found it too demanding to continue to pastor the local church, in addition to the responsibilities he had been given as the national superintendent of the Church in Mozambique. My prayer is that God's perfect will may be done in my life and that He will be glorified through me.

Sierra Leone

Healing is one way God often confirms His grace (cf. James 5:15). In areas where hospitals and medical facilities are not readily available, this seems to be especially true, as in the first story following. In the second story a young man is "shanghaied" into a military force. This practice is common in Africa where the military groups will sometimes "capture" a secondary school or a town (as in this case) and conscript all the young adults into their movement. Escape is seen as desertion and the penalty is death, whether the "recruit" believes in the tenets of the movement or not.

Up from the Dead to Life

Bintha Mansaray

I lived in Kamabai, one of the first stations of The Wesleyan Church in Sierra Leone; but I was a Mandingo. All over Sierra Leone, and even beyond, the Mandingoes are reputed for their belief in Islam. So one can just imagine the climate in which I was brought up. At the age of two, I lost both parents in a road accident. I was raised by my paternal grandparents, who were very careful to keep within the confines of the Koran. However, all my schooling was through Wesleyan schools, and God came in and snatched me for His own.

My grandmother, Ya Fatu Jalsie, had a dream that disturbed her all night. In the morning the dream became a reality. She complained of a severe pain across her throat, much the same way she had felt during her dream. She screamed and called for help. She was rushed to the hospital, but she could not be helped. She was taken to the best hospitals in the country, but all the X rays showed nothing. Finally, they resorted to an African healer; this also proved futile.

When they had exhausted all possible means, Ya Fatu was taken to Kamakwie, her hometown, to die. By this time she had lost a considerable amount of weight. She could not eat much. One had to come very close in order to hear her voice. All hope was given up. During this crucial time Rev. Momoh D. Koroma (commonly called MOK), a student at Sierra Leone Bible College, was sent to the Wesleyan church in Kamakwie for a pastoral internship. One of his assignments was to establish a morning prayer group in Kamakwie II, a section of the township that was predominantly Muslim. It was in this community that I lived with my sick grandmother. Our house was very close to their prayer meeting house.

I love to sing and hear Christian choruses. So whenever I heard the bell, I would sneak from bed and join the prayer meeting. I was always thrilled by the testimonies of the people. One day I asked the group to visit my sick grandmother and pray for her. The entire group consented. The next day all of us gathered at my house. I had informed the neighbors the previous day, so those who were willing came out when the group arrived. When it was prayer time, Pastor MOK laid his hand on Ya Fatu and assured us that today God's power would be manifested. He prayed aloud, and before we could understand what was happening, everybody in the house was trembling, including those who did not come out.

Ya Fatu pushed up from our hands and asked for a cup of water. She gulped one or two times, handed the cup over to me and joined us in praise.

34

On Sunday both of us went to church, where she gave a testimony of her experience in the prayer meeting. News of this event had already circulated throughout Kamakwie. She only confirmed it. She ended her testimony by saying, "Now I know that Jesus truly lives because He has relieved me of my burden. I cannot give up my religion now; I fear that consequences would follow. But let me freely tell you that from this day on I am a Muslim on the outside, but a Christian inside. This is my guarantee. I am freely giving this girl to you. I will continue to associate with Christianity as long as I live." The entire church applauded. The Christians welcomed us and after church some church members accompanied us home (an African custom).

After two weeks we returned to Kamabai. I continued with the Wesleyan church in Kamabai. My grandmother was there to defend me. After I had been baptized and received into membership, I went to Freetown. Although I did not continue with The Wesleyan Church because there wasn't one near my home, I joined the Assemblies of God church. I faced all sorts of embarrassments and provocation from my cousins, but I was resolved that I would never give up—especially when my grandmother encouraged me not to give up whenever she wrote to me.

Today I am happily married and my husband and I pastor an Assemblies of God church. My husband is very grateful to the Wesleyans for nurturing me. I, on the other hand, am grateful to both the Wesleyans and my grandmother for leading me to the Christian faith. I often say that "God restored her that I could receive Him! Praise God!"

The Rebel's Pastor
• •
Sullay

It is baffling! It is amazing! It is ironic! Even in a rebel camp, God still has His workmen. Listen to my experience in a rebel camp.

I was born in a village known as Kamaranka, 38 miles from Makeni, the capital city of the Northern Province. My family is Muslim. After my primary and secondary education, I went to live with my uncle in Kabala, about 110 miles from home.

When the rebel soldiers attacked Kabala in 1994, I was one of the many abductees. The experience I had during this attack contributed largely to my decision to switch to Christianity. Kabala is the home of the Tamaborohs—a group of local fighters believed to possess supernatural powers against any weapon. It is interesting to note that the head of all the Tamaborohs (who is said to be most powerful) lost his life in this attack, and a lot of other Tamaborohs suffered too. From this point on, I started questioning the sincerity of the Islamic faith, because most of these fighters purported to get their powers from this faith.

For six days we walked the long distance from Kabala to Kailahun where the rebels had their main base. The experiences of the journey are traumatizing to this day. Many of those who were captured in Kabala lost their lives on the way. When we finally reached our destination, we were presented to Corporal Foday Sankoh, the leader of the Revolutionary United Front (RUF movement). He welcomed us and then proceeded to give us the philosophy of the movement. He was a good orator.

Three days after our orientation, those of us who had been earmarked to be combatants started training. The exercise lasted for six weeks. I excelled in the training and was subsequently compensated with the rank of "Commando."

My final exercise in this training disturbed me for a long time and I thank God that I am a Christian now. Six red dots were painted on the wall a reasonable distance from one another. I was to shoot all these red points, which I successfully did. But alas! All the red points on the wall marked the heads of victims behind the wall. After the exercise my bosses cheered for me and took me behind the wall. They pointed to six bodies lying in pools of blood. I had unknowingly shot six people. I screamed on seeing them. "This is the result of your good marksmanship. From today you are a Commando," the leader of the team told me.

It was difficult to dismiss it from my mind. When we went behind the wall, one or two of the six were still struggling to get up. One was a six-year-old boy. They tried this trick on me because on several occasions they had asked me to kill people, but in each case I had refused. I was always ready to give my life instead.

For several days I was alone. For the first time I felt a sense of severe guilt. I did not want to talk to anybody. My appetite completely left. I did not want to go to the Imam (Islamic religious leader) of the camp. The brief moment I had met him, he seemed to be worse than most of the rebels. I wondered why he was ever called an Imam. He was the complete opposite of his Christian counterpart, the pastor of the camp.

I tried to dismiss this ugly experience from my mind, but I could not. However, my bosses treated the situation with some amount of understanding. Still traumatized by my ordeal, I sat down one afternoon and for the first time realized the counsel and comfort of a still voice. "Take courage, boy! All will soon be over. You can still make it up." These words kept on ringing in my ears for three days. They helped greatly to relieve me of my burden.

Sometime later I discovered an old friend of mine in this camp. His name is Foday Kamara. He told me that he had just arrived from Koribondo on operation.

Although he was a Muslim, he had been converted to Christianity in this camp. It was the lifestyle of the pastor in this camp that helped him. We shared several experiences and then we went to bed.

One afternoon, Foday asked me to accompany him to the pastor. When we arrived he welcomed us warmly and Foday formally introduced us. We discussed several things. By the way he talked, one could not doubt that he was truly a man of God. After some time, we bade him good-bye and went home. But before we left, he invited me to join them in their Sunday service. I gladly consented.

On Sunday I went to church. Although the service was brief and hastily done (because there were rumors of a pending attack on the camp), I enjoyed it. Two things captivated me in his message. He said, "You can meet with Jesus Christ anywhere, even here. And know that the Lord is always ready to welcome the worst sinner."

After the service I went to meet Pastor Brima and congratulated him. I promised him that I would continue to come to church except when I had an assignment. By this time I was gradually overcoming my ordeal. When I had been with the church for about two months, Pastor Brima called me one day and disclosed that he wanted me to assist him. It was difficult to give my word because my knowledge of the Bible was very narrow. I was more familiar with the Koran than the Bible. "Don't worry about anything. I will help you," he encouraged me.

When I informed Foday about it, he told me to grab the opportunity. "Everyone is looking for it." The "Pa" (Corporal Foday Sankoh) had passed a decree that all religious leaders should not go to war and when there was any attack they should be given maximum protection. The next day I hurried to "Mr. Pastor" (as he was called) and accepted the offer.

For eight months I read the entire Bible. Most of the things were not new to me. I had heard them in our Bible knowledge classes in school. I loved many Old Testament stories about how God had been good to His people. In the New Testament I was fascinated by the teachings and miracles of Jesus Christ and the life and works of Paul. Before I finished reading the Bible, I opened up and allowed Jesus Christ to come into my heart. I came to realize that "if anyone is in Christ, he is a new creation; the old has gone, the new has come" (2 Corinthians 5:17). And, "If we confess our sins, He is faithful and just and will forgive us our sins and purify us from all unrighteousness" (1 John 1:9). Jesus says, "I stand at the door and knock: If anyone hears my voice and opens the door, I will come in and eat with him, and he with me" (Revelation 3:20). I confessed the sin that had haunted me all this while and prayed that God would take full control of my heart.

We were finally released. I went to Makeni and stayed there briefly and later went to Manaranka. I disassociated from the RUF movement immediately. The opportunity I was seeking came at last. My people were thrilled to see me back because they had received news that I had been killed.

In Kamranka I associated with The Wesleyan Church. This was to the dismay of my family. They took it all as part of the effect of the rebel life on me. At first the church members discriminated against me, but when they realized that I had a good knowledge of the Bible, I was finally accepted. They now call me "Pastor." Presently I am one of the Sunday school teachers in the church. I am also very active in reaching out to the surrounding villages.

Please help me in prayer as I plan to serve the Lord full-time.

Witchcraft plays a large part in Zambian society. Sometimes Christianity is seen only as a "hedge your bet" proposition. You hold to one religious philosophy as primary, while hedging your bet with the other. Breaking with witchcraft, especially when one is as deeply involved as Kenny is in the first story, is a major step of faith. In the last story in this series, polygamy plays a major role in the story but is introduced as a passing moment of inconsequential logic, ". . . so I married both of them." Since polygamy is a common practice in Africa, this type of circumstance and its acceptance is not out of the ordinary.

Witch Doctor's Apprentice

Kenny Simbwalanga

efore I became a Christian my life was very bad. I committed a lot of sins in my life. I did not want to listen to God's Word. I was a stubborn boy. I feared witchcraft, so this made me trust in charms and witch doctors. I trusted in my charms very much. I committed a lot of sins like stealing, insulting, fighting, fornication, adultery, disrespecting my parents and worshiping the ancestral spirits of my forefathers.

I was an apprentice to a witch doctor. We used to go about together and do different kinds of activities, like digging roots from the bush for use. I trusted this man because he told me that he would protect my life from witches. We also had a gathering room where we used to meet on Sunday mornings. We used to call it *Mizimu* ("spirit") *Church*.

I was a fornicator and had a lot of different kinds of girls in my life. I thought it was a good way to live. My parents used to warn me about the danger of being a fornicator, but I didn't listen to them. I continued with my bad life. One time I got sick because of all the sins I was committing. At that time I remembered my parents' words and how they used to warn me. My life was in bad shape. They provided treatment for that disease, but after I became well, I continued sinning.

I got married while I was still sinning. I used charms for protection from witchcraft. Since I was friends with a witch doctor, I wrote down some roots and their uses. I was an expert in digging roots. The witch doctor instructed me to gather these roots while naked, which I did.

One day the witch doctor told me to look for hyena and vulture skins so that I could start practicing witchcraft among the people. There was a certain village where I heard that they had killed hyenas with poison. So I went to that village to look for hyena skin. When I reached that village, according to custom, I first had to see the old men of that village. I started asking them about hyena and vulture skins. These old men questioned me as to where I was taking those skins that I requested. I told them there was a certain sister of mine who was sick and she was at the witch doctor's house. The witch doctor sent me to look for these two kinds of skins. These old men told me, "We have these things you requested from us, but you cannot have them for witchcraft." I returned home without getting anything. When I arrived at the witch doctor's house, I told him what had happened on my journey.

The witch doctor then planned another way of getting me deep into his witchcraft. He told me to look for water monitor (a large lizard) skins. He told me to remove the tail skin if I caught one. Then after removing that skin I was to release the monitor back into the water. He promised to make me a *voodoo* if I took that skin to him. He told me, "This voodoo is to make you dream what will happen tomorrow."

After this discussion, I went along the river to look for water monitors in the place where they pass by when coming in and out of the water. I found such a place and laid my traps. Then I hid and waited.

I waited for some hours, then I went to check. I found one in the trap, so I removed part of the skin from the tail and released the water monitor alive. I took that skin to the witch doctor, who made me a charm to wear around my arm when I went to bed at night. I wore it for many months but nothing happened to me.

One day while lying in my bed, I was listening to the radio. I heard the people talking about Jesus Christ. That discussion touched my life. That night I couldn't sleep because of the name of Jesus. At that time there was a revival meeting at Muntuwamasiku Pilgrim Wesleyan Church. Early in the morning I went to where the revival meeting was taking place. There I met Jesus Christ through the man of God, Rev. Mwiikisa, who spoke from Mark, chapter 5, about the madman who used to live in the tombs. I learned how Jesus saved this man, so I gave my life to Jesus. From that time I stopped being afraid. I also stopped fornicating, fighting, stealing, worshiping ancestor spirits and trusting witch doctors and charms. From that time up to this day, my life has pleased the Lord.

I don't trust charms for protection nor practice the traditions of my forefathers. I am trusting the Lord Jesus as my personal Savior, because He has made me free from the fear of witchcraft and death, and destroyed the power of the devil in my life (Hebrews 2:14, 15).

Baptism Doesn't Bring Salvation

Meddy Sinabanza

I was baptized in 1989 by Rev. Mudenda. At that time I just knew about baptism without knowing what it really meant. I saw many people being baptized, so I thought about taking the step also, but without the truth in my heart. I just wanted to join the choir. I am saying this because at that time, even though I was baptized, I lived a bad life. I was still a thief. I was still in darkness. I know this because I can see the difference between the life I used to like before and the one I'm living since I have known the truth.

It was in 1994 that I came to know the truth. I was called with my friends by our district superintendent, Rev. L. Siamalambo, who asked us a lot of questions about our lives and how much we knew the Lord. Since I was baptized, my answer was that I was a true Christian because I knew that anyone who was baptized was a Christian. So my answer was that I was saved. I tried by all means to defend myself, but at last I came to know that I was lost.

I was convinced that the life I was living was not a good one. I asked myself, "What will this life benefit me?" I thought I was cheating other people, but I was cheating myself. Then I took a step and said, "I will follow my Lord." I confessed, and from that time I feel I'm free from sins. Because of this I have freedom. In the past I would think that maybe someone would come and say, "You've stolen this and that." But now because I am free I know no one will come to say this, for I am no longer a thief.

As a Christian, I have many friends who help me in times of problems and, because of this, I see the goodness of being a Christian. I am happy because I know even if I die I still have eternal life.

Sickness Precludes Ambivalence

• •

Siamoongwa M. Sialuumba

I was born February 12, 1974. My parents were not Christians and I never wanted to become a Christian, because it meant nothing to me. The life of sin in which I was involved was very good to me. I did not think of becoming a Christian because I thought that my future would be disturbed if I followed Jesus. I participated in all kinds of sins. My aim was to build up my reputation by sinning, yet I destroyed it completely.

Fornicating, stealing, fighting, insulting and hating were the major evil acts that I enjoyed very much. I had the spirit of unforgiveness. Whenever something went wrong for me, I could be very angry for a month or more. I used to sleep out with my friends who also loved the world and its evil. My life was very detestable in the eyes of God. If I had died during that time, I would have missed the way into heaven. I never wanted my parents to rebuke me when I did what was wrong. My life was in ruin because of my former group's influence. Not a day passed by without me committing sin.

When I was doing my junior secondary school education, I became very sick. My sickness greatly troubled me for a prolonged time. During that period of being sick, the Lord began to speak to me. I also started to realize the consequences of sin in my life. One man came to me and told me that the sickness I experienced was the result of the sins I had done. Still my heart was hardened all the more, so that I did not even think of repenting from sin. One day some Christians came to pray for me when I was sick. As they finished praying, I began to see the need of Jesus Christ in my own life. I realized that God was not happy with the way I lived. Being sick for a prolonged period challenged me. I made a promise that if only I could recover from my sickness, then I would repent and confess all my sins. I did not keep that vow because as soon as I recovered, I changed my mind and continued with the life of sin. That became a pattern every time I got sick. I vowed to become a Christian, but as soon as I got well, then I would say no, because the devil was ruling my life.

When I recovered, I became a very serious church attender. I thought that since I went to church every Sunday, that was good enough for me to be saved. I got involved in Scripture Union at school and always attended the prayer meetings, but I was still a sinner. I joined the singing groups and I

42

began to attend Bible study, but still I had no peace. God used to speak to me in various ways although I was resisting. The Lord spoke very clearly to me on March 10, 1995, when the gospel of salvation was preached during a revival meeting at Choma Secondary School. Pastor Alex Mbewe was preaching a message entitled "The Destruction of Sodom and Gomorrah" from Genesis 19:1-29. As he was preaching he began to mention the evil things that I used to do. I tried by all means to harden my heart and ignore the message, but the Holy Spirit was convicting me. Then I realized that something unusual was going to happen in my life.

My eyes and mind were opened. I thought deeply about my life because it was as sinful as that of the people of Sodom and Gomorrah. After hearing the message on salvation, I did not hesitate. I gave my life to Jesus Christ and received him as my personal Savior and Lord of my life. I repented and confessed all my sins to God in prayer. I asked Him to forgive me for all the sins I had committed. I believed in God and by His grace through faith I was saved. Now I am a new creation and a brand new man in the service of the Lord. When the preacher made the altar call, I just went forward to praise God for the new life that He gave me. I rejoiced before my God for His forgiveness of my sins.

Afterward, two men of God began to help me grow spiritually as a new convert. These men were Mr. Fred Mikesell, former sponsor for the Wesleyan Students' Fellowship at Choma Secondary School, and Mr. Samuel Mudenda, a teacher and member of the Brethren in Christ Church. I received baptism in the manner of Jesus to show the world that I had really repented and changed, and that I no longer belonged to the devil and the world. Now I am led by the Holy Ghost and I'm a child of God (Romans 8:14, 16).

My brothers and sisters can affirm that the testimony of salvation that I share with you is true. The Lord is mightily using me now. I am always prepared to work for Him. Wherever God leads me, I will obey. Where He sends me, I will trust and go to do the work of my Master. My life now has totally changed. I preach the gospel to the lost. I love the Word of God. I love the Christians. The good that I hated, I now love. The evil that I loved, I now hate, because the Holy One, Jesus Christ, lives in me forever.

The Polygamist

•••••••••••••••••••••••••

Sinabanza M. Pavlet

I am now twenty years old and before I met God my life was bad. I did not fight, murder or do other bad sins. My sins were prostitution and stealing. Family members would tell me, "You're a thief," but I did not accept it. I would say, "I am not stealing but getting."

At this time I also went to church because my parents told me to go. In 1990 I joined the baptism class and was baptized in 1991 during camp meeting at Chababboma by Rev. Musune Musange. At that time I had not yet received Jesus.

In 1994 a girl became pregnant and I was found to be responsible. In 1995 another one became pregnant, and again I was responsible, so I married both of them. In 1996 I was still with them and that is when I started realizing the importance of being a Christian. I looked for a way to escape polygamy, but I had no way out.

On her own initiative, the senior wife decided to leave, for she said she could not manage to share one husband. I had started seeking the will of God before this time, so when the senior wife left, I confessed my sin to the Lord. I started leading a worthwhile life.

In October, seeing that I was being faithful to the church, the leaders decided to have me back in the work of the Lord. In November I started my work and was appointed as secretary of the church. I also became the Christian education director in our local church in January 1998. I am now walking with my God continually and my God is able to do all things.

My daughter often suffers from malaria. One time this almost made me lose my faith because she wasn't healed, even though I prayed. We would take her to the clinic and there she would be admitted for a day and then she would be dismissed. One thing usually happened. She would be out of the clinic at around 9 a.m. and around 6 p.m. she would be seriously sick again. This happened two times, and the third time I said to myself, "Why am I suffering this way? It's as though my God was not living." And so at night I decided to pray, but I didn't tell my wife that we were to pray for the young one. I just told her, "Let's pray." And these are the words I used. "Lord, I thank you for our lives and for the guidance of the whole day. Father, You have seen how much we have suffered. Have mercy on us tonight and let Your will be done." And this was the end of my prayer. In the morning when I woke up, I put my hand on the baby's body to feel the temperature. It was okay and again I told my wife, "Let's pray." And again I said these words, "Lord, I thank you for hearing my prayer. May You continue being with us in our lives and let Your will be done. Amen."

Asia

Cambodia

I n 1975, Pol Pot and his Khmer Rouge army took control of Cambodia. More than a million Cambodians were executed (estimates run as high as three million) and almost the entire population was displaced. Phnom Penh, the capital, was totally evacuated in three days and anyone left behind was killed outright. Every Cambodian who lived through this terrible period which lasted until 1979 has a tale to tell. This period of time is often referred to in the following stories.

First Wesleyan Pastor in Cambodia

Chhin Ho Saing

I thank God for this special privilege to share my testimony. I was born in a war-torn communist country and was raised in a Buddhist environment. My mother was killed by the Khmer Rouge during the reign of the communist government under Pol Pot. I first heard about Christ through my father. He became a Christian through reading a gospel booklet given to him by a pastor. He prayed for us, his five sons, to become strong Christians too. God answered his prayers. All of us five brothers are Christians and are actively serving the Lord.

I accepted Christ as my Lord and Savior in 1990 through the ministry of Far East Broadcast Company. This was also the time when I received God's call to full-time ministry. At that time there were no Bible schools in my place, so I first went to a secular college. Then, in 1992, a Bible training center was opened and I studied for two years. God opened a way for me to study also in Thailand for one year. In 1995, God sent me to the Philippines to continue my Bible school training in the Wesleyan Bible college in Rosales, Pangasanan.

When I became a Christian, God changed my life. From being a sinner, God made me one of His children. When I was in Bible college, God continued to work in my life. He changed my bad attitude and strengthened my Christian character. I learned to live a holy life—a life that is totally committed to the will of God. I have just finished my field training here in my country. In my first year as a pastor of Good News Wesleyan Church in Phnom Penh, I realized that being a pastor is not easy. I have been through tough times and God has allowed me to experience different difficulties. I thank the Lord because He never leaves nor forsakes me. My father told me that if I ever got out of Cambodia, I should not return. But God put the burden in my heart for my countrymen. I want them also to hear and know about this Jesus who has the power to transform lives. Please pray for me that I may be a humble and patient minister of Christ. As John Wesley says, "I will make the ministry my business, and the world my parish."

Death Brings Life
● ●
Chia Bow Lehk

My name is Chia Bow Lehk. I am a thirty-six-year-old man and married. Before I believed and accepted the Lord in my life, I was a person full of hopeless anxieties. I was a troublemaker, always fighting with my neighbors and family members. I had a very bad relationship with my wife and the people around us. I was also hooked on gambling, drinking and smoking. Almost all the money I would earn would go to my vices. Most of the time, nothing would be left for my wife and my children. I became worse and my wife became angry and bitter at me. We always fought and these things made her life so miserable.

Near the end of 1995, around 1 p.m., while I was in the field, I heard the loud cry of a girl coming from our house. I went to check what was happening. When I arrived at our house, I saw my wife lying on the ground, unconscious, with insecticide coming out of her mouth. I called out for help and we brought my wife to the nearest hospital. She was already dead when we arrived at the place. She had committed suicide. I didn't know what to do at that time. I was blaming myself for all that happened. At her burial, around 3 p.m., three men came to console and comfort me and my children. I did not know them. They introduced themselves as Christian workers and missionaries from The Wesleyan Church. One of them started sharing the Good News to me. I remembered him encouraging me to give God a chance to work in my life. He shared God's Word for a couple of minutes and all the words I heard started comforting and enlightening my heart. I heard about Jesus Christ, and how He would give me hope and forgiveness. At 4 p.m. that day, I prayed and received Jesus Christ as Lord and Savior of my life.

After a week, Pastor Kong Kim San (the Wesleyan pastor who shared the Good News with me) came back and started sharing more about the Lord Jesus and about God's Word. From that time on, he regularly visited me, teaching me the Bible and discipling me to serve God. My life was completely changed. I became a gentle person, all my sinful vices were gone, and the loneliness brought by the death of my wife was replaced by joy and hope because of Christ. I decided to follow Jesus no matter what happened. Truly, God has changed me!

I regularly attend the Wesleyan church. I have been nurtured and discipled (and I am continually being discipled even now). I am now one of the laymen in our church here in Phnom Penh, the Good News Wesleyan Church. I am also one of the students at the Bible League Church Planter Training Program with three others from our church. I am involved in almost all the activities and ministries of our church—doing evangelism, participating in the worship program, visitation ministry, leading small groups and taking care of church properties. God has also blessed me with a new wife. We got married just last year. She is also faithfully attending our church now.

I strongly believe that the Lord whom I trust will never leave nor forsake me. I am hoping and praying for God to continually bless me and my family. Praise God!

Death to Life

Dey Sokha
(told by Jun Rafael)

Dey Sokha grew up in a strong Buddhist family. His parents are Chinese-Cambodian, so his Buddhist faith was a combination of these two portions of his life. Sokha was a very quiet young man. Inside and outside his home, he rarely talked. He was afraid of everything, afraid of people. He just stayed at home most of the time. He was so unhappy. He did not have hope in his life and was considered the least in his family. He also knew he was full of sin.

In May 1997, the Wesleyan church in Phnom Penh rented a place near Sokha's house as a pioneer church. This area is called Budeng. Aside from worship and other church activities, the church also opened a small English class. Sokha joined this English class. He was very interested and was never absent.

After almost a month, Pastor Chhin Ho invited him to attend the church. The preaching during that service was about sin. The Holy Spirit spoke to Sokha so after the service, he approached Pastor Chhin Ho and asked directly, "If I am a sinner, can I not go to heaven?" The pastor told him that surely he could not, then started explaining and dealing with this young man concerning his need of forgiveness. Sokha accepted the Lord at that time.

After his conversion, Sokha faithfully sought the will of God in his life. Through God's grace and power, this sad, fearful young man who seldom talked became a very joyful and good young person of the church. Because of his love for God, he faithfully attended all the church activities. His life was changed so that even his family was surprised by the changes. He became very obedient to his parents.

The Lord gave Sokha a servant heart. He extended his help to the church regularly—from cleaning, to running errands, to any other menial jobs he could do. He arrived the earliest for almost all the activities and services. His life was a blessing to everyone.

He died just last March 13, 1998. He was eighteen when he died. Before he died, he confirmed his faith and undying devotion to Christ. Sokha now is in heaven with our Saviour and Lord Jesus Christ.

Single Mother, Heavy Load

Kaew Sam At

My name is Kaew Sam At. I am forty-eight years old with two children. I am a single parent, since my husband left us for another woman. My life was so full of problems—problems we were not able to solve. The worst was when my husband started taking this other woman into his life. I felt I could not bear that trial. I did not know what to do. I did not know what to think. I asked help from Buddha, offered sacrifices, and did other acts of worship but nothing improved. I was so hopeless.

During that particular situation, I remembered people who often shared with me about their new life and hope, which was brought about by faith in a certain God. I was reminded of some messages they were trying to share with me from a certain book. I was searching in my heart until one day, a friend came to our house with some missionaries and their pastor. She is a Wesleyan member and she made an appointment to visit me when she learned I wanted to know more about their God. Pastor Chhin Ho shared the Word of God, focusing on His greatness and power. This God is Jesus Christ, who is much more powerful than Satan or Buddha or any other gods in this world. He also said that Jesus is the only true God and that He loves me and died for me. After hearing these truths and being convicted of my sins, I confirmed my desire to accept Jesus Christ that night of November 26, 1997. I was also instructed to remove any amulets I was wearing at that time. One of the missionaries helped me remove them. I was led to pray the sinner's prayer. We also removed and gathered a sack full of Buddhist altars and idols around our house. All of these were burned later.

After I received Christ in my heart, I had peace even though there were still problems. I know where to go and what to do. I always go to the Lord and pray. My mind is also enlightened. I know I have hope and a good future. If sickness comes to my family, I go to God and ask His healing power. One time, my body was in such pain. I prayed to Him and He answered immediately. I was healed. Also, there were times we didn't have money, even rice to eat. We always prayed and God always helped us.

I have a strong belief in the Lord Jesus and I respect Him wholeheartedly. I will not ever turn my back on Him and will not worship any other god again. I will only worship my Savior and Lord, Jesus Christ. I am now a member of the Good News Wesleyan Church here in Phnom Penh, Cambodia. I used to sing for weddings. Now I will be using the gift in singing for His glory. Let Him be glorified!

No Help in Buddha!

Kaw Chay Hieng

My life was full of suffering and pain. I felt in my heart that I probably had more burdens than any person throughout the world. Things became worse when my child and my grandchild died. I asked Buddha why he allowed all those things to happen to us. I said to myself, "I am not a bad person at all." Worse came to worse when my husband Tu Tem started having an affair with another woman. Before that, I had tried to just endure and close my eyes to all my husband's vices (drinking, smoking, gambling), but having another woman was just too much for me. We always fought. I felt my life was hopeless and useless.

We were living that kind of life when a friend of mine visited me one day. She is a Christian and a member of the Good News Wesleyan Church here in Phnom Penh. She shared with me her newfound faith and brought me to Pastor Kong Kim San. The pastor shared with me about salvation through Jesus Christ and then led me in prayer. I accepted Christ and surrendered my life to Him that February of 1998.

My life was dramatically changed. The burdens I had before were taken by the Lord and He filled my heart with peace and joy. There are still trials and difficulties, but God is helping me and strengthening my family. I also want to thank the Lord, for my husband is also now a believer! Both of us are faithfully coming to the church. We were just both baptized this year. Workers and missionaries of our church are regularly coming to our house to conduct Bible studies. We desire to know God more and to serve Him.

Waylaid by Faith

Tu Tem

My name is Tu Tem. I was a very sinful, wicked man. I was also inconsiderate and a mean husband to my wife. I was an adulterer, a chain smoker, a gambler and a drunkard. I made my wife's life miserable and difficult. We always fought because of my wicked ways. It seemed really impossible to remove my vices and I had already determined in my heart that these were part of my life and that nobody could stop them.

One day, somebody shared a new kind of faith with my wife. She convinced me to welcome these people into our house to share with me also about this new faith. One Sunday noon in February of this year, people from the Wesleyan church came to our house and started sharing with me about Jesus Christ. I realized all the sins I had been doing. I was especially moved when they told me that Jesus Christ could change my life completely. I felt the love of God and my need for forgiveness. I accepted Jesus Christ as Lord and Savior of my life that day. I also learned that my wife had really invited them for the purpose of tearing down all the Buddhist altars we had. The church members, workers and missionaries, together with my wife and me, broke down all the altars and idols at our house.

After this experience, things happened fast. My sinful vices were just gone. The urge of doing wicked things against my wife wasn't there anymore. I am now concerned with her welfare and interest. I left my other woman and together with my wife, began attending the Good News Wesleyan Church here in Phnom Penh.

Truly, God is a powerful and forgiving God. I thank Him for how He is changing my life.

When Fathers Lead
●●●●●●●●●●●●●●●●●●●●●●●●
Kong Kim San

My name is Kong Kim San. I am a family man. I have been through the communist time of Pol Pot. We were in the province during that time. That was a very difficult life for us and every time we slept, how we wished that we would wake up realizing that those experiences were only bad dreams. But we survived those dreadful days. I moved to Phnom Penh with my family and I started working in an electric company in 1982. During those days, I had a lot of friends and we loved doing bad things. My friends always invited me to gamble, drink wine and smoke. I always thought of stopping my vices because they were not doing my health any good. Every time I tried, my friends would start to tease me and I would return to the same lifestyle again. I also began to notice my beautiful wife deteriorating, becoming sadder and older because of me. I saw she always cried. My children were not doing well at school and were being affected by my wrongdoing. I was very miserable. Sometimes I was happy, sometimes I was hopeless. I always asked myself, "Who can help or deliver me from this pitiful situation?"

In 1991, I learned that one of my friends became a Christian. He talked to me and invited me to attend a Christian church. I was hesitant at first since I was Buddhist, but I decided to go anyway. When the pastor finished his message, he invited people who wanted to accept Jesus into their hearts as Savior and Lord. I didn't hesitate to respond. I accepted the Lord Jesus in my heart and surrendered my life to Him. I knew then that He is the answer to my question. He is the One who can deliver me from all my vices.

My life then miraculously changed! God has given me joy, hope and wisdom. My vices were gone, instantly! My wife was so happy for the changes she saw in me. Once again, I saw her beauty glow and her radiant smiles. Another miracle the Lord did was to give wisdom to my kids at school. Since that time, when they also accepted the Lord in their heart, they began to do well in their studies. I really praise God for sending His Son Jesus Christ to die for my sins.

My entire family (wife and four children) became Christians after me. In 1996, I got involved with the Wesleyan church here in Phnom Penh. I became one of the leaders of our church and started leading a small group. In 1997, I left my job at the electric company and began full-time work in the ministry. I am now studying in one of the Bible schools here, and at the same time team-pastoring Good News Wesleyan Church with Pastor Chhin Ho Saing. To God be the glory!

Soldier Comes to the Savior

• •

Nit Ban Yen

M y name is Nit Ban Yen. I am forty-nine years old, and the father of nine girls. I was twenty years old when I stopped going to school and started working. The government sponsored me to study in Thailand and become a soldier. I was trained in Thailand for six months. Not long after I came back to Cambodia, the Khmer Rouge began fighting against the government until they successfully occupied the whole country. Life during the Khmer Rouge regime was like a nightmare. I experienced a lot of difficulties. I was separated from my wife for a number of years. Life was so miserable that all I hoped for every time I woke up was that I was only dreaming.

In 1979, after Pol Pot was overthrown, the government hired me to work for them as an employee. I served the government until 1992. During those times I felt I had no freedom, that I was a slave of somebody. Even though the oppressing rule of communism had ended, I still felt hopeless with no freedom. I always argued with my wife and children (I was rejoined with my family after the Khmer Rouge fell). I had friends who always invited me to drink wine, to gamble and to go to places where I slept with prostitutes. I always cheated people. I didn't have love and concern for others. This situation had been so depressing for me. I tried to always think of good things that I wanted to do, but I could not do them. I was even persecuting and laughing at people who were calling themselves Christians. I was so enslaved by sin.

In October 1993, a certain man from a Christian church was able to share the Good News with me. While he was sharing the gospel, I kept on telling myself that I already had a god (Buddha) and I didn't need another god. But this man patiently and continuously shared the Good News about Jesus Christ to me.

One day I went to a province 300 kilometers away from my hometown. I stayed with one of my relatives who happened to be a Christian. I again heard something about Jesus Christ. My sister-in-law prayed for me and asked God to speak and work in my heart. The following day was Sunday, and they invited me to attend their church. That time I felt God working in my heart. The pastor started talking and dealing with me and shared the love of God. At that very moment, I opened my heart to God and accepted Christ in my heart. That was October 17, 1993.

The Lord changed my life since then. I felt the joy coming from the Lord. I stopped all the bad things that had enslaved me before. I became a happy person. Every day I read my Bible and meditate on it. I will never exchange my life with Christ for any other thing in this world. I thank the Lord so much for hearing my prayers. In my walk with Him, He blesses my endeavors. Even though I lack wisdom and strength, He is faithfully helping me. I am now pastoring New Life Wesleyan Church in Siem Reap. I pray for God to protect and empower me to do His will and remain in Him.

Daddy Learned Best

Sothkann

My name is Sothkann. I used to work in an electric company until 1991. I had experienced lots of difficulties and lived a wicked life centered on worldly things. I drank wine. I gambled a lot and had no concern for my family. I only thought of myself—how to make myself happy and satisfy my desires. Every time I was drunk, I cursed my wife and children. I always noticed their faults and was so cruel to them. I argued and fought with my friends when I was drunk.

Deep inside me, I was full of worries and difficulties. I felt I had no hope in life. One day, a companion at the company I was working for shared with me about Jesus Christ. He didn't say a lot. He only said to me that I should believe in Christ. At that time, I didn't know if God could help me with anything, but I asked Him to help me anyway. I went to church with my friend that Sunday,  August 11, 1991. I met several people at that church that day. They welcomed me warmly and I felt their sincere love toward me. I sat and sang with them and heard the pastor preach. When the pastor invited people to accept Christ, something inside me pushed me to go and respond to that invitation. I accepted Christ that Sunday. I have gone to church regularly since that day. I had a new desire to read the Bible. I was so amazed how the Lord cleansed me from all my sin. He then changed me little by little. I experienced joy in my heart. My family was also happy. I became concerned for their welfare. I stopped drinking wine, stopped gambling, stopped smoking and other bad things I used to do before. Almost every day, I read from the books of Proverbs, Psalms, and the Gospels. I liked studying God's Word. If I didn't understand something, I would ask my pastor. I also praise the Lord for opening opportunities for me to attend various Bible seminars. I really wanted to serve Him. I shared God's love to others, visited people and helped in the church as much as I could.

In 1993, I was appointed as one of the leaders in that church. My family also began attending services until all of them accepted the Lord Jesus Christ. In 1996, I became involved with the Wesleyan church here in Phnom Penh. I became one of the first leaders of the emerging Wesleyan church here in the city, though only part time. I worked full time at FEBC (Far East Broadcasting-Cambodia) which is a Christian radio station. I am helping Good News Wesleyan Church every Saturday and Sunday and in my free time. I also minister to our new outreach in one of the provinces with the missionary on Sundays. I praise the Lord who saved me and my whole family. All of us have the desire to serve the Lord.

Northeast India

O nly one of the following stories is about the salvation of an individual. The others are included because they tell the history and philosophy of salvation. "The Peace Sacrifice" tells of bringing the salvation message into the context of the people being reached. A number of the other stories stress the need for a holistic message and practice in order for salvation to be real.

Healing Brings Spiritual Health

• •

Good Deed

(told by Dr. Lalkhawlien Pulamte)

Had this incident not happened in South Manipur, the history of the church could have been entirely different from what we see today. Wherever the mission of the Church in Manipur is referred to, this specific incident has to occupy an important place as a reminder that God is still in control of history for His own glory.

When Christianity was brought into Manipur state in the 1920s, there was a great need for clinics for the poor villagers, since there was not a single government-run hospital in the area. Accordingly, the mission started health clinics in two places. Through medical ministries, several hundred people became Christians. People believed that the medicine used for their physical ailments had a kind of magic power to heal. Therefore, medical aid given them was called *damdawi*, which literally means "magic of healing." Medicines were given carefully to the patients only after prayers were offered. The non-Christians who were healed became Christians. Thus the number of new believers swelled in many villages.

As the mission expanded its work in Manipur, the missionary in charge, Mr. Coleman, approached the *Raja* (king) of Manipur to allocate a plot of land. The Raja, being a Hindu by faith, didn't appreciate the expansion of Christian work in the state. Under normal circumstances the Raja would have refused the request of the missionary. But God had his own way of solving the problem.

At that time one of the daughters of the Raja became seriously ill to the point of death. The Raja promised Mr. Coleman he would give land for the mission if the doctor could heal his daughter. This offered the mission not only a good opportunity, but also a great challenge. After much prayer, a missionary doctor, Dr. Grozier, took up the challenge and attended the daughter. The Raja's daughter recovered. Upon seeing his daughter healed, the Raja granted the mission a large plot of land which was named Churachandpur, in honor of the Raja Churachand Singh. The mission headquarters and hospital were established there. The missionary work was carried on and the present population of Christians is the fruit of the good deed shown to the Hindu Raja.

Power Encounter

●●●●●●●●●●●●●●●●●●●●●●●●●●●

(told by Dr. Lalkhawlien Pulamte)

Power encounters between Christians and the animists of the Hmar people in 1910-1945 were common phenomena. Mr. Khuonga, one of the early Hmar converts, wrote the following incident in his diary.

"Once a couple who had a *jhum* (rice field) near ours stayed all night in a small hut built in the field. One of the followers of Nelhau, a spirit called *Rawt Rawt*, came and frightened them. The couple almost died from fear and sickness. I told them that I wanted to challenge this spirit.

"The couple advised me to put out the light from the fire and the spirit would come immediately. I followed their instruction, and sure enough, I soon felt the floor shaking, but I kept silent. A noise came saying, 'Rawt Rawt,' but as I raised my head up, the sound moved away. Again I slept in the darkness, and again another sound came.

"A few minutes later *Rawt Rawt* stepped onto the roof and it was about to collapse. *Rawt Rawt* tried to frighten me, but to no avail. Suddenly I got up and called upon the name of Jesus. The spirit quickly moved away and then I prayed.

"I told the couple that the spirit had been defeated. 'You can come and stay and nothing will happen again.' They were comforted and later the couple became Christians."

Reconciliation Is More Than Spiritual

●●●●●●●●●●●●●●●●●●●●●●●●●●●

(told by Dr. Lalkhawlien Pulamte)

Northeast India consists of seven states. Though they are very small in size, they produce a lot of noise in the ears of people around the world. This tiny corner of India is infested by two deadly diseases—AIDS and insurgency. The former invades a large number of young people.

It is estimated that within the next ten years, several thousand will die of AIDS. The latter, equally damaging, brings tears to hundreds of thousands of families.

Professing oneself reconciled to God or designing a perfect course on the theology of reconciliation is one thing, but practicing reconciliation in a hostile environment is an entirely different thing. It involves risking even one's own life. But for God's children who take this truth seriously, there is no alternative.

There was a shooting incident between two factions in February 1997, the day before I was to arrive at a village to attend a very crucial meeting. I stayed overnight in a small town to spend time with the Wesleyan church members on that particular night. The next morning when I was about to leave the town for the meeting, my dear Wesleyan families, sensing the danger ahead, pleaded with me not to proceed any further. But I told them that I had come to attempt reconciliation and I would not be stopped just then. On hearing this, they bade me farewell with a word of encouragement saying, "We now understand your commitment and if you are killed, you will be a martyr for the glory of God."

Immediately after that I proceeded towards the village where the shooting incident had taken place the previous day. As soon as I arrived, I met the commander of one faction and shared my purpose for coming there. I confronted the groups and told them to stop the shedding of blood.

While we were having this discussion, the leader told me that they held three fighting men of the other faction in their custody in the jungle. These men were to be killed at noon that day. I immediately responded that they should not carry out the death penalty imposed upon the prisoners. At times the discussion became very heated.

At last they were convinced and they promised to hand over these three persons with one condition: I had to meet the other group, which had retreated from the spot of the fighting, and persuade them not to attack again. Unfortunately, no one knew the exact location of their hiding place. The only clue I had at my disposal was that they had moved up to the top of the mountain. With that little information I took one person and headed immediately in that direction. It was already dark and no one knew where we were going nor why we were going there.

It was a bit chilly since the winter season was not yet over. I needed to be constantly vigilant on the way. The flashlight I had in my hand was no use in this kind of dangerous situation. We have a saying that those who come for peace or emergency reasons must use our traditional lamp (dry bamboo sticks lit with fire). So I followed these instructions and carried the twenty-foot-long burning bamboo. I had to look for other dry bamboo on the way to keep the flame burning. Sweat covered my whole body as I walked up a small footpath. I stopped several times because I was so exhausted—no water to drink, no food for my empty stomach.

After walking with difficulty the whole night, we arrived at one village about fifteen kilometers away at the top of the mountain. We met the leaders of the village and we were informed that the people we were looking for were hiding in the jungle and no direct communication was possible. We sent an emissary with a letter explaining my purpose in coming this far. I had to wait patiently for the response. At last a positive reply came through the emissary, and the time and place of the meeting was fixed. The leader and his guards entered the village carrying sophisticated arms. After intense negotiating for some time, a meal was served. To my great relief, they agreed not to fight with the group down below.

At about 8 a.m., I had to return to the village where the rival group was stationed. Mentally I was well-prepared to go down. My heart was filled with joy because reconciliation had been achieved. But physically I was not fit to walk down a narrow footpath because my whole leg was swollen from the night's long walk. In the meantime, my heart was heavily burdened with the thoughts of what might happen to the three persons on death row. The commander had promised to hand over these prisoners to me upon my return. Would he really honor our points of agreements or would he betray me? With slow paces I arrived at my destination around 4 p.m. Right after a simple evening meal, I met the commander of the faction. I gave him the assurance that the opposing armed group would not come to fight and followed with my demand to release the three accused men to me. He agreed to my request. Because night had fallen and I did not have a place to keep the prisoners overnight, the handing over of the three was put off until early the next morning.

At the appointed time, the three persons were escorted out of their temporary imprisonment in the jungle across the river. As soon as my eyes caught a glimpse of their physical appearance, I struggled to keep myself from crying. One person in particular had obviously been seriously tormented—his body was full of scars, lesions and swelling. He could neither eat nor drink. The condition of the other two looked much better. I still can vividly remember our brief time together inside a small hut. The most severely mistreated victim expressed in a low voice his appreciation for our efforts to save them from death, saying, "God sent you here to save my life and henceforth I dedicate my whole life to serve God."

They were secretly taken to the appointed location to avoid public notice and then safely to their final destination. It was obvious that God made all those things possible because He can change people's heart.

A year after that (May 2, 1998), I had a chance to meet the most injured person in his village while I was distributing rice purchased with the financial assistance of the Eastern Ohio District of The Wesleyan Church. It was a joy for me to talk to him personally—this man who had narrowly escaped death. In appreciation of that effort, he and his whole family had joined The Wesleyan Church and are now church members.

Reconciliation is not just a sound biblical truth to be subscribed to but must be practiced even in very hostile environments. It is worth taking a risk to demonstrate God's solution of reconciliation for lost sinners in our mad world.

Note: For security and related reasons, names of the persons and villages are kept secret. All the incidents took place within the state of Manipur, India. This is a true incident from the reconciliatory ministry of Rev. Lalkhawlien Pulamte, Regional Superintendent.

The Peace Sacrifice

● ●

A Tribal Analogy
(told by Dr. Lalkhawlien Pulamte)

The Hmar people had passed through the bitter experiences of tribal wars with many of their neighbors. Peace was made between the warring tribes or villages along boundary lines, using a process well-understood and accepted by all. Watkin R. Roberts (an early missionary from Wales), after his failure in attempting to persuade the people to accept the gospel, was helped by his interpreter to make use of the culturally acknowledged peace-making process to illustrate the gospel of reconciliation and redemption. Roberts accepted the suggestion and began to make use of the following cultural analogy.

When two tribes are at war, the party who wishes to make peace goes to the hilltop at sunrise and beats a big war-drum three times. If the other side responds by doing the same thing before sunset, that is the sign that the offer for peace was acceptable and that the agreement would be settled at the boundary line. The chief who wanted to make the treaty slaughtered an animal and let the blood flow over the boundary mark. The two parties put their hands on the victim while negotiating and making terms and conditions for the treaty. This was followed by embracing and sharing in the peace meal on the same spot.

Roberts then explained the gospel message with this backdrop. God sent His Son to die on the cross in order to reconcile man to God. The Bible is a record of God's treaty with man and His invitation for man to come to the boundary and accept God's sacrifice for peace. Roberts claimed that it was the most effective means of communicating Christ to the Hmar people. Soon the chief of Senvon and four Hmars accepted the gospel invitation. This was followed by a group conversion. The word spread fast about the conversion of the chief Kamkhawlun and his people. The young converts went about telling people of the joy that was theirs. The tidings swept across the hills like a mighty storm, and amazement and awe filled the hearts of all who heard it.

All the evangelists took their cue from Roberts and emphatically presented the message in the same fashion. As a result of the hard labor of such evangelists, about 70% of the Hmar population turned to Christ before the end of 1940.

The Risk Taker

● ●

(told by Dr. Lalkhawlien Pulamte)

Rev. Lientinkai, one of the early converts in South Manipur, took drastic steps which annoyed the other villagers. The same day he became a Christian, he removed all the fetishes from his body and burned them in the presence of his nonbelieving relatives. The family strongly objected and pleaded with him not to do this. They said that magic or the influence of evil spirits would come to him and kill him within three months. But Lientinkai stood firm and nothing happened to him. Seeing this, the villagers came to him with a message that his God truly kept him alive and that they too wanted to become Christians.

Another time, while witnessing for the gospel, Lientinkai met a hunter with a gun. The hunter loaded the gun and pointed it at Lientinkai, threatening, "Pathien thu Awipa" (You who are obedient to God's Word, you will be shot dead). But Lientinkai bravely told his would-be assailant that without God's permission, the gun would not work. The hunter became indignant, unloaded the gun and moved away. Amazingly, two or three months later the hunter met Lientinkai again and told him that since Lientinkai was not afraid of him, he thought that Lientinkai's God must be the true God because He had protected him from death. So the hunter decided to follow the God of Lientinkai. From that moment the hunter became a Christian. This incident encouraged Christian workers to face the challenge of the devil, and by faith the early Christians overcame such challenges through the power of the resurrected Christ.

As a result, the non-Christians not only came to doubt the authority of their spirits, but even the very foundation of their system of belief was shaken. They surrendered their lives to Christ, whose power cannot be challenged.

Rice Wine

• •

Evangelism
(told by Barry and Margaret Ross)

D r. Lal Pulamte, regional superintendent of The Wesleyan Church of northeast India, was invited to visit some of our churches in very remote villages. Buses rarely travel these days to such remote areas because of the ever-present danger of holdups, looting, demands for money, and even killings by underground groups armed with sophisticated modern weapons. Yet, this day a bus driver dared to go. Lal, pushing aside his own fears and concerns for personal safety, was fortunate to get one of the few remaining seats. The road was very bad as well as deserted. Though Lal's destination, Senvawn Village, was only a 150-mile journey, the bus took fourteen hours to reach that last bus stop. Lal still had ten miles to travel by foot. But the strength of the Lord sustained him. When he reached the village, he felt as though he had traveled only a few yards.

Finding that the church had prepared programs for him to preach three consecutive nights, concluding on Sunday, Lal waited upon the Lord for what he was to preach. As he sought the Lord's guidance, an expectancy came into his heart that something special was going to happen among these people who had gathered under great hardship to hear the messages.

Yet God acts in His own time. At the conclusion of each of the first two night meetings, there was no unusual response from the people. Lal wondered if he had correctly sensed the Lord's promise. On the final evening, however, the church building was fully packed. Those who couldn't get inside filled all open spaces outside. So many were eager to hear the message! Lal preached from Luke 4:16-18. He urged the church to invite unto Christ the downtrodden, the wretched, the brokenhearted, and the people society had rejected and branded as the vilest of sinners, that they too might become transformed persons. People responded to the message with "Hallelujah," "Amen," and "Praise the Lord."

At the conclusion many responded to the message in commitment to Christ. Among them was a man some 70 years old. This man was regarded as the vilest and most infamous person in the village. He had started a business of preparing and selling homemade rice liquor. This liquor business angered the local armed underground rebel group. They kidnapped him from his house and took him outside the village, intending to shoot him dead. Fortunately, for no reason it seems, they spared his life and let him return home. But God knew the reason.

While listening to Lal's preaching, God opened this vile man's heart to the message of God's love for sinners. That night he became a new man in Christ, transformed by God's Holy Spirit. What a merciful God we have!

Early the next morning this transformed man came to the house where Lal was staying. To Lal's surprise, he invited Lal to a meal in his house. After a few minutes he stood up, took the Bible, read a few verses, and started talking about his past life and how God had changed him the previous night. He then confessed before God that he had repented from his sins and again committed the remaining years of his life to Jesus. Lal later said, "The meal we later shared together certainly could be smelled in eternity. This man's family now lives in a different atmosphere."

Central India

nly five percent of Indians are Christian. In central and western India, less than one percent of the population is Christian. While the Hindu religion accepts thousands of gods and people may worship a special one in their household, there is generally a territorial god worshiped in an area. Christians who refuse to worship any god except Christ are seen as bringing the wrath of the regional god upon the community. If Christians would agree to worship the regional god as well as Christ, there would be no persecution of Christians. This break with regional gods, a huge step of faith, is prominent in the stories from central and western India.

The Wesleyan Church operates a number of social and philanthropic institutions around the world. The following story is an example of the results we desire—the healing of the soul, as well as of the body and mind.

Leper Finds the Lord
●●●●●●●●●●●●●●●●●●●●●●●
Manju Deshlahres

I was born to a Hindu family in the village of Tiroda in the state of Maharastra. I have seven sisters and two brothers. I contracted leprosy at the age of twenty. My parents were worried and spent a lot of money, but there was no improvement. We came to know about the leprosy hospital run by the Wesleyan mission and I was admitted there. One of the nurses, Miss L. White, spent a lot of time in counseling. Her love and behavior attracted me and I started to like this hospital. Mr. Deorath Lal used to conduct the daily morning devotion by singing hymns and reading the Bible. Something started working within me. I started praying and this led me to life in Christ. At the entrance of this hospital there is a board on which John 3:16 is written. This verse talked with me and I became a believer of God.

I was in this hospital for five years and got my physical and spiritual healing. I have accepted Jesus Christ as my personal Savior. Then the question came about baptism, which is necessary according to the Bible. There were so many hurdles in the way from my relatives and parents. The Lord helped me in this matter and answered my prayers. I was baptized on August 5, 1979.

During my stay at the hospital I got acquainted with Mr. Tiharu Deshlahre, who was also a patient here in this hospital. After getting cured he started working in the hospital as a work supervisor. We got married here in the Hospital Chapel. I thank God for giving me a good born-again Christian husband. We are still here on staff and living in the staff compound at the hospital. We have been blessed with a son and two daughters who are studying in the Wesleyan English Medium Higher Secondary School.

My sincere request to you all is to pray for me and my family so that none of us may lose the salvation.

Hindu Roots Untangled

Dayaram Sahu

I was born March 26, 1971, in the village of Paniajab at Congargarb Tahsil in Rajnandgaon into a staunch, orthodox Hindu family. After finishing college, I am at present a student of a Bible college.

From my childhood my mother had taught me to worship *Tulsi Mata* (a sacred plant) daily after washing my face. She said, "Your brother daily worships Tulsi Mata and passed with a good division in school. Therefore, you must also do accordingly." So I developed the habit of saluting the Tulsi Mata daily. When I was in seventh grade, my brother married into a very religious Hindu family. They inspired me to recite the verses of the *Ramayan* and *Yayatri* daily.

I got interested in my studies and finished secondary school in the first division. But after finishing, I started worrying and thinking about my future. I got very upset. In March 1988, two Hindu holy men came and fooled people by telling them about their future in order to get money from them. I got very angry and tried to drive them away. Somehow they guessed that I was upset, frustrated and worried. They asked me to give 25 rupees to get peace. I had only 21 rupees, which I gave them. No one else knew about this except for my sister-in-law. But after offering this money, instead of getting peace I became more worried and disturbed. Through it all I wrote and passed my matric examinations.

After passing my examinations, I tried various other competitive examinations. People made me more worried by telling me that even with high qualifications people were unemployed. I was disappointed and tried to enroll in the military services. In the selection process I was disqualified. Some of my classmates who were not good students got jobs. I became still more worried and frustrated.

I observed that my people and the villagers who toiled the whole day seemed to be without worry and tiredness. But I felt tired and could not sleep at night. I was depressed and sad. I was studying in college, but I was internally very tired and frustrated. I thought of committing suicide, even though I knew it was cowardice. But there was no peace in my mind and it wandered aimlessly.

On August 1, 1990, I wrote in my diary, "Under all circumstances I shall try to live. In case I have no desire to live, I shall go to a distant place where no one knows me. I shall lie down on the rails of the train and commit suicide and there end my life." I was in search of a peaceful life. During my period of studying in college, I was worshiping gods and goddesses and reading *Ramayan* as usual, as well as other Hindu writings.

In March 1991, I found a red-covered book, the New Testament, and a small tract about the good news. It drew my attention since it was new to me. I asked my brother where he had found them. He said, "A Christian preacher who preached about Christ gave them to me." I informed my brother that I was taking those books and he could get them when he felt like reading them.

I took the New Testament and the tract to my room. I read the first two chapters of Matthew and found it uninteresting. I closed the book to read it after the exams. I read the tract also, and carefully put them away. After finishing the second part of my exams, I came across these books again. In one place it was written, "If you want to know more about Jesus' life and His sermons, we shall send you a correspondence course free of cost." The address of the Bible Society in Jabalpur was given.

I sent a postcard ordering the correspondence course and saying, "Privately I wish to know more about Jesus Christ." I thought some books would come to me free. After a week I received and read a book called *Jesus, the Savior of the World*. I read the book and sent the answers to the questions. After some days I received a magazine and a certificate along with it.

On July 16, 1991, God's servant came to meet me in the afternoon. He told me about Jesus' life, His sacrifice and the salvation of mankind. He also prayed for me. When he went away, I laughed and felt happy realizing how much they do for their God. After this these servants of God visited me regularly on Sunday evenings. They gave me God's message and had fellowship with me. After this they invited me to come to the church services held each Sunday. In the fourth week I went to the church, but returned after reaching only the gate. God's servant invited me again. In the eleventh week, I attended the church and met many other members of the church. God's servants started visiting me three times every week and we had fellowship together.

I started reading the Bible regularly which, at first, seemed like a story to me. I was a staunch Hindu. How could I leave my religion which I followed with great respect? But when I saw the faith and love for Christ in the lives of the Christians, my faith and belief in Christianity started increasing. It was the great faith and love of the believers for Christ that encouraged me.

Daily I got up to study at 4 a.m. In 1990, I discovered a program on the radio called *Dedication,* relayed from Sri Lanka through Trans World Radio. Because it was a Christian program I ignored it and, instead, listened to Hindi film songs. Finally in July 1991, I decided to listen to the *Dedication* program.

On that program there was a challenge: "If you are tired in the walk of life and feel like committing suicide, immediately come to Christ who will give you rest and comfort." Upon hearing these lines, I felt that there was real comfort in Christ. From that day I felt my burden was lessened, and my faith in Jesus Christ became strong and solid.

On September 2, 1991, as every year, I kept the fast on *Janmastoni* day (birth of Krishna). This I did from my childhood. I felt guilty, as I had accepted Christ in my heart, and here I was fasting for the Hindu god, Krishna. I was in a fix. I had two paths to follow—first to walk behind Christ with the cross and, second, to believe in the Hindu idols and their pictures. The whole day I was upset and there was turmoil in my heart. In the evening I went to my room and accepted Jesus Christ as my individual Savior. I confessed all my sins and prayed to God to be forgiven. I fully dedicated myself to God. I promised to do His will and walk according to His wishes. Thus I dedicated myself to the Living God.

When I disclosed this to one of my college friends—that I believed in Jesus Christ and had accepted Him as my Savior—he said that all gods are one. There is only a difference in names. He said that the principles and teachings of Christianity are good. But I could follow my Hindu religion as well. Then I remembered the verse in Acts 4:12 from the Bible: "Salvation is found in no one else, for there is no other name under heaven given to men by which we must be saved." Some friends said my studies would be disturbed if I entangled myself in the religious affairs concerning God and soul. They advised me that first I must stand on my feet and then seek God. But the answer to this I found in Matthew 6:33: "But seek first His kingdom and righteousness." After caring for no one's advice or suggestion, I dedicated my life to God, leaving all desires of life and body. I decided firmly to lead a spiritual life in Jesus Christ.

At home I confided only to my sister-in-law that I believed in Jesus Christ and He was now my Savior. I asked her to take down all pictures of the Hindu gods and goddesses from the walls of my room or else I would tear them down and burn them myself, as they had no meaning for me. I did burn some pictures myself. She told this to my brother. In my absence they took away all the pictures and the *Ramayan* from my room. When my family members came to know about this, there was a great chaos and they treated me as an outsider. My father stopped paying my college fees. He even tried to snatch away my Bible. I told him if he took away one Bible from me, I could get ten more the next day. He returned the Bible to me and insisted again on hanging the Hindu gods and goddesses in my room. I strongly opposed this.

On October 7, 1991, my maternal uncle called and tried his best to entreat me. But before everyone I gave the living witness of Jesus Christ. My brother told me, "From today all our family relations are broken and you'll not get even a gram of rice to eat." In spite of all this, I stayed on in my house.

Three days later, they brought my father-in-law. He was of a very religious temperament. He had inspired me to read the *Ramayan* regularly. He tried his best to explain things to me. His arguments could not satisfy me. My faith and belief increased. My father told me that I had crushed down his family's name. He said I must leave his house. Because of me the family will be looked down upon in their Hindu society. He said, "You have brought ill repute to the prestige of our seven generations. So we can't have you in the house."

My father determined to use his last weapon on me. He asked me to recite before the *Panchayat* (a committee) that I had no right to his movable or immovable property and I could go wherever I desired. On October 11, 1991, a meeting was held. The elders of the villagers urged me to remain in my own Hindu religion. I told them that I had decided firmly to leave the Hindu society and had accepted Jesus Christ.

All present there were wonder struck when I declared my decision. There were tears in my mother's eyes. I prayed to God as I was leaving this house of mine. I asked for His help and guidance for my future. The next morning at 8 a.m., I left my house and family and went to Dongargenh and started living with the believers. Even here people of the Hindu Council gave me trouble. They tried to explain things to me. My professors said that I was hypnotized. My friends also advised me not to take this step. But Jesus Christ gave me the strength and courage to remain in faith.

When I asked the believers of God to baptize me as a real witness of God, they advised me to wait and consider more fully my decision. I told them I had fully thought over the matter. After coming to light, I didn't want to return to darkness. When I was going to the court to have my affidavit made, again God's servants pressed me to think before taking this step. I told them that I would not go back and was even willing to die if I had to in order to take this narrow path.

I was baptized in witness to Jesus Christ as my Savior. On January 1, 1992, I became officially "a Christian" and a member of the congregation. Before I had accepted Christ, I had walked with a great burden. I had tried to fulfill the desires of life and I felt weary. Now I feel Jesus Christ is with me and He has carried away all my burdens and worries on Him. Now I feel lighthearted and happy. I have dedicated my whole life to His service. I am trying my best to walk in His steps, carrying His cross.

At present, I'm a Bible student in a Bible college. I request you to remember me in your prayers, so I may grow more and more in His faith and glory every day. May God's name be praised and glorified.

Western India

T he Wesleyan Church in western India has recently experienced several incidents of religious persecution. One of the things that especially upsets the Hindu extremists is the salvation and staunch faith of common people—fishermen, bus conductors, watchmen, leather tanners, policemen, factory workers, clerks. When a tanner, who is of the lowest caste within Hinduism, accepts Christ and staunchly and fervently serves Him, it upsets the balance of the local Hindu community. Christianity gives a dignity to a low caste person that is often appealing to others of his caste. The result is often a Christian group that no longer kowtows to members of a "superior" caste. This is an undercurrent in almost all of these following stories. On the other hand, when an upper caste person accepts Christ and "stoops" to associate on an equal basis with low caste persons, this is insulting to the all-pervasive caste-consciousness in India. This is a primary undercurrent in the case of the Wapi GID Church, although it is not specifically stated. A Hindu person who becomes a Christian goes against the weight of community and religious mores. Burning household gods and ignoring "omens" of death or "bad luck" add to the surety of the opposition. All of these things may be seen in the following stories of faith in India at the local level, which is the place where faith really counts.

Hindu Gods Lack Peace

Atul Church

(told by Dr. Samuel Justin)

In Gugarat conference there are thirteen churches in the cities and towns. The Atul church was organized in 1974. There were some old Christian families in that area, but I want to tell you about one of the new families that came to Christ. The name of the husband is Raju and Jaya is the name of his wife. They were Hindus, but they were coming to the worship every Sunday. They thought that if they would accept the Lord Jesus Christ, there would be change in their lives. When they were Hindus, there was no peace in the family. They quarreled often among themselves.

The pastor of that church worked with them and tried to teach them, and for many months they attended the worship services. After six or seven months they were baptized. A great change came in their lives, and there was peace in the family. They really accepted Jesus, the Prince of Peace. They are very regular with their family in all the church activities and meetings. Jaya and Raju are true Christians and they often give their witness. If they had not come by faith to Jesus Christ, there would have been no peace in their family life. They would have probably been separated, but now they are living the true Christian life. They are very active and strong in their Christian faith, and in all things they are praying. They have become knowledgeable in the Bible and their children have become strong in the faith. They have also brought two other families to the church through their testimony of what God has done in their life. We know that when Jesus comes into a life, even the family life is changed.

Fishermen Find Faith

Dandi Church
(told by Dr. Samuel Justin)

D andi is a fishing village and most of the people of that small village go into the ocean early in the morning and come back late with fish. They have boats and depend on the fishing business. For many years we have had a church there. We had missionaries and medical work there. But the area was dry. The missionaries and the national workers labored together, but the fruits were few. We continued to pray and worked hard and within just the last few years we have seen the harvest.

There was a man named Natu. He was a Hindu man and every day he was going to the ocean to fish. I think in 1992 Dr. and Mrs. Ross came to visit our Wesleyan field from Japan. I arranged a meeting for them at Dandi. This man came to that worship service. He came to me after the service and told me that after two days he was going to put a new boat into the water for fishing. So he asked us to come and pray for his new boat. So I said yes, we would come and pray for his boat. I asked Dr. Barry Ross to go on the seashore with some of the church people to pray for the boat. So Dr. Ross put his hand on the boat and prayed for God's blessing. After two days Natu put the new boat to sea. He got a big catch. When he came in the evening, he called the pastor to the seashore and said, "This is a miracle. That missionary prayed for my boat and this is the biggest catch I have ever gotten." So he continued to participate in the church services. Sunday morning he did not go to the sea, but came to church with the other Christian fishermen. Pastor taught him and after a few months he was baptized. Today, Natu and his wife and son are members of our Dandi church. Whenever we go to Dandi we meet him and he reminds us of that wonderful day when his boat was blessed and God gave him a big catch. Once he said he would never forget that day, but the better day was the day he and his wife were baptized.

Now I will tell you about a man who was the Saul of Dandi who became Paul. His name is Premu. Many years before this, his father had become a Christian (and is still a member at Dandi) but this eldest son of the family hated Christianity. Some years before this, Premu's son, Bharat, and his wife became Christians. But Premu was not pleased with his son. He always troubled them. He would also harass believers who were not yet baptized by throwing stones at them when they went to church. Sometimes he would try to stop them on the way. In the Dandi church people gathered every day in the church for prayer from 7:30 to 9 p.m. Premu was causing problems for the church people and

 when they would leave church, he would often be drunk and curse them. But all these years his son and wife were praying for him with tears, every day, that God would win him for His glory. Finally, the Lord heard this prayer. One day Bharat came to Pardi with the good news that his father wanted to be a Christian. I could hardly believe this statement. But the pastor said it was true. In that week Premu began to come to church. He became so humble and broken and came to the evening prayer meetings. We fixed a date for the baptism and about 400 people gathered to see this baptism. Even some of Premu's friends who had been persecuting Christians came because they thought something would happen. When we went there I saw that not only Premu but also his wife was there. He said his wife had also asked to be baptized because she was so astonished at the change in his life. She never believed that her husband would become a Christian. It was a big festival, and other Wesleyan churches also came to be a part of this festival. He testified before this big group and he asked to go around to all the churches and give his testimony. So I arranged and went with him. He is a bus conductor and he told his officers in the bus depot. Sometimes he gives his testimony to the people on his bus. He is so happy. He left drinking, he left smoking, and now he is a true Christian. Last year he was elected to represent his church as their delegate to the district conference, and he gave his testimony to the conference. He is very articulate in prayer or in giving his testimony. He says that he is a regular reader of the Bible and gets strength from it for the day. He has really become the Paul of Dandi Church.

Ramish Bari has been pastoring in the Sukish church. When he accepted Christ, his whole family turned against him. Even his own father put a price on his head. He declared that if someone would kill Ramish, he would give him 25,000 rupees. Many of Ramish's relatives accepted that challenge. Ramish lived in Dandi and was working in the government office about 40 miles from Dandi. He had to travel by public transport. His father arranged with some people to attack him. But God protected him every time. Yet his father did not give up. So finally, Ramish had to move to another place. He left his village and his house, his fields and his two fishing boats. His father blackballed him, telling people they should not fish or work fields for him. Then his father took his boats and property. Still Ramish continued to serve the Lord Jesus with joy. He lost everything, but Jesus Christ is with him. For the last two years he has been a lay person. He now lives near Pardi. He says that what he now has is worth far more than his fields, boat, and house. He is well educated and has a very nice Christian library in his home. He has been elected as our conference secretary. Don't forget to pray for Ramish. He is a precious soul in our church. God is going to use him in a mighty way in His Kingdom.

Fire Worshiping Parsee at Pardi

•••••••••••••••••••••••••

(told by Dr. Samuel Justin)

I want to tell you the true story about our Pardi Church. There is a man whose name is Kaki. His ancestors were from Iran and he is a Parsee. He was staying near Pardi in a village where his parents lived. His father was a rich farmer. From his childhood, Kaki went in the crooked way. During his school hour he was wandering here and there with bad company. He became a smuggler, gambler, drunkard, and eventually a gang leader. His gang was robbing the people and breaking into houses. They often beat people and took their ornaments and other precious things. Finally he left for many years. People thought that Kaki had died. But after fourteen or fifteen years he returned. One evening I was sitting on my porch and I saw a man coming toward me. He asked me, "Who is the pastor here?" I told myself, "Ask him where he's coming from." He said, "You don't recognize me? I'm from this area. I'm from Sukesh. My name is Kaki." Then he began to tell me he was not the Kaki of days before. He said he was a new Kaki. But I could not trust him. His jeep was outside the church compound and I saw someone in his jeep. I asked, "Is someone there with you?" He said, "Yes, I have family." His wife and four children were there, so I invited them to come in. Then he said, "You have heard many bad things about me. But God has saved me and I want to stay in this area and join the Wesleyan church." I asked, "Why?" He said he was from the village of Sukesh where The Wesleyan Church is well known. But still I didn't trust him. I asked him where he was going to stay. He said he had bought a big house in Valsad. This is about eleven kilometers from Pardi, and he invited me to come to his house. So I went with my wife and talked to him and he asked that we come every week to visit and pray with him. I asked him how this change came about.

He said that he had become a smuggler, gambler and drunkard and it was difficult for him to stay in this area. He left and went to Bombay and from Bombay went to Saudi Arabia, where he earned very good money. So he came back after some years to India. He was staying in the city of Bangor and then he met a girl named Rada. Rada was from a high caste Brahman family. She promised him that she would marry him. They were married and one day a Christian evangelist came to their home. Rada was baptized and became a Christian. Kaki was still not living the right way. When Rada was reading the Bible, he would turn on the radio and make a racket to disturb her. Whenever they would pray in the home, Kaki would leave and would not join. Rada was praying and praying for him. They had a good family life but Rada was not satisfied. After a few months Kaki became seriously ill and was put into the hospital. The doctors told Rada that within a few weeks he would be dead. But Rada had faith. She told the Hindu doctor that she had one God, Jesus, to whom she would pray and that Jesus would heal him. The doctor laughed at her. She asked the doctor to keep him in the hospital, so the doctor allowed this request. And every day before his bed, Rada prayed with tears. Then one night Kaki was worse and told his wife that something would happen. Rada was fearful and again began to pray earnestly. About midnight or one o'clock, the hospital room was filled with light. Kaki looked and Rada was asleep. Kaki tried to see the source of the light, but there was no source. He couldn't understand. Then he listened and heard a sweet voice, "Dear son, you will be free from your sickness and you will be My witness. I am Jesus." He woke his wife up and told her all he had seen and heard. The next day the doctors were surprised at his improvement. The same doctor that had predicted his death was astonished. Rada told him that Jesus had talked with her husband and promised he would be healed. After a week Kaki was discharged and today he is so happy. He was baptized and is now with us in our area.

Kaki and his whole family go in his jeep every Sunday after the morning service to the villages and take the gospel message, tracts and Christian literature. He went to his own village where he was brought up, but the people there would not listen. Kaki told them that Jesus had changed his life, that he was no longer a smuggler, gambler or drunkard. But people could not believe. They said, "Kaki please don't try to con us. After many years you are here, but we know that a person cannot give up those kinds of habits." But Kaki continued to go back for many Sundays and witnessed to them. Finally, they began to listen to him. He went to the people of his own caste, the Parsee people, Iranian people, and distributed Bibles and tracts. But these people hated him. They drove him out of their houses. These Parsee people worship fire and they said, "We have our god." Kaki still continued to witness to them.

The whole family is regular in church attendance and outreach. He is very regular in his giving. Pray for Kaki and Rada and their family. Pray for the Pardi Wesleyan Church.

Adopted as a Son

Samuel Justin

In 1929, a Wesleyan missionary lady took three orphans from the Bombay government orphanage. I was one of them. Rev. C. M. Justin and Daiah Justin adopted me. I think this was God's plan. My adoptive parents were workers in the Wesleyan church in Gujarat and they had four sons, but they all died. If they had not lost their own children, they would not have adopted me. I was six months old, but I had such bad sight that I was almost blind. By the time I was five years old, I could not see past three feet. But my dear parents prayed and prayed for me. When I entered school I got glasses. The teacher thought I could not study, but my parents were praying and praying and my sight was improving. I finally was able to graduate from secondary school.

At that time I was thinking of joining the railway service. The British were here and the railway service was a place of honor. It had a good salary and there was good housing and so it had an attraction. But my parents had dedicated me for the Lord's ministry from the beginning, and God heard their prayer. I was in a convention after graduation. In a morning prayer meeting, I felt God touch my heart and call me to ministry. When I came from there, I applied for training.

At that time there were many missionaries and a missionary administration in our church. One of the missionaries who was in charge of administration told me that first I needed to work in our mission school as a schoolteacher, which I did for four years. Then God told me it was time to go for training. So I applied again to the conference and I was accepted as an evangelist. My heart was full of joy. My eyesight was not as good as others, but I could function better than before. I could ride a bicycle or motorcycle. Then for many years I was an evangelist. In 1967, God gave me a ministry in a different way. I am so glad that my two boys are also called to ministry.

Fifteen Gods Burned
•••••••••••••••••••••••••
Sukesh Village
(told by Dr. Samuel Justin)

W hen our conference started the church in this area there was much opposition, but after many months of struggling God opened the way. One family came to the Lord Jesus Christ. They were a husband and wife and a small child. The husband's name was Bavabhi and the wife's name was Kekubai. They were both worshipers of different idols. They were tanners, and sold skins and made sandals. In India, the tanners are the cobblers and are lower caste people. When our conference started the church in Sukesh village, it was about nine miles from Pardi. The missionaries and the Indian pastors took a tent and started the work.

The result of the labor was this family coming to the Lord. The other people of their caste opposed them when they became Christians. The Christians told them to burn all their fetishes and idols that were made from wood. Bavabhi thought it would be difficult for him. No doubt he had faith, but he was afraid to burn the Hindu idols. But the missionary and the national workers encouraged him; they told him to stand aside and they would burn his personal temple with the six gods and nine goddesses in it. So he announced to the village that on the next day at a certain time, the missionary and national workers would come burn this temple and burn these wooden idols. So many people gathered over there—more than a hundred people. The workers were afraid in the beginning because there could be a riot. They prayed in Bavabhi's home and they prayed in the compound. They went to the small temple where all the wooden gods and goddesses were fixed. Again they prayed there. None of the tanners were Christians, and they wanted to see what would happen. After prayer one of the pastors put the fire into the small temple. After a half hour all the gods and goddesses turned into ash. The people didn't speak a word. But they were whispering among themselves that the gods and goddesses would punish Bavabhi and the Christian workers. They scattered from there out of fear of what would happen, but nothing happened. The people began to drop by from time to time and ask, "Has something happened?" But when they asked, they discovered this couple was so happy; they had joy in their hearts and they had no fear, not at all.

This couple gave a piece of land to build the church building. Then three more families were converted and were baptized. Today in Sukesh there is an organized church with a church building and a pastor. There are about forty members in that church. Our God is wonderful. In the beginning, our workers were afraid of attack because of burning their gods. But nothing happened and our God, the Lord Jesus Christ, became the victor. Bavabhi, Kekubai and their son are still members of the Sukesh church. They are helping us in evangelism and church activities. Their hearts are full of joy and peace and they are satisfied. Now the church is growing to the point that not only are we building a pastor's house, but we are going to have to build a bigger church building.

Trying Salvation for Free

Talasari Village
(told by Dr. Samuel Justin)

We organized the new church in Talasari four years ago. They have about sixty members in that church now. One morning one of the tribal people came to the church and said that he wanted to accept Jesus as his Lord. Then the pastor asked, "Why?" In that church's area, there is much opposition to our Christian work, and it was possible that this man was sent as a trick to cause trouble. When we were building the church building, people opposed us and applied to the police department and to the government to try to get the building stopped. The government took some actions, but we thank God now that we have a church building and are able to have regular church services. Many people have joined that church. So this tribal man came and the pastor asked him, "Why do you want to have joined the Christian church? We are not giving out anything."

There were some Roman Catholic churches in that area giving the people free grain and clothes. They gave free books and uniforms to the students in order to attract the people to their institution. But we Protestants are not working in the same way. The pastor was trying to be careful in asking these questions. He told the man, "We do not give grain, or a piece of cloth, or something for your children." This man replied, "These Catholic people give us all the material things but they cannot give us peace. Me and my family want real peace. One of your church members came to my house and told me how God was giving him peace. God is giving him joy." So the pastor invited this tribal man to come to the worship service. Then the pastor took time to explain the gospel message to him and told him to bring his wife and three children. The next Sunday the whole family came.

The Catholic priest insisted that this man should not come to our church. He told him that he would give him more than he had been given in the past. He told him that if he needed money, he would give him money. He told him that if he needed more grain, he would give it. He would give more clothes. This tribal man would not agree. He said he was looking for real peace, not some "things." After three months his whole family was baptized and his three children were dedicated. They are now full members of the Talasari Church.

People are so hungry for peace, real peace. They don't get peace from material things. They are not satisfied with the grain or the clothes, but some people want the real peace in their hearts. We are so thankful to God that He can give that peace.

The Policeman Who Prayed

●●●●●●●●●●●●●●●●●●●●●●●●

Tulsi

(told by Dr. Samuel Justin)

In the Dagamar Wesleyan Church where Rev. Joel Justin is the pastor, a policeman in uniform entered the church during a morning service. After the worship service he expressed a desire to accept Christianity. Joel asked, "Why do you want to join Christianity? Why do you want to accept Jesus Christ as your Lord?" The policeman told him that after two days he would return and tell him. Then the policeman returned with his wife and children. They decided to become Christians. Again the pastor asked them why they wanted to become Christians. Then this policeman, whose name is Tulsi, said that he had read much about the Lord Jesus Christ. He was a person of literature and he told Joel that he had a New Testament that he had gotten somewhere and had been reading about the life of Christ. And then the Lord Jesus began to work in his heart and told him to accept Him. So he came to the Dagamar church for that morning service. The pastor taught them about our doctrines, biblical truths, and about Jesus Christ who gives forgiveness from sins. He taught them for six months about the things they needed to know. Thus, the family was very well prepared for baptism. The day came and we had a big convention at the Pardi Wesleyan Retreat center. The Asian area director, Dr. Barry Ross, was there. Tulsi and his wife were baptized with other Hindu people in the presence of about 300 people that day. We praise the Lord that God worked in his heart.

He came and told the pastor that he did not feel he could continue to live the Christian faith and be a policeman, because policemen sometimes have to do many wrong things. Sometimes there was the temptation of taking bribes and speaking a lie. So it was very difficult for him because when he was not a Christian he had experienced all of these things. But now Christ was working in his heart and Tulsi didn't know what to do. The pastor encouraged him and told him to pray. He told him, "When you have a temptation to take a bribe, or to do the things that are not right, you pray to the Lord Jesus Christ. You must work faithfully and with justice in the fear of the Lord Jesus." So Tulsi went back. After a few months he came back to meet with the pastor privately because he was being transferred. But he and his wife would often return and participate in the church. They continued to hold their membership there also. One day he gave his testimony. He said God was helping him to do the policeman's work as a Christian. He said it was difficult and that he had made mistakes. But he would always go to God and God had forgiven and strengthened him. They are still strong in faith and faithful members of the church. We are so very thankful to God that He is using a policeman to witness for Him. Tulsi has declared in his department that he has become a Christian. He has endured much ridicule but he is still strong in his faith.

Brothers in Christ
• •
Wadafalia Church
(told by Dr. Samuel Justin)

We recently had the dedication of the beautiful church building at Wadafalia. In 1962, two other workers and I fixed our tent in that village and we began to preach about the Lord Jesus Christ. The village was a stronghold of Hinduism. They did not oppose us at that time. We had evening service with the "magic lantern" (strip slides on a pressure lamp projector) of the life of the Lord Jesus Christ, the Good Samaritan and other Bible stories. One night after the service, we were ready to go to sleep when two men, Garnabhai and Chandabhai, came to our tent and requested to speak with us. That night we had shown the story of the prodigal son. These two brothers thought they were the prodigal sons. When we showed the picture on the screen, the Holy Spirit was working in their hearts. They wanted to know what they could do to come out from all the evil things they were doing.

 They told us they were gambling, drinking, stealing, and breaking the commandments. We told them, "Don't worry, the Lord Jesus Christ came to take us out from all these evil things." We were there for fifteen days. Their family members also were with them and accepted the Christian teaching after the night service. We stayed up late into the night teaching them. These two brothers and their wives were baptized.

In 1962 we had not organized a church in that area, but these people were very faithful. In 1990 we organized a church there. From 1962 to 1990 these two families did not sit quietly, but they witnessed to everyone about the joy and peace in their hearts. They went from house to house and told people of their joy. After a few years, other families joined in the worship of the Lord Jesus Christ. Today we have twelve families who were once Hindus in that church. They have been baptized and have all suffered much persecution from the people in that area. In the beginning, all the children were coming to the Sunday school. Then other people began to encourage the Hindu children to persecute the Christian children. But these children are also strong in the Christian faith. And now once again they have begun to come to the Sunday school. Even some of the non-Christian people have begun to come to the church. Some years before this area was hard, but now we see hope for the growth of the church. There is not even one family in that church who has transferred from another Christian church. They have all come from Hinduism.

Many of the officials of The Wesleyan Church in America have visited this church and have seen the hardships we have overcome. Now we have a very beautiful church building which was dedicated June 8, 1997. We thank God that He supplied our need and that we were able to build a very beautiful church building. Presently, ten ministerial candidates with Hindu backgrounds are being taught Christian doctrine.

The political atmosphere has changed and there is now much political opposition to the Christian work. But we know our God is an almighty God. So we have a good hope that many with Hindu backgrounds will come to know the Lord Jesus.

The Test of a Child

• •

Wapi Wesleyan Church

(told by Dr. Samuel Justin)

We have two Wesleyan churches in Wapi. One was organized in 1991 and since then, five couples have been baptized. I will tell the story about one couple.

They were Hindus and they were working in a paper mill. They were baptized and joined the Wapi church. After three months they lost their only daughter, who was two years old. The father and mother worked in the paper mill and this girl was cared for by a neighbor. The little girl was outside the gate playing with other children and a big truck ran into them. The little girl died. They informed the parents and they rushed from the paper mill and saw that their dear child was very badly crushed. The truck driver ran away. So they called the pastor and there was a funeral at the Wapi church. But some Hindu neighbors told them, "Jesing Bai and Husung, you know why this thing happened? It is because you have given up your Hindu gods and they are angry. This is why this has happened."

In the beginning they were upset. But the church people continued to visit and pray for them. Finally they answered those neighbors, "We will never believe that this is the punishment because we accepted the Lord Jesus Christ. No doubt we have lost our daughter. But we will never forsake the Lord Jesus Christ. He has given to us and now He has taken away." This couple is now strong in the Lord and in their faith, and they again have the joy of the Lord in their hearts. They are quite new; they have only been baptized about a year and do not have much spiritual experience. Their simple faith is commendable.

Jesing is telling people that death is coming to each house, to each family, whether Christian or non-Christian. In the same way death can come to our family, but we have a hope that goes beyond death.

Japan

T he salvation experience is not the same for every individual; each is unique. Often the Lord uses cultural expectations to break through the barriers which would hinder an individual from coming to Jesus, as in the story of Mrs. Inage.

Mrs. Inage Comes To Jesus

Toyomi Inage

(told by Barry and Margaret Ross)

M rs. Inage came to our home on one of those evenings when she wasn't supposed to be there. At least we had made no plans for her presence. You see, it was a summer Sunday evening when there was no evening service at our Japanese church. We were free! And three other nearby

86

missionary families were also free. Together we were to meet at our home for our once-a-month Sunday evening missionary fellowship time of singing, praying and studying the Bible in English. You see, all of us worked daily with the Japanese people, speaking the Japanese language, pushing aside our American ways as much as possible. This fellowship on one Sunday evening a month was a needed time to be ourselves, in our own language. So we do not invite any Japanese to this meeting. But God had another plan for this summer Sunday evening. At 2 p.m. the phone rang.

"Hello, Margaret. This is Lucy."

Lucy is a lovely Korean lady. She had become a Christian out of a Buddhist background just a few months before. Every month she came to Margaret's cooking class and Bible study and was attending Immanuel Church.

"Margaret," she continued, "I'm coming to your house this evening. And I'm bringing my Japanese husband. And, by the way, Mrs. Inage is coming too, with her eighteen-year-old daughter, Akiko. Can your husband meet Mrs. Inage at the train station at 5 o'clock?"

"Who is Mrs. Inage?" Margaret asked.

"Oh, don't you remember? I've talked about her before. She's my dearest Japanese friend. She lives not far from your home. Her husband is an alcoholic. There's much trouble in her home. She's terribly unhappy. She's seen a change in me since I became a Christian and is wondering what has caused my new happiness. I've told her that if she will only come to Margaret's home she will laugh again. So I've invited her to your home tonight!"

"No, no, this can't be," thought Margaret. "This is our evening. Lucy is the only one of the four coming who speaks English. We'll have to use Japanese." Silently she prayed, "Dear Jesus, what would you have me do?"

"Okay, Lucy. Please come. My husband will meet your friend at the station. We'll have a good time," Margaret enthusiastically answered.

The four guests arrived. The six other missionaries came, with three very undisciplined children. It was a fun evening, but one of those times when in our hearts we doubted that God could have spoken to these unbelieving Buddhist hearts. We sang Christian songs in English and Japanese. We talked in both languages. One missionary told nonstop jokes in Japanese. The uncontrollable children ran up and down the stairs, in and out the door, shouting in through the windows from the yard. To us, the evening was a mess! But Mrs. Inage and her daughter began to laugh, and laugh, and laugh. They joined in the songs. They seemed to be having a good time.

By 10 p.m. everyone had left. Margaret and I straightened the furniture, washed up the dishes and fell into bed. Before dropping off to sleep, I prayed, "Oh Jesus, could you have used such an evening to speak to a broken, hurting heart? Couldn't the evening have been more spiritual?"

Monday morning at 8 a.m. the phone rang. It was Mrs. Inage.

"Thank you, thank you," she began. "Last evening was the best time I've had in a long time. This morning Akiko is even singing some of those church songs around the house. She says she remembers singing some of them in a Sunday school she attended a few times when she was a little girl. Thank you for such a wonderful time!"

I hung up the phone and prayed, "Oh, Jesus, You were here last night. A seed has been planted in Mrs. Inage's heart. Can you make it grow?"

Mrs. Inage began coming to our church. She heard Pastor Joshua Tsutada preach about God's love. She came to our home again and again. We tried to show her God's love. But she continued to be a very troubled woman. She and her two daughters moved out of her home to be away from her alcoholic husband.

Early one Thursday morning near the end of the summer, Mrs. Inage called. Excitedly she began, "Pastor Ross, a strange thing happened to me in the night. About 4 o'clock this morning, 'someone' came into my room. I awakened, but could see no one. There was a strange light in my room. I was frightened at first, but then there came to me a feeling of 'love' in my room. And into my heart came the thought, 'Pastor and Mrs. Ross love me. Lucy loves me. The people at the church love me. Pastor Tsutada talked about God's love. Could this be God's love in my room? Could it even be God himself?' There came to my heart a great peace. Pastor Ross, I think I'm a Christian now."

I related this story to Pastor Tsutada. I asked if he thought God would make Himself known to someone in this manner. He urged me not to doubt that God has many ways of coming to people. The next Sunday after morning worship, Pastor Tsutada taught Mrs. Inage the steps to becoming a Christian. He told her of Jesus' death on the cross and His resurrection. He told her the meaning of sin and explained her need to repent from her sin and turn in believing faith to Jesus. Mrs. Inage prayed a clear prayer of repentance and belief. At 12:32 p.m. on that Sunday, Mrs. Inage became a Christian. She will often refer to that special day and that exact time as her spiritual birthday.

Myanmar

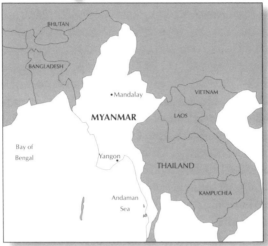

The country of Myanmar (or Burma, as it is commonly known) is primarily Buddhist (above 90%). They boast of one million pagodas—one of which is layered with seven tons of gold and topped with 5000 diamonds—and one million Buddhist monks. While Buddhism is not officially the state religion, it is equated with nationalism. There is a common understanding that says you can't really be a patriotic person without being Buddhist. Therefore, Christians are often seen as outsiders, or nonpatriots, and evangelism is viewed as an antipatriotic act.

Buddha Has No Way
••••••••••••••••••••••••

Maung Chit Ko Ko

I grew up in an extremist Buddhist home. My father was a part-time monk. He had strongly accepted Buddhism and sacrificed for his beliefs. In the year 1993, I became interested in knowing about the Christian religion. I visited around to the churches and participated in their worship. I was easily convinced by their worship and the free and happy fellowship they enjoyed.

During 1995-1996, the year I was employed in the engineering department of the Government as departmental officer, I studied the Bible and was influenced day by day. One day I saw a miracle of God upon a paralyzed man through prayer. It was so amazing and I understood that prophecies of the Christian book were coming true in my own sight, in this new era.

I wanted to be a Christian at once and I received Jesus Christ as my Lord and my Savior. I have attended and participated in regular church worship, which led me to have a strong faith and peace in my inner spiritual life for everyday life.

Because I was not well-grounded in the Christian doctrine, I followed an evangelist in his camp meeting services and crusades in many villages around Kalemyo Township. I was very happy in this ministry serving among Myanmar Buddhists of my own nation. In this ministry we visited house to house, witnessing from the Bible, praying, giving testimony, and giving tracts or Bibles in the Myanmar (Burmese) language. We were friendly and helped them with their physical needs. I followed this man for forty days.

After I became a Christian, I did not suffer physical opposition from my family or neighbors. They did not physically beat me, but they threatened me verbally. My father did not like that I was a Christian, giving my whole life for the gospel. He wanted me to help him in our household, especially since I would be the house-holder after he died. But I could not accept the aims of my father and his will because I have sacrificed my whole life for the gospel. I especially wanted to preach to my own people of Myanmar who are Buddhists. Because of this, I dare not think of my relationship with my family. However, I wish that my parents and all of my brothers and sisters will become Christians some day and that we will live and worship together.

I knew that I would be facing many kinds of problems after some days, because even though Buddhism is not legally nationalized in Myanmar, almost all strong nationalists of Myanmar are Buddhists. There was one Myanmar nationalist who was converted from Buddhism to Christianity, and from his experience I understood that it would not be easy for me to minister to Myanmar nationalists. I also recognized that I needed to join with a church immediately. I came to know about the Wesleyan Church of Myanmar and its plan for ministry in new areas, especially among the Buddhists of Myanmar. They were in the process of training nine people for film ministry. I was pleased to know that there is a church that has a real ministry among the Myanmar Buddhists. I am now a part of that ministry to Buddhists.

The One True Religion

Win Maung

A mong the populations of the world there are four main religions: Islamic, Hindu, Buddhist, and Christian. I had thought that the worship of Buddha was the only one true religion. I have now come to understand that the only true religion is Christianity. One of the people who brought me to this conclusion was Mother Teresa. Because of reading about the life and service of Mother Teresa, I had a mind to study the Bible to understand what a Christian was.

As I read the Bible in the beginning, there were many verses that I could not understand. But I met some Christian friends who were able to explain the Bible and the doctrine of Christianity to me. I was baptized on December 27, 1995, by Rev. Kyaw Tha Aung. I was so happy that I had become a Christian and a new man.

I did not dare tell my parents or my brothers and sisters that I had become a Christian and had accepted Jesus Christ as my Lord and Savior. They began to see the changes in my life, especially that I began to attend church every Sunday. So problems came from my family more and more. My heart was very heavy and I thought that the best thing for me was to die. So I drank some poison at night, but I did not die. My God did not allow for me to die and spared my life for His Kingdom. After I had drunk the poison, my family and friends tried to persuade me to turn again to Buddhism, so that I would live with them more easily. But I was persuaded by now that I would be a disciple of the Lord Jesus, my Savior, and I would serve His Kingdom. I began to feel that God wanted me to preach the good news among Myanmar Buddhists. On March 18, 1996, I left my family in love and in peace. I also left my friends and hope of any earthly inheritance.

I knew that my first task was to train for the ministry. God answered all my prayers in this when I joined the ministerial program for Christian life and Biblical training. After the training, I started the ministry in Kusein village. I also had a circuit in other villages of that area.

I did not have full support in my ministry, but simply served by faith. Sometimes I was weak and nearly wanted to go back home, but I knew that God was with me and gave me compassion to serve my people.

At first I visited house to house and gave little tracts in the Myanmar language. I prayed with people, read the Bible and explained its meaning, and discussed the difference between Christianity and other religions. New believers were added day by day. We have now started to build a little church in Kusein village. I have taught these believers to practice their Christianity as soon as they become Christians.

Many times and in many ways, I met problems and difficulties in my ministry. But I am happy and pleased that I am able to preach the gospel to Myanmar Buddhists. The problems that I met helped me understand that I needed to join with the living church, which would be giving me support in my ministry. Therefore I came to Tahan and met with the leaders of the Wesleyan Church of Myanmar. I believe that God gave me guidance to meet with the Wesleyan Church of Myanmar because they had a strategic plan of ministry in new areas—especially among Myanmar Buddhists.

Pakistan

I n many rural areas religion is mixed. While people may call themselves "Muslims," "Buddhists" or even "Christians," their religious practice may actually be a mixture of animism (worship of spirits and metaphysical powers) and another major religion. This is the case in many of the following stories.

Idols and Charms Cannot Save

●●●●●●●●●●●●●●●●●●●●●●●●
Anwar Masih
(told by Rev. E. Bahadur)

Anwar Masih was born into a Christian family. But when he grew up, he left his village and went to the city in search of a job. After a lot of disappointment and hardship in the city, he met some idol worshipers. He started wearing amulets around his neck because he thought wearing them would help him find everlasting life and give him his desires. But when he was still not satisfied, he returned home after many years. His family was horrified at his condition and agonized over the amulets that he wore. A Wesleyan pastor shared the Bible with him and showed him how he could have salvation and peace of mind. When Anwar Masih studied the Word of God, he found that whatever he wanted in life was found in the Bible. He changed his way of life and became a true Christian. He knows he has found the way to salvation.

Conversion Brings Freedom

●●●●●●●●●●●●●●●●●●●●●●●●
Aslam Masih
(told by Rev. E. Bahadur)

Aslam Masih is a middle-aged man and lives in Sharakpur. He was involved in adultery and illegal trading. In his early life, he used to go to church along with his parents who were good Christians. As he grew and became an adult, he entered a company of people who were carrying on criminal business. They influenced him with the glamour of money, selling liquor and other crimes of debauchery. He continued fearlessly to commit various violations each day. But one day he was in deep trouble and his life was in danger.

He approached Rev. E. Bahadur and wanted him to help him find a way out of the darkness. He knew that the law enforcement people were after him to throw him behind bars for the rest of his life.

Rev. Bahadur had a counseling session with him and explained how he could get rid of his past life by accepting the Lord Jesus Christ as his Savior. They both prayed and the Holy Spirit touched his soul. He promised never, ever to go back to his past. Today he is an active Christian leading a life full of joy.

Life of Sin Exchanged for Peace

Barkat Masih

(told by Rev. E. Bahadur)

Barkat Masih lives in the village of Essan in Sheikhupura District. He was deeply involved in various crimes for pleasure and money. Although he was born in a Christian family, his way of life did not reflect his Christian training. Whenever the local pastor of the church invited him to join in prayer meetings, Barkat would simply laugh at him. This worried the pastor and he continued to pray for Barkat.

One day Barkat was very upset and terrified because he had done something wrong. He was constantly bothered by his conscience and was searching for a way out. The pastor of his church had arranged a youth meeting one evening to pray for the sick and downtrodden people. When Barkat heard of this meeting, he came along with the rest of the people of that village. The sermon that evening was from Matthew 11:28, "Come to me, all you who are weary and burdened, and I will give you rest." He was deeply touched by the Holy Spirit. His burdens and worries were gone, and he felt peace inside. He testified about his experience of repentance and acceptance of the Lord Jesus Christ as his Savior. He is now an active Christian.

Magician - Sleight of Heart
••••••••••••••••••••••••
Boota Masih
(told by Rev. E. Bahadur)

Boota Masih of More Khunda was a magician. His family had created their own god out of clay and worshiped it in their home. When Boota became older, he started training in black magic and soon was selling amulets. Lots of women used to visit his home to get amulets so that they could bear a child. Others came because they wanted help finding a job, recovering from sickness or marrying a desirable girl. But then Boota's son became sick for two months. He tried all his magic and amulets, but nothing helped. One day, Boota visited the camp meeting at Wesleyan Headquarters with his son. He also came to one of the services and heard the Word of God. After the sermon, an altar call was given for those who were sick or far from God. Father and son both went to the altar. His son was healed and Boota promised to give up magic arts and idol worship. He accepted the Lord Jesus Christ as his Savior, became an active member of the church and has left magic arts forever.

Pakistani Pagan Prays
••••••••••••••••••••••••
Jano Bibi
(told by Rev. E. Bahadur)

Jano Bibi lives in Kalalwala, Punjab, Pakistan. Two years ago one of the Wesleyan pastors visited her house and invited her to Sunday service at the local Wesleyan church. She said, "Pastor, do not pray, I shall be facing off with the church." The Pastor was quite concerned about this woman. He knew that she was involved in idol worship and he wanted to save her life and bring her out of the darkness. But she would not respond to the Word of God.

The Wesleyan pastor did not lose heart, but continued praying for her life. During those days, the Women's Conference took place at the Sharakpur Wesleyan Headquarters. The subject of the conference was "What is the Role of Women According to the Bible?" Jano was invited again to attend the conference but, as usual, she was unwilling to go and hear the Word of God. The same day the conference was taking place, she had to come to Sharakpur to do her shopping. Since a group of women was going to the conference, she joined them to travel to the market. When they reached the conference venue, she somehow changed her mind and came to the meeting. When she heard the Word of God from the Bible, the Holy Spirit worked and her life changed then and there. She accepted the Lord Jesus Christ as her Savior. This woman had never prayed in her whole life and never went to Sunday services, but when she learned about Jesus Christ and His wonderful work and the role of women at the Crucifixion, it entirely changed her heart.

Jano Bibi is one of the most active members of the church and is living a life in Christ. She is blessed and saved.

Converted Bootlegger

Mani Masih
(told by Rev. E. Bahadur)

Mani Masih lives in Sharakpur, Pakistan. Three years ago, he became a saved Christian. Before that, he was involved in the illegal trading of liquor, an offense against the state law. Since he was making a lot of money through this business, his attitude was criminal. One day police raided his place of trading and he was caught selling liquor red-handed. He was put in prison and the police had all the evidence to send him to jail forever.

In the meantime, his wife contacted Rev. E. Bahadur to seek help to save the life of her husband. Rev. E. Bahadur managed to get permission from the local police officer for permission to counsel with Mani Masih. On meeting Mani, Rev. E. Bahadur shared with him the gospel from Acts 16:31 and reminded him of the promise God has made to us. They prayed together and the Holy Spirit touched his heart. He accepted the Lord Jesus Christ as his Savior.

Later Rev. Bahadur arranged a solicitor for him who, with the help of God, got him released from the custody of the police. He promised to never sell liquor again. Today he is a true Christian, growing in the Lord Jesus Christ, and an active member of the church.

Deliverance from Demons

Sardar Masih

(told by Rev. E. Bahadur)

R ev. Sardar Masih of Basara had five male members of his church whose wives were captive to bad spirits. Rev. Sardar was quite concerned for these families. He knew that only through the Word of God could he help them. Rev. Sardar told these women that only through Jesus Christ could they find the Savior. He counseled with them each day for ten consecutive days and the Lord blessed these women. The evil spirits released them, and they accepted the Lord Jesus Christ as their Savior. Now these men and women are the most active members of the Wesleyan Church. The Word of God shared with them was Mark 5:1-20 (the Gerasenes man) and Mark 16:17, "In my name they will drive out demons."

Sri Lanka

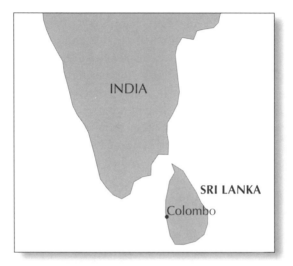

ri Lanka is a relatively small island at the southeastern corner of India. It was governed by the British as a colony under the umbrella of the Indian administration. Sri Lanka is primarily a Buddhist nation (only five percent Christian). One of its main treasures is a tooth thought to have been Buddha's. While Sri Lanka prides itself on its tolerance of religious plurality, religious conversion is discouraged and converts come under intense pressure to return. Buddhism espouses peace as its major tenet, but it is always in the future or in another lifetime. Real peace in this lifetime is not seen as a possibility. Peace, therefore, is a major theme in the following stories.

Birth of a Home Church
● ●
Calista Jawardena

The Wesleyan Church at Kolonnawa, the only established Wesleyan church in Sri Lanka, was born in my house three and a half years ago. At that time I was a nominal Roman Catholic, going faithfully to church with my two sons. I married a Buddhist who first became a Roman Catholic and subsequently a believer of the Lord Jesus Christ at an evangelistic meeting. However, I did not become a believer at the same time, although I attended meetings with him. Later my husband went overseas to work while I remained in Sri Lanka caring for my children.

While I was living my life without much to get excited about, Pastor Cedric, whom both my husband and I had known for quite awhile, visited our home. During his visit, he asked if he could start a Bible study meeting at our home. Without hesitation I agreed to the idea. The first meeting was conducted with just me and my two sons. As time went by, I began to understand the way of salvation and I fully committed my life to the Lord. My eleven- and twelve-year-old sons also committed their lives to the Lord. In the meantime, I also invited other people I knew to come to the meeting at my home. The group was growing in numbers, as my sons and I were growing in the Lord. Eventually we quit going to the Roman Catholic church and identified ourselves fully with The Wesleyan Church.

As I look back, I praise the Lord for saving me and my two boys, and my husband many years ago. I also praise the Lord for the fact that through our salvation, the Wesleyan church was born in my home. Today we are all walking with the Lord, happily and actively serving him through the week. May the name of Jesus be praised forever.

The Widow's Might

•••••••••••••••••••••••

H. W. Gnanawathie

At age forty, with three young children, I was suddenly widowed. I loved my husband very much and still weep over his death. I did everything I could to save him from the sudden illness that finally took his life. The tragedy left me utterly hopeless and unable to face life. I was just living a sad existence in order to bring up the children.

My mother began to attend the Wesleyan church. One day Pastor Cedric went with my mother to visit my son, who was in a prison sixty miles away. This was the first time I met Pastor Cedric. My twelve-year-old daughter, Sudarshani, and I joined them for the trip. While traveling, Pastor Cedric told us about Jesus. We stopped at a restaurant for a cup of tea and Pastor Cedric shared in more detail about the hope and freedom one can experience through Jesus Christ. Having heard for the first time in my life about Jesus in this manner, I asked my mother why someone didn't tell us about Jesus many years ago. A few weeks later, I allowed my daughter, Sudarshani, to go to church with my old mother. Sudarshani was, like me, a very devout Buddhist. She began to go to church faithfully from that time, although I still did not attend. She completely lost interest in all of her old ways of life and religion. She was drawn to Jesus like a magnet and not even I, her mother, could stop her. My daughter's life change left me surprised. I knew something really powerful had happened to her. My daughter was very lazy and uninterested in anything before she met Jesus. But I worried as to what sort of group she was getting sucked into. I decided I should check the group out.

As I went for the meetings, I found comfort, solace and, most of all, hope for my lonely soul. I attended the 1998 Family Camp with my three children. There I understood the need to surrender my life to Jesus, and did.

Now I do not feel desperate and utterly hopeless anymore. Recently I lost my job, but I was not in panic. I now knew Someone bigger and stronger to tell my problems to. I found a job in answer to prayer. Praise the Lord Jesus!

Saved and Lifted
• •
Jagath

My name is Jagath and my wife's name is Wasana. We were both Buddhists and we are both from the village. We went to school in the village and grew up in the village. We were barely twenty years old when we fell in love and got married. After our marriage, we had to leave the village and go to the big city of Colombo in search of employment. We found some employment and also a very small house in which to live. Nevertheless, we were a very depressed and unhappy couple. We had no furniture, and our little shanty home was flooded by the slightest rainfall. We were also feeling very lonely. During this time, we happened to hear of a Bible meeting close to our home. We normally refer to Evangelicals as "Bible Christians." We began to attend these meetings conducted by a group calling themselves "Wesleyans."

My wife was really getting involved in the teaching of these Bible people. I was not that quick to believe what they were saying. My wife became a believer and started growing in the Lord. I was not quite prepared to make a real commitment to the Lord until, one day, I was touched by the preaching in a very special way. Something began to happen in me and I began to believe in the Lord Jesus Christ in a new way.

When we both became believers and got baptized, our lives also became brighter. I soon learned the importance of giving to God and tithing faithfully. We have subsequently moved to a better home, and now we have a son and a better standard of living. We are much happier and at peace with each other and with ourselves.

Our friends and family saw our new prosperity and the way God had blessed us and made accusations that the church was giving us incentives. They said that is why we were prosperous and were calling ourselves Christians. But I have told them repeatedly this is not true; in fact, rather than the church giving money to me, I am giving tithes and offerings to the church. This is something they cannot understand. The fact is that the Lord Jesus Christ has changed our hopeless condition to one of hope and blessed us immensely. Glory be to the Lord!

Many Gods Cannot Save
●●●●●●●●●●●●●●●●●●●●●●●
Roshan Kumar

My life was very mixed-up religiously and I dabbled in both Hinduism and Roman Catholicism. Hinduism allows many gods, and Catholicism worshiped many gods (saints). My life was also mixed-up socially. I associated with drug addicts and other social misfits. I lived a dangerous life, getting into fights and arguments. I harbored a lot of anger directing it at my parents and the whole social system, which I felt had treated me unfairly. I got kicked out of school because I hit a teacher.

I knew something about Christ from Catholicism, but I attended the Wesleyan church for some meetings because my mother wanted me to accompany her. Slowly it began to dawn on me that the teachings I was hearing were truth. I saw the light as I attended church, week after week. With great caution and after much deliberation, I accepted Christ. This was not an easy step for me, since I do not accept emotion as a reason for action. Action must be based on reason as well as emotion. Pastor Cedric reasoned with me and led me to the full light of Christ in my life.

God helped me to get rid of all sorts of evil dependencies and bad habits. Now I find it difficult to go back to my former lifestyle and my old friends have forsaken me. I have new friends and meaningful relationships with God's people in the church. My life has changed dramatically for the better. A few months ago I found employment at a construction site. I was paid reasonably well, but I was not happy because something within me was pulling me more towards the church and its activities. So I met with Pastor Cedric and explained my dilemma. Pastor Cedric urged me to pray and find out from the Lord as to what He really wanted me to do. Finally, three months later, I felt strongly that the Lord was calling me to ministry. At this point I am not sure exactly what I will be doing in the future. Nevertheless, I committed myself initially to go to Bible college as a part-time student and work in the Church helping in various ministries. I praise the Lord for saving me at age seventeen.

I want to follow Jesus. Now I believe, not because my Mom told me, but because I have experienced Him.

The Shy Witness
• •
Thakshila Disna Kumari

opelessness marked my life and everything I did. I was a Buddhist who lived in mortal fear of the end of the world and disasters that could happen. My life was controlled and paralyzed by fears. Fear of failure was paramount. I would not talk to anyone other than my family. I was especially gripped by the fear of failing in my secondary school tenth-year examination. I would follow any tradition, worship, or lifestyle taught in the Buddhist way of life, just to make sure I was covered from faults that might send me to hell or a worse life to come.

One day I went to the Wesleyan church for a prayer meeting held in a house, just because my sister and brother-in-law were going. My idea of religion was somber, intense and quiet worship. But the people at this meeting were having fun! They were singing, clapping, playing instruments and virtually dancing! I thought, "How absurd! Religion is not supposed to be fun; it is a duty!" I thought to myself, "What a bunch of clowns. My sister is a fool to get caught up in such nonsense. I will never get caught up in such lunacy." The pastor invited me to come again, but I only chuckled to myself. I argued with my sister at home about evil spirits, reincarnation, and other Buddhist beliefs to which I held.

In 1996, when I was nineteen years old, I attended the Wesleyan family camp to help my sister out with the baby. But as I listened to the teaching, something began to happen in me. I couldn't believe the joy I saw in the people. My heart began to melt and my eyes began to open. On the return journey, the pastor's wife, Sharlini, talked to me. That conversation was the turning point in my life. I told her that I would like to join the "group," but felt so fearful of my relatives who might get furious at the prospects of yet another member of the family betraying the Buddhist faith! However, the pull of the Holy Spirit was too great for me to resist. I talked to Jesus in the only way I knew, saying, "Jesus, please choose me for this new thing, if that's okay with you!" And Jesus accepted my prayer. I began to hide in corners and pray secretly.

I sat for the 'A' Level examination through prayer. Instead of fear and panic, this time there was faith and comfort. I passed the exam! I wish I had known Jesus before. I wasted a lot of years gripped in fear and unnecessary anxiousness. I do not shake anymore when I have to talk to someone. As a matter of fact, I can now stand in front of a crowd and give my testimony and I am able to pray in public. To all who knew me before, these are miraculous achievements. I lost my job four months after baptism. God helped me to face it with courage through prayer. I found another job that is much harder. But I can go to work cheerfully. I often have to work at night packaging tea. This gives me endless opportunities to talk to my workmates about my faith. Most of the girls look forward to work, so they can talk about Jesus. For one who used to faint at the thought of talking to strangers, God has given me power to witness. I have been able to tell about five or six people about Jesus. Someone is giving me amazing words to speak. I praise the Lord Jesus that one has already accepted the Lord. Isn't God good?

Europe

England

Sixpence Worth of Sin

Lois Ruth

I was born in St. Andrew, Jamaica, and came from a Christian background. I attended Sunday school and had always received prizes for perfect attendance. I loved Sunday school and children's church on Sunday evenings. Sometimes we would just stay through the afternoon until the evening service.

One Sunday afternoon, when I was eleven years old, my friend and I were roaming around the interior of the church, waiting for the evening service to start. We came across the offering plate with loads of money. Someone had forgotten to put it away and had left it in the pulpit. We decided to take some of the money and treat ourselves to chocolate. We each took the same amount. We were fearful, but went to the shop and bought our sweets. The very moment I got mine, all my appetite and excitement was gone. A weird feeling of sadness and guilt came over me. Although it was only sixpence, I didn't spend it all, but took the remainder back to church and put it in the plate.

During the evening service I felt so very miserable and sweaty. Then I heard a voice saying within me, "You must confess; you must confess." I was sitting in the second pew near the aisle. Suddenly I was on my feet, facing the congregation with tears gushing from my eyes. I told the church what I had done and that I was truly sorry. The pastor and other members came and prayed with me at the altar and I gave my life to Jesus.

After that, I had surgery on my left big toe which kept me away from Sunday school and day school. During these times when the family would attend weddings and other places, I was left all alone. One day the pain in my toe became so severe, I cried and prayed to God to heal me and promised to serve Him for the rest of my life.

My mother, who was a very dedicated Christian, kept a scripture text box on her dressing table. So I went and took out a card and I could not believe what I was reading from 2 Kings 20:5b: "I have heard your prayer and seen your tears; I will heal you." I had no knowledge then that such words were written in the Bible. I showed it to my Mom who said, "Find the Scripture and read all about it."

From that moment on, I was on the mend. Within a short time I was able to attend Sunday school and day school again. After five years I totally committed my life to Jesus, was baptized, and started working for the church in various positions. I immigrated to England in 1962 and continue in the service of the Lord. I give Him praise, glory and honor.

God has blessed me with a marvelous husband, four children and grandchildren. I have never been sorry that I obeyed the voice of my conscience, "You must confess; you must confess." Thanks be to God.

Conversion Doesn't Always Bring Physical Healing

●●●●●●●●●●●●●●●●●●●●●●●●

Margery Elizabeth Hitchman

I live with a big family of three sisters, Mum and Dad. I am the last child and, unfortunately, I was born disabled with a muscle disease causing deformity in my face and neck. I had an operation when I was eight years old and I was in the hospital for six weeks. Even at that age I felt a presence with me, although I never went to Sunday school. My Mum and Dad had grown up in church and they taught me about God.

My two middle sisters got saved first and wanted me to come to church. But I was more interested in drink to take the physical pain away because my muscles hurt a lot. One day I decided to go to a meeting with them in London. A missionary from America was present. That is when I started to believe in God because I saw people getting healed. I got saved at a concert. Two years passed and I wondered why I had not been healed. So I left God.

But the people at my church were praying. I purposely ran away from home, got a job far away and started to drink again. When I could not stand it anymore, I went back home and joined the Wesleyan church again. Then I realized I had a lot of unforgiveness in my heart and so at a mission's week, I asked for forgiveness. The next year my healing began.

I have now finished two years of studying at a Bible school in London. I am completing a course at Wesleyan Bible Institute now and am enjoying it. In the other course I studied, God sent me to Albania and Belfast.

Even though Christianity is fun, you have to take the rough times with the smooth. I have become ill again but I will never leave the Lord ever again. I would advise anybody who is thinking of leaving the Lord that it is not worth it. God bless you all.

Germany

ermany is probably the most difficult field in which The Wesleyan Church works. While things are changing in Germany, people are self-sufficient and satisfied. The majority were baptized as babies and will return to the church to be buried as Christians. For many, infant baptism, marriage and burial will be the only time they attend church. The official church is supported by the government and has no need for attendance and commitment in order to operate. Christianity has been secularized and anyone who would suggest that the average person is lost and needs salvation has an uphill battle. This attitude with regard to Christianity is evident in each of these stories of grace.

"Christian" Is Born Again

● ●

Klaus Weidlich

I am the pastor of the Wesleyan church in Munich. The Lord blesses me and uses me. When I look back, this isn't natural. It is a miracle.

I grew up in a normal German home. My father was a baker. My mother trained us three brothers. We were baptized as babies and were members of the Protestant national church of Bavaria. I went regularly to church. Therefore I thought everything was all right. I didn't accept Jesus as my personal Savior. I thought that I was a Christian.

At our village there was a parish priest who persuaded me to read the Bible. I started at the age of twenty with the books of Moses and I found a holy God there. His expectations of His people were very high. I was happy that I didn't belong to the people of Israel. For the Christian it is different, I thought!

I visited a group of people who were "born again." I didn't accept these believers and I hastily left this house. The pastor's wife told me she would pray for me till I came back. After three months I went back. I had a girlfriend during this time and went to her house every weekend. I felt that my relationship wasn't right with God and that there was a wall between God and me. I also knew that this wall had to do with my relationship with my girlfriend. For the first time, I prayed for help and the Lord helped. This friendship with my girlfriend ended a day later. I asked God for forgiveness and I felt better. From this day on the Lord began to convict me of sin after sin. I then asked for forgiveness and felt better. After about a month, I really wanted to live completely with the Lord. Then I learned that God's forgiveness for my sins was mine for the asking, because Jesus had died for me. I was born again and the Lord put something into my heart—it was the desire to serve Him as a pastor. I spent another three years in that congregation, during which I married Heidrun.

I completed four years of training at a German Bible school. Seven years after my decision for a life with Jesus, we arrived in Munich. We became members of The Wesleyan Church and I later became a pastor under Dr. Ken Blake. The Lord is good and keeps His word!

Little German Girl Finds Jesus

•••••••••••••••••••••••

Claudia Weidlich

I am twenty-nine years old and married. I would like to tell you now how I found Jesus. When I was ten years old, I went with my mother to a Christian vacation place called Michelsberg, a camp for women and girls. Up to that time no one had told me how to include Jesus in my life. This camp had a children's hour while the adults had their devotions. I always liked the children's hour very much. I could hardly wait from one to the next. The games, songs and stories which we heard were terrific.

An older woman I liked and respected sat at our table. At the end of the camp I was alone with her in a room. She asked whether I would like to ask Jesus into my heart and into my life. I wanted this, so I prayed and accepted Jesus as my Savior. I felt quite carefree and happy after this. But the vacation and the beautiful camp came to an end.

After this, I went back to the everyday life of school. There were some Christians there, though they did not get along well together. But I found it easier to be with this group than with others. I was glad that I had Jesus as my Lord. He would always listen and I could entrust anything in my life to Him. Often there were fights in my life which had nothing to do with being a Christian, but which were the result of my stubbornness. I was very impatient. I had been a Christian for quite some time when I fell flat on my face. I was very sorry for this, but I thought I could never be restored to righteousness again and I became depressed. I thought Jesus could have prevented this and was also mad at God. Then it became clear to me that Jesus wasn't at fault; it was me, and I asked for pardon again. I then thought, "Why did Jesus still help me when I was to blame for the situation?" It was a lesson I needed to learn. It has taught me the need for personal responsibility in the Christian life.

I want to do what Jesus wants me to do. I am glad and grateful that Jesus died on the cross for the sins of mankind. Jesus has a good plan for everybody. I would like to encourage everyone to include Jesus in their life. He is a strong anchor in life and He is a loyal friend. Jesus died on the cross for you and me. He wants us to take His death as a gift, because everyone with faith will not be lost, but will have eternal life.

Shock of Death Brings Sanctity of Life

•••••••••••••••••••••••••••

Kerstin

I received a call in August of 1995 from a colleague informing me that my former boss had been killed in a motorcycle accident at the age of 39. Friction in the workplace had started at the beginning of the year. My boss was a doctor who had begun practice in the fall of 1993. He had taken on too much financially. Therefore, he wanted to dismiss one of us. Because I had been ill during that year, he dismissed me instead of others over whom I had seniority on the job. We didn't part amicably. When I heard about his death, it was a blow. Even though he had sowed discord in my life, I hadn't wanted his death.

My cousin Karin opened her heart to Jesus in August 1995 and, by the providence of God, invited me to the thanksgiving service at the Wesleyan church. I took this as a good opportunity to talk with somebody, even if God wouldn't answer me. I didn't hear God's voice, but I know now it was because I didn't expect to hear Him. I felt better after this service and left with the warmth of a loving reception from the congregation.

On the following Wednesday I went to the cell group and again felt well and safe. Three weeks later, Pastor Klaus said that if we had anything on our hearts, we could share with the others. After I had collected all my courage, I said that the iron bracket around my heart needed to open. The group prayed for me. It was the first time that anybody had prayed for me out loud. I had tears in my eyes. With great emotion I drove home in that great hug of love from God and His people. It was close to midnight when I fell on my knees and submitted my life to Jesus at home.

Salvation Works

•••••••••••••••••••••••••

Olga

(told by Brigitte Schoebinger)

Olga was a young woman from Kazakhstan, now living in Germany. Together with Sasha, a Christian student from Kiev, she visited our services, enjoying them, but always staying at a certain distance. Then Sasha left Germany and shortly after that Olga went back to Kazakhstan for a three-week holiday. We didn't want to lose contact with her, so we searched in our cell group for possibilities to get to know her better and to show her love. Kerstin and Brigitte, two of our church members, visited her before she left, gave her some flowers, and wished her a nice holiday.

The day after Olga returned to Germany, she called Brigitte because she needed to talk to someone. This was the beginning of a long story that had God as the Author. Soon it became clear that she had gotten into some great problems. We learned that her husband was living in Kazakhstan with little chance for a transfer to Germany, and that she had gotten pregnant. It was not to be an easy pregnancy. Moreover, she had still not finished with her education. This was a great challenge for our cell group.

We started to do two things. First was prayer. We took her in our midst and started a fight for her life and soul, praying for her seven days a week. Each day was covered by one of our members. The second thing was practical help. This was undertaken for the most part by Kerstin, Heidrun and Brigitte. We helped Olga find a doctor who cared for her baby, we visited her several times in the hospital where she had to stay for some weeks, and we managed things with her employer and the health insurance. We went with Olga to the administrative authorities for foreigners, and in other ways we tried to help her. Above all we shared our faith and prayed with her.

About three months after the process started, Brigitte had the chance to share John 3:16 with Olga. Shortly after that she invited Jesus as Savior and Lord into her life and was converted. Her problems hadn't disappeared, but God cared for her and we experienced many wonderful things. God did some great wonders.

Today Olga is the mother of a one-year-old boy, Denis. Andrei, her husband, is living with them in Germany. One day while pastor Klaus was talking with Olga about baptism, Andrei showed a great interest in faith. Today he is a Christian too and they have both been baptized. They live as a Christian family in Germany, though still having great problems with finances, language and other things. The story is not yet finished; it is going on. But the best thing of all is that God is involved.

More Than Head Knowledge

Brigitte Schoebinger

I grew up in a family where everyone did what was common practice in our church. I visited Sunday school, went to a Christian youth group and was involved in many other things, believing myself to be a good Christian. When I was about thirteen, I was teaching younger children in Sunday school, even though I was not living in a personal relationship with God. I did not feel satisfied with my life and I was restless. It was about this time I began to wonder whether my parents or my church had a heart relationship with God.

At the age of eighteen, during a youth camp, I finally realized that my Christianity was missing many things. I discovered this as other people talked about themselves as children of God. I remember very well one evening when I was so depressed about myself and my situation, that I began to have a lot of pity for myself. I retreated from the group to my room and there God spoke to me out of the silence around me.

God gave me one verse, 2 Corinthians 8:11: "Now finish the work, so that your eager willingness to do it may be matched by your completion of it, according to your means." This verse hit me. Even though I had knowledge of Him, now I understood that this was not enough. He wanted to be Lord! So I took the step to the Cross, laid my heart down and gave Him my life. He healed me at once and set me free from jealousy, shyness, envy and gave me joy, freedom, and self-assurance.

After that evening, a turbulent time started in which I daily experienced the power of God and His leading and guidance. During this time I became aware that our youth should leave the church. After some time of weekly meeting in a garage, we were able to establish an independent church and met in the Church of the Nazarene.

I am very thankful for these experiences and the certainty He gave me during the following years. Some years later God led me to Munich. I couldn't understand and didn't want to go to this big city where there were no Nazarenes. But I have to confess that His ways are the best. A year after I arrived in Munich, Americans Ken and Marilyn Blake, from The Wesleyan Church, came to establish a church in Munich. Then it became clear why God wanted me to be in Munich. He put me into a new work and gave me a new spiritual home. I am joyful about the fact that He considers me to be worthy to serve Him as a part of this church for His glory. He blessed me personally in a new way and brought me forth. As long as He wants me to, I'll serve Him here faithfully, obediently, and in love.

Russia

ommunism taught that there was no God. When the communist curtain came down and western Christians began to go in, they found a population with no frame of reference for religious belief. Evangelism thus often takes forms that will lead first to friendship and then to Jesus. Short-term missionaries have often been at the forefront of this thrust. This friendship evangelism has been the backbone upon which the church is being built in the former communist states.

Ping-Pong Tanya

Tanya Rodina
(told by Richard Lively)

Tanya spent her life in denial of God. Having been taught that He did not exist, this was not a difficult position to take. When she was a young girl, she was a "hooligan" who liked to win at all sports. It was this love of sports that led to her eventual occupation as a table tennis instructor and successful competitor on the national level.

In the spring of 1997, missionaries visited the club where she worked as an instructor. After playing Ping-Pong with the children, they invited the children and Tanya to visit the church where they had a table as well. Tanya visited merely out of curiosity; she had never heard of a church with a Ping-Pong table before! One of the missionaries asked her to return to church and offered to give her a Bible to read, but she refused the Bible, stating that she had no need of one. She did, however, take another book, *More Than a Carpenter*, and read it immediately.

After several weeks of the missionaries visiting the club, Tanya agreed to visit church again, and even to accept a Bible. This led to more visits and questions. One of the missionaries wanted to take Ping-Pong lessons and asked how he could repay her for the lessons. She responded, "You teach me about God and the Bible, and I will teach you to play Ping-Pong." By summer, Tanya had become a Christian, interacting with Christians from the church and regularly attending Bible studies to learn more about God. In the fall of 1997, she enrolled in the Bible school where she is currently a full-time student. She now speaks of wanting to serve the Lord with her life as a youth pastor. She doesn't want young people to make the same mistakes she made with her life before coming to Christ.

Little did Tanya or the missionaries know that a day at a Ping-Pong club would lead to this. Little did Tanya know that God does exist and that He loves her and has a wonderful plan for her life. But she knows now and wants to make sure others know it as well.

South America

Costa Rica

This is one of our newest fields. The Church in Costa Rica specializes in reaching the people on the lowest rungs of society. These are stories of absolute hopelessness, poverty, and sin in its worst forms.

A Lesbian's Testimony

Ana Isabel Vega Rojas

From the time I was a little girl, I lived a life of loneliness, bitterness, sadness and suffering. I knew only to do bad things and nothing that I ever did came out right. I was a problem child in grade school and high school. At the age of eighteen, I began to live the most bitter days of my life. I had a boyfriend I really loved, as every girl wants, but the day came when he let me down. This hit me so hard I couldn't stand it. From then on really hard problems began with my mother, and I left home.

I found a house where homosexuals and lesbians lived. There were drugs, alcohol and sex everywhere. I really wasn't familiar with this world. I had tried drugs and alcohol but had never been around the other things. In a few days, I was like everyone else. I began to use drugs and the addicts took me to the place where homosexuals and lesbians lived. This really made a big impact on my life. Since I had never felt loved or received any affection, I thought this was the answer to all my problems. I fell into lesbianism a few days after visiting this place and everything became worse—it was a world of pain, deceit, hypocrisy, and false love, not any genuine love. I became so depressed that soon my relatives came and took me to a mental hospital. I didn't know what they were going to do with me, but I felt I needed to be cured, so I agreed to be admitted into that horrible place. I was in treatment with psychologists, psychiatrists, pills and all kinds of stimulants. It was horrible for me to realize I was in an insane asylum when I knew I wasn't crazy. My situation was sexual deviation, because I didn't know if I liked guys or girls. It was so hard and I rebelled against everyone—my family and myself. When they let me out of the hospital, I got worse. I went with my parents, but became more involved in drugs, alcohol and lesbianism.

My parents suffered so much that my father said he would sell all he had to see me cured. Then one day, I wanted to die. I was taking care of my grandmother at the time. She was the only person I loved and that I felt loved me, and she was dying. I thought, if she dies, what will become of me? So I went into my room and took out an old Bible I had saved back from Catholic school days, and I prayed a prayer to the Lord. "Lord, I want to tell you, I am just trash. I have drug and alcohol problems, and worse, I am a lesbian. I am nothing, but please don't let my grandmother die until I know I am loved." And so it was. God began to deal with me in a marvelous way. I didn't want to smoke or drink or be with my girlfriends. One day a guy saw me on the street and began to tell me of God's love. A few days later, I went to a revival meeting in a church. Today I am in the Wesleyan church called the Sun of Justice in Grecia, Costa Rica.

I was so touched by the testimony of this man. I didn't wait to tell him how touched I was. Six days later this same preacher was in my house and I had the most wonderful experience I had ever had in my life. Jesus touched me. I felt peace and I realized my heart was cleansed. I got up, lifted my hands in the air and could only laugh. I felt like the happiest woman in the world. From this moment on I belonged to Him. Now I can say I am completely free. Right now I serve the Lord in song and worship in a beautiful music group, and I am also in a group called "Friends of Jesus."

This group works with drug addicts, homosexuals, lesbians and prostitutes. I have belonged to Jesus for seven years now.

Jesus Knows My Name
• •
Anonymous

I grew up in a very big family of eight boys and six girls. We were so numerous my parents really didn't have time for us and really didn't show us any love. I remember that when I turned eight years old and was in second grade, my parents told me that they had to take me out of school. My mom needed me to help her around the house and to take care of my siblings. My parents always fought. My dad abused my mom physically and always threatened to kill her. The situation became so bad that my mom left our home when I was just barely nine years old.

At this young age I began to take responsibility for the household, like taking my dad's lunch to him where he was working in construction in Cartago or San Jose. My dad would take advantage of me and sexually abuse me now and then until I was about fifteen years old. I felt so depressed, especially when I saw my girlfriends with their boyfriends or with their fathers, knowing I would never have a relationship like that with my father. I kept the situation to myself and never said anything because I was afraid.

When I was sixteen, I went to live with a good family. They were the parents of a very good friend of mine. The father had a dance hall and asked me if I could help him in the business. Time passed by and one day the father offered me twenty pesos if I would have sex with him. I told him yes because I felt no self worth. About this time his wife found out and threw me out of the house.

From that moment on, I began to go to dances and go out with both single and married men. By the time I was twenty, I was working as a barmaid from 3 p.m. to 2 a.m. From time to time, I would visit my mom and give her money. She asked me to move in with her, and we moved to Conception of Three Rivers.

I continued to live a very sinful life. Some friends offered me various types of drugs and this led to addiction and drug trafficking. I went to jail several times. I couldn't live at home anymore and so I slept in coffee fields or in whatever place I could find. I met a man and became pregnant. This man's mother told me to come live with her so that I would have a room to sleep in and a place for my baby. She treated me well and gave me clothes, food and a room. She also began talking to me about God. I accepted the invitation to live with her and also accepted the Lord as my Savior.

After we got married in the church, my life began to change. I felt good and happy about the birth of my child. However, the baby lived only a few minutes. This was so hard on me and I knew it was only God's mercy that I too still lived. God blessed our home two years later with another little girl. Now I have three beautiful children, a wonderful husband, and have been married fifteen years, thanks to the mercies of God.

Recently I went to visit my dad. I found out that he was in the hospital and they would be amputating his leg. I went to visit him and told him of God's Word and what had happened to me in the last few years. I told him I forgave him, and prayed God would have the same mercy on him as He did on me. Today, thanks to that divine God and His love, I am serving Him. It has been the best decision I have made all my life because only God could change my life and bring me true happiness. And I want this for you, too.

Up from the Gutter

Heiner Martin Ballestero Alvarado

I came from a very poor family. My father was an alcoholic and my mother a housewife. I am the oldest and have five sisters. My childhood was bad from all aspects. I shined shoes to earn a living. When I was eight years old, I went to reform school and from then on began a criminal life. I escaped from the reform school and continued roaming around. After some years, I was sent to the Central Prison in the first section for theft. I had already learned to smoke marijuana, drink liquor and use whatever drug that appeared. I was beginning to find out what this life was all about. I was in prison for many years. By my actions, I was constantly betraying any confidence put in me.

While I was in St. Luke's Island Prison, I went without seeing my family members for many years. I felt so alone and so empty that I began to inhale a liquid that you use to preserve wood. It is called "lacquer." I was always looking for something to get drugged on. On occasions when I didn't have money to buy drugs, I would look for spider webs and smoke them as if they were marijuana. The day came when I was sent to a halfway house. I worked in a greenhouse during the day and then went back to the prison each evening. But on one occasion I didn't return. I continued to look for drugs. But it was worse this time because it was cocaine. I again became a thief. I smoked rock in a tube, pipe or beer can. Every day I stole money to smoke. I slept in fields, caves, underneath trucks or wherever. I was well versed in all kinds of vices. I drank liquor, alcohol and persuaded others to do it too. I cut my arms and stomach to get attention.

Now I want to tell you how I came to the feet of Jesus after being a con artist for Satan. After so much sinning, one Sunday I felt so bad I told myself I had to seek help or I was going to die. The first thing I did was to look for Jesus Christ who has so much love. Today I am the happiest man on earth because Christ did a miracle in my life. The Holy Spirit was the One who really took me to church. I feel completely changed by His power; what I do now is testify to all His wonders. I give to others that I might receive. I can testify with all security and conviction in my heart that His is the living hope for all who look for Him and fall in love with Him. Now I am more than a conqueror. He that is in Christ is a new creature. All the old things are passed away and everything made new.

Street Child

●●●●●●●●●●●●●●●●●●●●●●●●●

Ismael Angel Cascante Vasquez

From the time I was just a small child I was a bad influence. At only five years of age, I began sinning. One time I looked for a way to rob my own grandfather of his week's salary. As I grew up, the sinning increased. We were very poor and I was in school. At eight years of age, I had to find a way to eat and help out at home. My dad made me a shoeshine box to shine shoes. His intention was that I would shine shoes and make some money honorably like himself. In the shoeshine business, I began to run around with other guys and became quite disorderly. I began to smoke cigarettes, marijuana, drink alcohol and get messed up with prostitution too.

When I was eleven years old, these guys took me to a brothel. I was really nervous, but every time I drank or took drugs the nervousness left me. So with the shoeshine money, I went to the brothel and began to drown myself in alcohol, prostitution and theft. I couldn't study in the state I was in. I was rebellious and disobedient to my parents, full of anger and violent behavior. I really suffered when I was finally put in jail at such a young age, remaining there through most of my childhood and adolescent years. I rebelled more each day and looked for ways to do bad things to everyone. For this reason no one accepted me. I rebelled against God and it offended me when people talked to me about God. I felt a terrible hate for my father, so much that I made his life impossible. I had many court hearings because of the aggressive behavior I directed at my father. I stole from my mother, sisters and brothers whatever I could to quench my thirst for the vices I was involved in.

I began to look like a beggar, sleeping naked on the sidewalks of the main streets of town. I didn't have the will to go on living; I didn't even have the will to keep on robbing. I was a wasted social outcast. I tried to commit suicide but it didn't work. The last time I was in jail for armed robbery, I could only think of five years that I wasn't in jail or a hospital or a restoration house for alcoholics and drug users. Nothing helped to change my life and I was dying little by little. I went from jail to the hospital to maximum security. But one day, some men arrived at the prison to talk about what God had done in their lives. Even though I was very sick and without the will to live, I listened to these people tell about the "Good News" of salvation. I accepted Christ and I told Him if He would heal me and change me, I would follow Him the rest of my life. Days passed and I began to study the Bible. I didn't miss one meeting and my life began to change so much, it scared me. I didn't blame God anymore. I didn't smoke and I didn't use foul language. I felt a peace in my heart. When my family came to visit me, I told them I was free and very happy. At this time the jail gave me peace and joy. Neither bars nor cells nor chains can detain the power of God.

Now I am serving as a leader in a cell group in the same neighborhood where I grew up. I am also in a Bible Institute program, preparing myself to serve the Lord as best I can. I am ready to work in His Kingdom for whatever He wants me to do.

Saved from Suicide

●●●●●●●●●●●●●●●●●●●●●●●●●

Jeudry Rodriguez Calvo

M y name is Jeudry and almost twelve years ago I had the most fantastic experience of my life. I remember it like it was today. I was in the backyard of my house and that afternoon I was so mentally depressed, nothing mattered in my life. By the time I was seventeen years old I had already tried many things that this world has to offer. I had made the decision to end my life, believing that doing this would end all the disgrace that I had been living in.

I was raised in a poor home with many problems. But the problem I hated most was my father's filthy alcohol problem. I saw how he would come home many times from the nearby bar and upset the table, or throw the food my mother had cooked at her feet, or just insult her. But what was worse was to see him physically abuse my mother. All this remained engraved in my mind from the time I was a small child, causing me to have a tremendous hate for my father.

When I was fifteen, my father and I were arguing and he shouted at me, "The day you get mixed up on drugs, I will do everything possible to put you in jail." He said it like it was some great thing, and I hated him even more for it.

I began to run with street friends and one of my youthful passions was "Break Dance Fever." I got so mixed up with this dance that I wanted to be the best dancer in town. I worried about it and just wanted everyone to see how good I was. My friends and I would go to a dance hall and begin to break dance. Many people would stop dancing to look at us and watch our acrobatics on the dance floor. I liked the attention. Because of my involvement with these friends, I began using drugs. About this time I also met a girl who would eventually become my wife. In looking for a way to get myself out of all I had gotten into, I went to live with my girlfriend. This did not work out because I refused to leave behind my friends and their stupid activities.

One Sunday morning, I went to see a soccer game. Instead, like a very desperate person, I ended up consuming a lot of drugs with my friends. I had never ever experienced anything like I did that day. When the drug took effect, it was like an explosion in my body. I wanted to die and my friends thought it was just a game. They laughed at me and began kicking and insulting me. Everything was horrible. One of them threw a brick at me and it broke in pieces on my knee. So with a little courage, I struck him like a crazy man. I took off running because it felt like my heart was exploding and my body was going in different directions. I arrived home and shut myself in my room and waited to die.

I fought with my wife over this and swore I would never do that again. I told her that I was going to leave those friends and that is exactly what I did. My wife was pregnant at the time, but the baby was born dead. The doctors in the clinic where he was born told us he had a congenital deformity because my wife's and my blood types were incompatible. This was a very low time in my life. I began to listen to voices in my mind telling me that I wasn't worth anything in life and now I wouldn't even be able to have children. I began to feel so alone and so filthy dirty that my only option was to do away with myself once and for all.

So on a Sunday afternoon I found myself in my backyard near a big tree and an inner voice telling me to hang myself with a rope. For a moment I sat on the ground and closed my eyes really hard, thinking—only thinking. And suddenly I felt a hand on my shoulder. A young man took me in his arms, hugged me and asked my name. Then he asked me something that really caught my attention. He asked me, "If you die today, where will your soul go?" I knew very well how awful my life was and I answered, "To hell." With love and wisdom he explained how awful hell was. He told me the solution was in Jesus Christ, and then I wouldn't have to go there. That very afternoon I received Christ as my personal Savior. It was the best thing that could have happened to me.

Today, after twelve years of following Jesus, I feel blessed by God. He has given me three children and a home full of peace and love. He has permitted me to serve Him for nine years in the music ministry of the Brazos de Amor (Arms of Love) church and many other places. I have had the opportunity to travel outside Costa Rica to testify to the world how marvelous God is. John 3:16 is my theme.

Note: Jeudry is one of the most gifted keyboard musicians and singers in The Wesleyan Church in Costa Rica. He works as a tailor for men's clothing and faithfully ministers in music and song at every church service.

God Reached Down and Picked Me Up

•••••••••••••••••••••••••••

Rita Maria Chanto Hernandez

My name is Rita and I want to greet you in the name of the Lord Jesus Christ. I now have the privilege of sharing my story with you.

My life was a little confusing, although I came from a well-to-do family and had all I ever wanted in life. As far as clothes, dolls, parties, and anything else, I just had to ask for them. It was like living in a castle; my parents were the king and queen and I was a princess. That is until one day as I was playing outside with a cousin of mine, and she told me, "You are just a pick-up." I said to her, "I am not a pick-up. I am Rita." But I was really frightened by what that word meant since I was only six years old.

Hurriedly I went to look for my mother but couldn't find her, so I went and hid in the corner of my room. When she finally came home I went to tell her what had happened, and she verified that indeed I was adopted, and that neither she nor my father were my blood relatives. From that moment on, a rebellious spirit entered my mind and heart and later in my teen years, I just got worse. I began to smoke at the age of twelve, and when I was fifteen I took my first drink. That same night, thinking I had nothing to lose, I had sex with a young man I had never met before and who didn't know me either. This young man was very surprised to find I wasn't a virgin. Since the age of twelve, I had been abused sexually. My parents would go out to parties, dancing and enjoying themselves, while we young people drank, smoked, rented porno videos and used drugs. It didn't matter to me that we were doing it in our own house because by then it was only a place where I ate and slept. I got really mixed up in alcohol and smoking, but even worse, I began to sleep with anyone. It got so bad, I quit school, began to frequent disco clubs and nightclubs in San Jose, and was under the influence of some really bad friends. I began earning money, but at the same time my adopted father stopped giving me an allowance each week. My mom made problems because I wouldn't go to mass with her. One night I heard loud noises coming from my mother's room and I investigated. I saw her lighting candles and placing different pictures around those candles. When I wouldn't join her in this type of worship, she got angry.

When I was eighteen, I decided to leave home for good. For a year I lived and worked as a waitress and cashier in a bar that also served as a brothel. One day the owner told me I could earn lots more money if I let her recommend me

131

to the men that visited there for sexual pleasure. So began my life as a prostitute. I began to hate myself and in one form or another it began to destroy me. I drank, I smoked, I slept with anyone and nothing bothered me. Later I met a Chinese lady who owned a restaurant. She also knew the martial arts and how best to use them. I decided this was a good thing to learn to protect myself, and I went to work for her. She began to indoctrinate me in martial arts and its religion. She also taught me to have fun in life—to dance, smoke and have men. I kept a close rein on the hate and revenge I felt in my heart.

One night I went to Conception of Three Rivers and met a young man named Arthur. In time we had a little girl named Tatiana. Little by little, we got to know each other and eventually married. I had to quit work because Arthur liked to find me at home when he came home from work. Arthur talked about God and, little by little, began teaching me things about God. He would sing about God in the house and although he drank and smoked he seemed to be happiest when he was singing about God.

One evening we were invited to a church to see a film. The church was so packed we thought we would have to leave, but a lady gave us her seat and we stayed to see the film. It was about a young man trapped by drugs, alcohol and sex, and at the end Billy Graham gave an invitation. I saw myself in this young man, and at the end my heart began to burst—it felt like it was breaking in two. So I went forward to accept Christ that night, and the people there tried to minister to me. Somehow it didn't work and I ended up with such a hatred in my heart for everyone and everything, including even a hatred for my sweet husband. It was so bad at night when I was in bed, that I had nightmares where I would gnash my teeth. Even though I tried to cover up the hate, it would manifest itself. The only thing that seemed to calm me was music. Every time I tried to be good, I felt like I was being strangled; I couldn't speak or even breathe.

I had a lot of confidence in the pastor's wife at that church, but she was on a trip and wasn't there to help me. The devil made me think that she, along with my mother and father, had left me and failed me. So I decided the best thing for me to do was to throw myself out in front of a car and that would be that.

The following Sunday at church, a lady had a vision in which she saw me being delivered from sin and knew that God was going to deliver me. However, I didn't attend that Sunday. My husband was very upset. I felt forgotten and my mind was so tired of everything. I told my husband that I was so tired of it all I just wanted to die. He said, "Let's go find the pastor first, because he lives nearby." I thought, "Right, we will talk about it and nothing will come of it." Just then Pastor Barrantes passed us in his car. We came to his house when he was just arriving home. When Pastor Barrantes prayed for me, it was as if a fire from heaven shot down clear through me and I saw a vision from God. It was the hand of God reaching down for me to free me from the bonds of Satan. That day God did a mighty work in me so that later I could testify to others.

After seeing His glory and after experiencing His great love, I encountered many problems. We had to move and live some distance from the church, and I saw my faith getting weaker. Finally I rededicated my life, asked God's forgiveness, and decided that nothing and no one would keep me from God's love. Now I am living completely for the Lord and, like Samuel, my husband and I keep watch over the house of God. God has given me a ministry in mime and pantomime drama. I am hoping to have another ministry, sharing God's Word with the men, women and children of Africa. God has promised me and I believe Him that He will never leave me nor forsake me.

Catholicism seems to have been mixed, on a wide scale, with various forms of animism (Voodoo) in Haiti. The paranormal is such a strong part of Haitian society that it is looked for and expected in all practical aspects of life. In the two stories from Haiti, you will see both of these aspects of Haitian life.

Dirty Clothes, Clean Heart

Christian Demero

I was born in a Catholic family. My family did not want anything to do with Protestant Christianity. When I was a very small boy, I longed to go to Sunday school with other children in my neighborhood, learn to sing the songs they sang, and hear the stories they talked about. My parents found out I wanted to go to Sunday school, and my mother would not wash my good clothes. One Sunday, I left the house in torn, dirty clothes and went to Sunday school anyway. After that, I started going with the other children, always in dirty clothes.

When I was a small child, I gave my heart to Jesus. Later, my parents became Christians. I attended the Wesleyan church regularly. I enjoyed the young people's group and the choir. I felt the Lord was calling me to become a pastor, but I was not able to go to Bible school. Missionary Dan McCandless encouraged me to enroll in the Theological Education by Extension (TEE) program. So I did. Missionary nurse Mary Osborne continued to encourage me. In the meantime, the pastor of the church I was attending passed away, and I became the lay preacher at the church.

The district asked me to take a different church that had been through some difficult problems and needed a shepherd. The first Sunday I was there, there were only two or three little old ladies and about six young people. God has helped me. The church is growing and today we have about 100 people who attend. I continue to study in the TEE program, and hope to be an ordained minister one day. I want to serve the Lord and The Wesleyan Church here in Haiti. I am thankful for a good wife and four children. God has done so much for me. Pray for me. The church is growing, and we need a bigger building and a new parsonage. I am trusting the Lord to help us.

The Lord Speaks through Dreams

•••••••••••••••••••••••

Saint Aubert

M y name is Saint Aubert. I was born and raised in a Catholic home where my mother worshiped images. She knew nothing about the reality of God, and had no relationship with Him. One day, when I was playing with a friend at her house, the pastor of the Wesleyan church in our town went to visit a neighbor, just on the other side of the fence of my friend's yard. I ran and hid inside the house, because I did not understand what he was talking about. I was fifteen years old. The pastor asked the neighbor if there was anyone next door that he could visit. I went further into the house and hid. I did not want anything to do with him or hear what he was talking about. The pastor left and went home and later, I did too.

That night, I had a dream. In my dream, I saw a man standing and talking to me. He said his name was Saint Paul. He told me I should have gone out and talked to the pastor. He told me I needed what the pastor was talking about. I didn't want to talk to the pastor. I knew my parents would not be happy with me. Then I had another dream, and I knew I should go to the pastor's house. I got a friend to go with me. When I got there, the pastor was not home, but his wife was. She told me they had been praying for me. That day, she prayed with me and led me to the Lord. I began attending the Wesleyan church. I got involved in the youth group and, before long, was singing in the choir. The Lord worked in my life, and I grew in Him.

Later, I joined the Wesleyan Women and within a few years, I was elected as the secretary of the local society. After two years, I was elected president of the local society. Four years later, I was elected the president of our district Wesleyan Women. God has done so much for me. He sent me a wonderful Christian man and we have three children. We attend the Wesleyan church as a family. I thank the Lord for sending missionaries to our country to teach us about God. The Ortlips, Vermilyas and Hartmans all had an impact on my life. Mrs. Hartman had a sewing school and taught me a skill that now helps me add to our family income with my sewing and needlework. Last year I was able to attend the International Wesleyan Women's Convention in Marion, Indiana. I have never been to anything like that before. I came home more encouraged than ever to serve the Lord here in Haiti, and to do my part to be a witness for Him. I could never finish thanking the Lord for all He has done for me.

Mexico

T he Wesleyan Church in Mexico is seeing growth through the able leadership of Rev. Edward Parman. Through these stories told by Ed, you see both his passion and vision for the lost. You will also see God working in miraculous ways to protect His messengers and the opportunities of grace.

Blind Thieves and Motorcycles

•••••••••••••••••••••••••

Evangelism

(told by Ed Parman)

In the church, we are working with a program of evangelism and discipleship that is currently in its second cycle. It involves three months of prayer for neighbors, family and friends (specific people), followed by an invitation to a special mini-campaign in church members' homes and at the church where the gospel is preached. We are praising God in heaven for the blessing He's given us in two main areas. The first is that the leaders that were in the cell groups of prayer have multiplied and new leaders are being raised up. In the last cycle there were nine leaders. Now there are 21 who have been praying in the groups during these three months. Perhaps the numbers aren't impressive, but in reality it is a marvelous achievement. For a very long time there was a certain apathy regarding God's work. Now God is touching hearts and giving them the desire to rise up and fight to win souls for Him.

At the beginning of this time of work, there were many difficult trials for our leaders—illness, family problems and tremendous attacks by Satan. But thanks to our great King, these brothers and sisters were able to have victory in Jesus. We are sure that this is a step in the spiritual growth of each one and we give glory to God for this. There were even several leaders returning home on a bus that was robbed. The muggers got on the bus and took everything the passengers had—money, watches, etc. But when they went by our brothers and sisters, they went by as if they didn't see them there. They were the only people on the bus who were not robbed. This has happened to several of our people on different occasions. It is a very practical way we can see how God takes care of His children when they are within His will. We give Him glory for His protection and blessing.

The second area of God's blessing is the souls who have come to Christ, making the most important decision of their lives. In the mini-campaigns, we have seen 38 people commit themselves to Christ; in the campaign at the church on Saturday and Sunday, six people have committed themselves to the Lord.

Two of the people who made this decision are a couple that live a block from the church. Two months ago their fifteen-year-old daughter died. One Saturday night she went out with her friends, but they turned out to be bad company. They were fooling around on a motorcycle and crashed just feet from her own house. The parents were traumatized. She was their only daughter. A friend spoke to us about this couple, Manuel and Ana Bertha, and we went to visit, not even knowing them. They opened their home to us, which is very uncommon here in Mexico City. We believe it was God's preparation.

While visiting with this couple, the woman commented that she no longer had the will to live, that she had been so close to her daughter. The husband told us that he was very worried about his wife and her suicidal comments. We shared God's Word with them and several leaders visited on different occasions to pray with them. They were very grateful for this prayer support. When we had our next campaign in the church, they were invited, and the two of them gave their hearts to the Lord on that day. We believe that God is going to lift them up and that soon they will offer their home for the next cycle of prayer. Glory to God for His blessings!

In one of our prayer cells, we were praying for a woman who was bedridden because of illness. Her family members, who are Christians, asked if she would like us to pray for her and she accepted. The couple who connected us to her, Nora and Eduardo, host a Bible study in their home every week. They had invited this woman's son, Angel, to come to the studies on several occasions, but he had always refused. The last time he was invited to attend, he said he would only go if he saw his mother healed. The prayers continued for this woman and God answered them. She was eventually healed and got out of her bed. This family was invited to Nora and Eduardo's home for a mini-campaign and the whole family came—the woman, her son Angel, and his wife. They heard the gospel and we were thrilled to see all of Angel's family and his mother embrace Christ as their Savior. They have been invited to begin a discipleship class and are now studying to better know the Word of God.

Abandoned and Found

Gloria Cuazitl Romero
(told by Ed Parman)

About fifteen years ago, Gloria was abandoned by her husband, who was a doctor. She was studying at this time to advance her education and bring herself up to the level of her husband. But he was unfaithful, even in their own house. He finally left to be with the other woman, leaving her with two children and her studies.

This began an even more difficult time for her and her small children, ages six and eight. Sometimes they didn't have any food or proper clothing. At this point she wanted to take her own life. She didn't feel like she had a reason to live. Many times she went to speak to her husband to ask him to return to their house. But he gave her the same answer—that he would only return to their home if he were permitted to bring the other woman, so that the three of them could live "happily." She did not accept this. She went so far as to have *limpias* or spiritual cleansing (a form of witchcraft) done on behalf of her husband so that he might return. But none of this worked. She passed some time in this situation.

On one occasion she was telling her story to a friend, who gave her a Bible. It was 1985 when she began to read her new Bible, though she did not know exactly how or where to begin. She began to feel that God was speaking to her through the Bible. For several years she continued to read, not knowing what it meant to accept Christ into her heart. She said to the friend who had given her the Bible, "Invite me to your church." The friend said she would take her, but unfortunately this woman traveled out of the city frequently and often was not there on Sundays. But Gloria kept insisting. Finally in February of 1998 she was invited to our church, where she felt a great peace in hearing the Word of God. She said, "I was motivated to stay— the church people treated me like a queen and it was so nice!" And she has continued to attend weekly without her friend. After about a month, she responded to the altar call to accept Christ as her Savior. Since that time, she speaks of the great joy and peace that comes from living with Christ. She has started bringing her son, a university student, as well as another friend who is going through some difficult problems.

She would like for both her children to come and experience what she has found. She is very grateful to God and doesn't tire of telling her story to any who will hear it! She praises the Lord freely, with the freedom we receive when we come to Jesus.

Puerto Rico

AIDS is a tremendous problem in many third-world nations. It is a vicious disease that some Evangelicals seem to exult in viewing as a deserving curse from God. But Christians should never exult over the effects of sin in another's life. Even in these things the Lord can be Lord. As in this first story, AIDS may intensify the surety of death and the need for life in Christ.

HIV Positive, but Positive in God's Love

• •

Ivette Gonzalez

My name is Ivette Gonzalez. I am twenty years old and my husband and I are both HIV positive. I have a five-year-old daughter who does not have the virus. I thank the Lord.

It has been five and a half years since I found out about my condition. Since the day I knew about it, I have been certain that God has a purpose for me. During these years, God has confirmed this many times.

I have always felt Father God close to me, but something was missing. In my prayers I asked direction in choosing a church. I wanted to belong to a church; I needed one. I received invitations to some churches, but I did not feel the desire to attend. It was then that a neighbor wanted to take my daughter to her church and I told her I would accompany them. What a joy that was! Once more God answered my prayers! I knew He wanted me in this church. That is how I arrived at the Wesleyan Evangelical Church of Caparra.

I felt the need to speak to the people about what God had done in me. I didn't find out about my condition until I was in my eighth month of pregnancy. I was not able to receive treatment so that my daughter would have a chance to be negative. But my God took care of that. Thank you, Lord! Thank you for my daughter! Thank you for her health!

I was depressed when I first learned about my condition. Those were difficult times, but my God took care of everything. He has been guiding me and making me understand that there was a purpose for everything that was happening. His guiding me to the church has made it possible for my faith to strengthen and for me to learn His Word. He has taught me to love and pray for others.

As part of my treatment for this condition, I periodically have laboratory tests that measure the virus count in my body. A count of 10,000 is considered high. Some patients have counts of 70,000, 100,000 or 200,000. These are very, very high. To my doctor's and my surprise, my first result was 742. When the second result was 400, the doctor's surprise was even greater. The new drugs were lowering the levels and bringing them to a zero count. This does not mean that the person is no longer positive, but that there is control over the virus, thereby prolonging the patient's life.

Why did my virus count diminish when it should have gone up? Why is this still happening when I am no longer taking medication? Only God has the answer. Once again He confirmed His purpose in my life.

After five months, I had the laboratory tests again. Remember that I do not take medication for my condition because the doctor did not think it was necessary. Therefore, my virus count should have increased. But, for the glory of God, these results were also negative!

Why is this so if I no longer take medication? It is because I have the best, the perfect, the all powerful medicine . . . my Lord! May He be glorified forever!

My life's purpose now is speaking about HIV/AIDS to teenagers. I take these seminars to schools. Another HIV-positive young mother accompanies me. We want to make young people conscious of what the HIV patient goes through. When you speak about these experiences, the listener is impacted in a more effective way. The name of our seminar series is *Proyecto Mensajeros de Vida* (Project Messengers of Life). I know the Lord blessed this project because I have never done this and He has been directing me. Many of the things written I received from the church.

The most important thing about *Proyecto Mensajeros de Vida* is that it is based on love. Love for oneself, love for others, and above all, love for God—love for God who has given us the gift of life and which we must take care of and value. I know my God accompanies me on this road that I have started to walk, and I know that only He can make success possible.

I know in my heart that someday I will be totally healed. I don't know if I am totally healed or not at this moment, but I know I am saved. I only know I love life, myself, my family and God. I am an instrument of God and all I do or say is for His glory.

Being HIV positive has not been a curse in my life, nor is it the end. It is a happiness that has started a life, a life with my Christ who gives me the strength and the confidence that with God all things are possible.

May You be praised forever, King of Kings! Thank you, my beloved God!

Atheist Outwitted by Christian Daughter

Maria Ricarda Cabello

I welcome this opportunity to witness how the Lord fulfills His promise, "Believe on the Lord Jesus Christ, and thou shalt be saved, and thy house" (Acts 16:31 KJV).

On this occasion I want to share the beloved experience of how my father became saved, and how this promise of the Lord became a reality in my life and in the life of my whole family.

My grandfather passed away when my father was the age of ten. He already was the provider for both his mother and grandmother. He lived in the capital of Puerto Rico, which is surrounded by the sea. Because he was a good swimmer, he went to the piers and with spectacular dives into the water, retrieved the coins thrown by the marines from the ships in the harbor. He also gathered coal from the ships that came from Spain. Later, he exchanged the coal for food in a Chinese restaurant in Old San Juan.

When his mother and grandmother died, he went astray. A helping hand was extended to him by the Socialist Party where, for a living, he rendered small services at their offices. There, in a very short time, he was transformed from an altar boy in the Catholic Church to a fervent socialist and atheist.

He never went to a formal school but learned to write all by himself. He became an avid reader and his best friends were books and newspapers. Set apart from his peers by his beautiful speaking voice, it became his most precious asset.

In the course of time, my father married my mother and in some way, at last, he had a home. I recall him as an excellent citizen, a compassionate man, a very good father and provider. On the negative side, he was a bit dictatorial at home.

As time went by, I accepted Jesus Christ as my Savior and became a member of the church. My father and I developed a very close relationship. We talked about almost every subject—politics and religion included. One day, he went back for a short time to his old tactics and "ordered" me to vote for the party of his preference. But, as we were on good talking terms, I asked him, "Did I ever tell you to 'vote' for Christ?"

He was surprised at my question, perhaps more shocked than surprised. I imagine him thinking, "Who is this young lady daring to ask such a question?" Nevertheless, I continued, "Let's make a bargain. If you ask me to vote for your party, I will have to ask you to 'vote' for Jesus Christ."

His reply was fast and to the point, "How can I trust you and be certain that you are going to vote my way?" I replied, "Because I am a Christian lady, and if I say that I will vote that way, you can be certain that I will do it." With a smile he said, "I accept." Immediately I thought about the forthcoming Annual Rally Day of my church, and I told him, "You can't go to my church at any time you want. You will have to wait till I invite you."

That momentous day came shortly. It was a very bright day and we had a splendid service. I recall it as the most precious service that I have ever been part of. Every detail was taken care of with exquisite precision. The church choir sang "The Holy City" with an excellence that touched my father profoundly. When the altar call was made, my father passed in tears to the altar. I cannot remember in my life a more emotional experience. I still see in my mind that obnoxious atheist, dressed in white, kneeling at the altar, giving his life to the Lord. Some time later my father told me that he regretted not having spent his life as a preacher.

My mother was also saved and most of my family. I keep rejoicing in His promise that all of them will be saved. Blessed be the Lord that keeps His promises forever!

Suriname

L evi Iengibe is the district superintendent in Suriname. Under his leadership, the church in Suriname has grown faster and planted more churches than in any other period of our mission history in Suriname. Many able missionaries and national leaders in the past influenced Levi and saw within him potential that he didn't even see himself. Now God has made him the person for the time.

Kicked Out, Knocked Down, Picked Up

●●●●●●●●●●●●●●●●●●●●●●●

Levi H. Iengibe

(District Superintendent)

At the age of thirteen, I was becoming a rebel in my village and in my school. It was a very terrible period of fighting and making trouble. I did not care about my life or what people would think. During those years, I was used by the devil to hold other people back from serving the Lord. Before this time I had been a very quiet boy, with respect for the things of the Lord. I used to go to Sunday school almost every Sunday. The hate began when I saw a few Christians who were very hypocritical in serving the Lord. That caused the bad change in my life. I could not see the love in them that the church taught. Fighting each other, complaining about church rules, gossiping, and speaking harshly about each other during the week, it seemed their holy talking and living was only on Sunday. This was not the Christian life for which I was looking.

I knew I was missing something. I was empty, without peace, and felt like no one loved me. I became sick and this also caused a lot of questions. If God was real why did He treat me like this? I was a good boy—I knew that—but even the bad people were happy. Why did God love others more than He loved me? Why was there so much hatred, trouble, turmoil, sickness and poverty? Why did God hate me? I became a rebel against Christians and things of the church.

Because of my behavior, I was thrown out of school. The main reason was because I sent a message to a girl named Maria that I would marry her. There was no place in this school for boys who wanted to marry girls. This was a Wesleyan school. My hatred against The Wesleyan Church increased. I did not want to hear anything about this Church.

My parents sent me to my brother, who was working for the large bauxite company, Suralco, at Paranam. He found a job for me in a local hardware store, in hopes that I could be enrolled at a different school in the coming school year. According to my school report card, it would be difficult to find another school. I was without hope, without love and without a future. All my illusions were gone. There was only one thing left, death. That seemed better than life. Killing myself seemed to be the only way. This became my plan.

On Monday, September 7, 1970, while I was working in the storeroom of Ilahibaks Hardware Store, I felt like somebody was talking to me. It was God. He opened my mind and my eyes and placed my real life before me. I knew I was a sinner. It felt just like I was in a cinema. The more He talked, the more I saw myself. I felt terrible. I wished I could hide. There was nothing else to do; the only possibility was to call on Jesus. I fell on my knees on a bag of rice, put my elbows on a few sheets of roofing tin, and wept. I asked the Lord to forgive me for all my sins. After that I was sure that my sins were forgiven. The Lord found me. The crisis in my life was over. There were no more hurt feelings. I became a new creation. The Lord had restored my life. The hope came in. My life was filled with joy and happiness as never before. I began to sing and my heart was filled with joy.

My boss saw a change in me and asked me why I was so happy. I told him about my conversion experience, and how Jesus had set me free. "No," he said, "Jesus cannot make people happy. He died. There is only one book that can make people happy and that is this book, the Koran. Do not fool yourself, boy. I am happy because of this book." I replied, "I'm not talking about a book. I don't know what kind of book that is, but I am sure of one thing. I have been set free by Jesus Christ. He died indeed, but He rose again on the third day. He died for my sins. I am sure my sins are gone." Then he went to his office. After that day he could see the difference. He became a good friend to me.

God made it possible for me to be enrolled in a high school in Paranam. The first thing I did was write a letter to my mother and my former principal, asking them to forgive me for the things I had done to them. The joy was great! The Lord found Levi. The Lord helped me in school. I was the best student in my class. That year I took the exam for the junior technical school and I passed. At the end of the year, the principal discovered that I was not officially enrolled in the school. But since my test score was so good, he was able to fix everything for me so that I could be enrolled in the tech school. I still had to face many problems, but the Lord helped me through all these things. After three years, He made it possible for me to go to college. It should have been impossible for me to go to college because I had no one to support me. But He found me a place in a dormitory where I did not have to pay anything.

I only had 80 guilders, but I needed to pay 150 guilders to be allowed to take courses in college. It was a time of deep prayer for me. One week before school began, the government dropped the tuition charges. I could go the school without paying anything! That year the school board decided to help poor students by giving them some support. They gave me 75 guilders every month. The Lord was very good to me. I was able to finish school within four years.

Another blessing of the Lord is the wife he gave me. My prayer was always that the Lord would make the choice for me. I had no idea who my wife would be but I wanted to marry a good Christian lady. He made my dream come true.

One night before I went to bed, I asked the Lord to tell me in a dream who my wife would be. This is hard to believe but it is the truth. The Lord showed me that my wife would be Maria. "That's impossible, Lord!" I said after I woke up. "They threw me out of school because of her. Anyhow, I don't think she will ever love me. But if this is true, give the same dream again." It was a Saturday night when I had the dream. Sunday after church I went to rest a little bit. Oh, what a miracle! In my dream the Lord gave me the same name again. "Your wife will be Maria." It was as hard for me to believe as it must have been for the Virgin Mary to believe that she would have a baby. But the Lord's promise was certainly true. We married on April 5, 1980. The teacher who threw me out of school was our special wedding driver on that day. We have a happy marriage and the Lord has blessed us with four boys. I have seen the hand of the Lord in my life and in my work for Him.

I was a member of the Sloot Wesleyan Church when the Lord called me into the ministry. It was on a Sunday evening, after an evangelistic service. As Maria and I walked home, the Lord spoke clearly to me. He had something for me to do, but I did not know what. I thought that maybe he would send me to Pelgrim Kondre in the interior, since Rev. James Leitzel, the pastor at Pelgrim Kondre, had asked me if it was possible for me to become the principal of the dormitory there.

The Wednesday after that, just before the service, Rev. L. van der Kuyp, the district superintendent, asked me if I would be able to help in the newly planted Wesleyan church of Flora, where we had just started services. I would be working together with missionary Steve Saunders. I had felt that was the work for which the Lord had called me, so I told him yes. It was a very wonderful time to work with the Saunders family. We worked very hard, but there was not much fruit after three years.

After the Saunders family left Suriname, the district board of administration (DBA) asked me to become the Flora pastor. I was still a student in the Bible school. I asked the board to give me one month to pray about it. I told the Lord that I would accept this challenge only if He would help. I gave Him three months to let me see results. In the next meeting I told the DBA that I was able to serve.

Indeed the Lord gave me the first nine members within three months. And from that day on, the Flora Wesleyan Church became a discipling church. After a few years I became the assistant district superintendent. We really began to see progress in the work of the Lord.

While our regional superintendent, Rev. Paul Downey, lived in Guyana, the Lord moved our membership from 93 to about 250 in three years. In 1993, I became the district superintendent. The Lord is still blessing the work here in Suriname. The membership is now almost 500. The Church had a hard time with growth at first. The membership was only 93 after 40 years. Now that has changed. The dead churches have been revived and the Holy Spirit is moving. Almost every Sunday new people come to Christ. Demon-possessed people are set free and the Lord is healing sick people. It seems that we are in the midst of a revival.

The Lord is blessing the Church in many ways. Property for the Bible school has been bought. After one week of serious praying and fasting, the Lord moved the resident "Bonu man," a wonder doctor who was a strong enemy of the Flora Wesleyan Church. The building that was used by Satan against the Lord is now the Bible school building. We praise the Lord for that victory. Our God is a very strong and wonderful God. The mission home is now Wesleyan property since Wesleyan World Missions purchased it one year ago. Five churches have been planted in the last three years. Our intention is to plant three more in 1998. The church in Suriname also feels that now is the best time to reach out to another country, French Guyana. God has called one of our pastors to go to this country. We are sure the Lord will provide all our needs to start a new work in French Guyana.

Pacific

Australia

Culturally, Australia is very near to North America. The church in Australia has grown dramatically because of an emphasis on evangelism. That emphasis is evident in these stories.

Angel Abused

Angela

Angela was born in Grassano, Italy, in 1951 and grew up in a large family of seven boys and three girls. They did not have much of this world's wealth but were taught the importance of love toward God, obedience to parents, and forgiveness toward others. It would only be through the grace of God that she survived the suffering in her life.

When she was just fifteen, her parents arranged a marriage with Marco. Although she felt he was a "bad man who didn't believe in God," she followed through with the wedding in obedience to her parents. "He treated me bad and made me suffer. But I never told anyone and just cried in my heart because I didn't want people to cry for me. I carried my little cross, full of pain every day."

One day he returned home to announce quite unexpectedly that he had booked tickets for the family to migrate to Australia. Leaving family and familiar surroundings, Angela dutifully boarded the boat with her two children, arriving in Australia in 1973. "I thought this may change my husband, but things grew worse. The sufferings came more, the pain came more."

In 1977, while working with her husband picking fruit, Angela, then about six months pregnant, realized something was very wrong. Frantic, she called to her husband to help her, or let her go home, but he ignored her and instead beat her, demanding that she keep working. When she was eventually taken to the local hospital, the police persuaded her to seek refuge with The Salvation Army. They gave her a room with the children, though she was ashamed to call it home. "But God blessed me there and gave me hope. They helped with food until I found a job." Not long after Angela left Marco, he was killed in a car accident.

Angela developed severe asthma and could not keep working long. She found life very difficult providing for her two children. About this time she met a Greek man named Jack. "I thought things were going to be better, but they didn't go well and I started to suffer again, every day." When she was eight months pregnant with his child, she went to the Housing Office in tears and asked for help. "God performed a miracle and I was immediately given a Housing Commission flat in Windsor. I love this area and have lived here ever since."

In 1988 Angela was in a car accident herself. Lying in a coma, she thought she was dead, but she felt God touch her and say, "No, you're not dead. I want you here." As she says, "I came back into life." She knew that God was taking care of her.

Once again, thinking things would be different, Angela married Barry in a Registry Office in 1989. Very quickly she realized things were not right. "He made me suffer, smashing and abusing me and my little boy, Jack." Then in December 1993, Sofia was born. Hoping that this new life would bring love into the family and stop the trouble, Angela was again disappointed. Barry only vented his anger on his little girl as well. In 1995, young Jack, always out for a "freebie" at the end of the day, met one of the pastoral team members of the local Wesleyan Methodist Church who was working in a pie shop. Through her encouragement, Jack struck up a friendship with another member of the team and soon the whole family started attending church.

Then late in 1996, Barry suffered a stroke that reduced him to a shadow. Fighting bravely, he attended church as much as he could and professed a faith in God before he passed into His presence in January 1997. After the funeral, Angela felt led to go and see one of Barry's friends, Phillip. She wanted to invite him to her church. He had met God thirty years previously and she wanted him to feel the love of the people who had helped her so much. "He loved God very much—then I found he loved me, too. Pastor Nalin married us on July 27, 1997. The people in the little church give me a beautiful wedding. They provided everything—flowers and bouquets, reception, video of the day to send to family in Italy—all the things I never had, even when I married the first time at fifteen." She was even able to wear again the wedding dress her grandmother had lovingly made for her first wedding. This time, however, she was marrying a man for love, a man who shared her love for God. "I will never forget my second family who marry me far away when my own family is missing." At the wedding some of Angela's neighbors remarked on the change in her. The change, she told them, was because she had grown to love God so much.

Life has not suddenly become a bed of roses for Angela and Phillip. Recently Angela passed into the dark tunnel of death, a tunnel to which she could see no end. When she was revived by the medics, she woke saying, "I am a fool for you, my God." No matter what life has thrown at her, Angela has kept her faith. With a quiet, loving, and attentive Phillip by her side, her love for God has blossomed. Now she has a joy that overflows and passionately shares Jesus with others. "Look what He has done for me. So many miracles."

I Am My Brother's Keeper

Bruce

(told by Alan Brown)

God is at work even when you are at Bible college—Kingsley College in Melbourne, to be exact. I thought that when you are studying that you were somehow "on the bench." But how wrong could I be?

Most students find the grind of study and their Christian service appointment enough to keep them occupied, but somehow I didn't quite agree. When a simple need to disciple a young teenage girl arose, my wife and I opened up our flat each Wednesday night. That didn't seem too hard, but suddenly there were more young adults turning up. We didn't have any exciting program. We just ate together, washed up together (suds fights were the norm) and sat down and had Bible study afterwards. God honors those who honor him. It was at this time my youngest brother Bruce, all of twenty-one years, was finding out that the life presented by the world lets you down. He had suffered a broken jaw after being bashed. He found out that relationships were fickle and that cities could be very lonely. Now as I talked to him by phone, I suddenly realized that God had provided me with the opportunity to reach out to my own brother.

"Would you like to come to a young adults group?"

"Yeah, sounds interesting."

Bruce lived on the other side of the city and it took one hour to drive over and another hour to drive home. He usually had to be out of bed by around 5:30 a.m. for work. But he came searching for God.

The first few weeks Bruce sat back and observed, but slowly he realized that these Christians still had struggles and lived in the same world as he did. Study by study God stripped back the layers until Bruce began to pray and to express a changed heart. Bruce got involved in Circle Church, a house church run by Dr. David Wilson. It was not long before baptism was organized.

I will never forget the day that we gathered at Eltham Beach as a huge storm blew up. Still, the folks being baptized really wanted to be baptized. But above all else, my very own brother had surrendered to God and had been changed forever.

Seven years later, Bruce is still involved in Circle Church, helping to run a fellowship at his place. But he now lives over near Kingsley College. Nearly all the young adults have gone on for the Lord. In fact, the original teenage girl, Rebbekah, married another group member, Kevin. God wants us to be faithful, no matter what circumstances we find ourselves in. He is able to do much more than we could ever think or imagine.

A Mother's Testimony

•

Carol Keilar

On August 12, 1984, God gave me a promise for our daughters. "I will pour out my spirit on your offspring, and my blessing on your descendants. They will spring up like grass in a meadow, like poplar trees by flowing streams. *One* will say, 'I belong to the Lord'; *another* will call himself by the name of Jacob; *still another* will write on his hand, 'The Lord's,' and will take the name Israel" (Isaiah 44:3b-5, emphasis by author).

I have to tell you that when God gave me this promise, none of our girls was walking with the Lord. They came to church on Sundays, grudgingly, because their father was the pastor. Our second daughter, Trish, was fifteen and had been suffering for two years from anorexia. At one stage she was so weak that I had to carry her around. Shortly after this she was hospitalized for two weeks. Then we were instructed by the dietician to note everything she ate and keep a constant watch over her.

Just after we arrived in Rockhampton, Central Queensland, to pioneer a church, Trish was hospitalized because her weight had dropped about forty kilograms and we could not get her to eat. We knew that she was at death's door and there was nothing we could do about it, except pray! At this stage we did not know that the doctors had no cure except to force-feed by tubes and release the patient when she was at an acceptable weight. Once home, she would again look in the mirror and announce that she was fat! It was a constant battle to make sure she was eating. Most times it seemed to be salads, vegetables and fruit, very rarely a decent meal. Then we had to make sure she did not resort to bulimia and lose it all anyway.

This put incredible pressure on the household and on our other children, Susan (nearly seventeen) and Cathy (nearly thirteen). It was at this difficult time that God gave me the promise for our three girls. We had begun to set aside Fridays as a day of prayer and fasting, particularly for Trish. Even though at the age of seven she had professed Christ and been baptized as a believer, she had rebelled and gone far away from the Lord. We felt that the anorexia was demonic because many times as my husband prayed for Trish, he felt like there was a wall in front of him, blocking his prayers.

Every time I started to feel desperate about the situation, God would remind me about the promise that He had given me, and I would reread it, meditate on it, and claim it for our girls.

In 1990, we were on the southeast coast of Western Australia pastoring an independent church in a small country town called Esperance. Trish was 21 and still battling anorexia. She had become desperately ill again and the doctor ordered that she fly to Perth and be admitted to the Fremantle Hospital. Her weight was again around forty kilograms. I flew up with her. It was a very harrowing time since the family also had to have a round-table conference with the psychiatrist who blamed the ministry for causing our daughter's problems.

Indeed, my husband lost his ministry position through this situation. The people in the church did not understand and kept making comments like, "The pastor needs pastoring—this is not professional behavior." It was not until a few months had elapsed that one of the ladies visited me and apologized. She said she did not realize what we were going through until her sister called to say her niece had been diagnosed with anorexia.

After being released from the hospital, Trish decided to live in Perth in a flat attached to a house where her oldest sister, Sue, and Sue's husband and son were living. We remained in Esperance until April 1993 because we were given another ministry there. Our youngest daughter, Cathy, remained with us, but attended the former church that we had pastored since all her friends were there.

One night, after we'd moved back to Perth, Cathy phoned to tell us that she had accepted Christ—despite once telling us that she would never become a Christian because she had seen how so-called Christians behave and treat their pastors! We were delighted that our youngest daughter had taken the step of faith.

In October 1994, we were called to pastor the Thorpdale Wesleyan Methodist Church in Gippsland, Victoria. Since this would be the first time that we would not have any of our children with us, I passed each one of them over to Jesus in my mind in the last service before we left Perth. In March 1996, Trish and her son came to Thorpdale because she was having marriage difficulties. While there, she attended church for the first time in years. Her three-year-old son said to her, "Mummy, when we go home can we go to church and can I have a dog?" After three weeks she did return to Perth and church became a reality, but the dog did not. Instead, Jordan got a baby brother later that year.

On May 3, 1996, we received a letter from Trish that said, "I have some good news about myself in that I recommitted to God on Sunday at the end of the service. It really had little to do with the message, although I found it a challenging topic that has kept me thinking. But the thing is that God has been calling me back to Him for a long time now, and up until last Sunday I continued to resist Him. I didn't want to give in to Him because I know that the cost of following God is great and it is no good being a hypocrite who says all the right things but whose life doesn't measure up."

Then in early 1997, we received another letter that told us that Jesus had healed her of her anorexia. She had waited this long to tell us because she had been expecting her second child previously and wanted to be sure it was not a food fad.

We were ecstatic and wanted to tell the whole world how God had saved and delivered Trish from anorexia and that, indeed, He was answering the promise that He had given me nearly thirteen years ago. Trish and Cathy were now walking with the Lord. In January 1997, my husband had the joy of baptizing Cathy at Thorpdale Wesleyan Church while she was visiting us on holiday. Since this time she has grown in leaps and bounds in her faith and service to the Lord. She leads worship services and Bible studies, has taught Sunday school, is a greeter at the door and has been involved in hospitality in "Newcomers' Dinners."

We had planned to visit Sue in December 1997 to be part of her thirteenth birthday celebrations. In September 1997, at the southern district conference, my husband was elected to the position of district superintendent. This necessitated us moving from the country to Melbourne and also finishing our ministry in Gippsland, but yet we knew we had to fulfill our promise to Sue and be with her at her party on her special day.

On December 28, 1997, my husband preached at the Bundaberg Wesleyan Church on the topic, "Where are You?" At the end of the service he made an appeal, and who should come to the front in response to God, but our daughter, Sue. She was crying, my husband was crying, I was crying, Cathy was crying. In fact I don't think there was a dry eye in the church. It was a wonderful day, a day we will never forget!

It had been thirteen years since God had given me the promises for our daughters, but praise His name, He fulfilled them and answered all our prayers. I want to encourage all pastors and parents to keep on praying for their families and to never give up, because we have a great God who is able to save to the uttermost. Even when things look impossible, God is at work.

The "Personal" in Salvation
•••••••••••••••••••••••
Dave Powell, National Superintendent

rowing up in a Christian home didn't assure me of salvation. My parents were Christian (Salvation Army), my dad's parents were officers in The Salvation Army and my mother's grandfather was an evangelist in England after being converted in prison. I remember Grandma telling me how her father took her to see General Booth, the founder of The Salvation Army, and to hear him preach. We went to the Army and to other churches regularly where I heard the gospel often. I witnessed people being born again. But during my teens I experienced a strong pull from worldly mates to "booze on," and I obliged quite happily. I had many opportunities to die by my stupid behavior and if that had happened, I would have been a salvation-knowledgeable resident of hell. The fact that being right with God was a personal thing just hadn't dawned on me.

It did however on January 1, 1971, at 1 a.m. As a church youth group we used to go to the Keswick Convention at Mount Tambourine whenever it was on. They reinforced how "personal" the gospel message was and how sinful man was. It began to sink in. Ivan, my brother, went forward at the altar call that night. A few hours later, at 1 a.m., I found myself with a group of young people who were praying for a certain girl. When it came my turn to pray, the Holy Sprit spoke to my mind. "Here you are praying for this girl when you are the one who needs prayer." I felt so dirty with sin in such a way that I had never felt before. Hearing the gospel so many times ensured that I knew what to do when I heard the call of God. Feeling so guilty, I sobbed it out to God, seeking His forgiveness and asking Jesus to come into my life. I sensed an urge to tell my church friends what had happened as a testimony to God. Sadly, my testimony at the time was better received by my worldly friends than my church friends.

Some years later I went to Tahlee Bible College, received some good training, found a lovely wife (Joy), and eventually entered the Wesleyan ministry where we have been pastoring and church planting. It is indeed a great joy to preach the Word of God and see people grow in the Lord. People respond to that which is good and their lives are turned around.

Brotherly Love Reigns

●●●●●●●●●●●●●●●●●●●●●●●
Francisco
(told by Alan Brown)

I met Francisco at the Gympie family camp. He was working at the farm where we camped in tents. God's timing was incredible since this man was visiting for only six weeks. Originally from Peru, he now made his home in New Zealand, but his English was still fairly broken. I was the guest speaker for the weekend. Francisco approached me after the first message and asked, "How can the people and you have such love for each other? You have only just met!"

I explained that we were all born-again Christians and it was the love that God provided that he was seeing in action. Perhaps more puzzled than understanding, Francisco headed off to do some farm work.

At the next session, Francisco decided to sit in and discover more of this God of love for himself. Afterwards he again spoke to me.

"Alan, I have been a Catholic all my life and my knowledge of God is a distant God. I want to know God like you know Him."

I was thrilled to open the Scriptures and point out salvation passages, allowing him to read them for himself. He jotted down all the verses so he could read them over again that night. I met with Francisco again and this time I asked him if he would like to ask the Lord that he barely knew to come into his life. "Yes, Alan, I want to do that."

"Then, Francisco, you must surrender your heart to Jesus and by faith allow him to live in you. But, there is one more thing. When you pray, speak in your heart language of Spanish." A large smile greeted my words. He knew that he was truly going to pray to his Savior and he bowed his head and asked Jesus to come into his life.

What a joy to see another soul come into the Kingdom! I asked Pastor Stuart Hall to give follow-up counseling until Francisco left the country. A video arrived in the mail some weeks later. I watched the baptism of Francisco in the Mary River as the Gympie fellowship rejoiced. I realized the power of Jesus' words, "They will know you are my disciples, if you have love for one another."

Waiting Room to Eternity
●●●●●●●●●●●●●●●●●●●●●●●●
Hugh and Lindsay Cameron
(told by Stan Baker)

I met Hugh Cameron in February 1981 while we were sitting in the waiting room at the Nanango hospital. He was waiting to see a doctor about a painful foot and I was with my oldest son who needed some medical attention. We began to chat and I discovered that he had come to town as a result of the building industry and was a plasterer by trade. I told him that I was the pastor of the Wesleyan Methodist Church, the church that sent a rather large bus around to collect the children for Sunday school every Sunday morning. He told me about his little girl, Kathryn, who was about three years old. He was obviously concerned that she had not been baptized.

During 1981, I visited Hugh and Joy's home several times. I remember being warmly received and enjoying some very meaningful discussions over a cup of tea. Hugh is the oldest of four sons, and it was towards the end of 1981 that I first met his brother, Lindsay. Lindsay obviously sought to enjoy life to the fullest and was on his way for a holiday in New Zealand.

On March 4, 1982, I started an evangelistic Bible study with Hugh and Joy. This Bible study continued for several weeks. On April 22, 1982, I visited Hugh and Joy and they told me that they had received Christ and testified to a real change in their lives. Even at that early stage, they began to talk about the possibility of attending Bible college. They soon joined as preparatory members of the Nanango Wesleyan Methodist Church, and by July 1982, they became full members. Sometime during this period, Hugh's youngest brother, Ian, who lived in Bundaberg, also received Christ as a result of Hugh's testimony and the change in his life.

On August 4, Lindsay Cameron came for tea. I shared the gospel with him and he received Christ. Lindsay was now working with Hugh in Nanango and they were warmly accepted and loved by the Nanango Wesleyan Methodist Church. They entered into its fellowship and became involved in its ministry. Lindsay became a full member on Sunday, March 4, 1984.

The Lord began to speak to both Hugh and Lindsay about pastoral ministry, and in February 1985, they both enrolled in Kingsley College for ministerial training. It was with mixed feelings that Nanango church bid them goodbye—sorry to see them go, yet rejoicing in this good fruit of its ministry and witness.

Following years of training at Kingsley College, both Hugh and Lindsay served in the Queensland District of the Wesleyan Methodist Church. When the new North Queensland District was formed in 1992, Lindsay Cameron was the first district superintendent. He was succeeded a couple of years later by his brother, Hugh. Hugh continues to minister in the city of Townsville. Lindsay is now a missionary, along with his wife Rosalea, to Mozambique.

Their brother Ian worships in the Bundaberg Wesleyan Methodist Church as does their mother, Mrs. Freda Cameron, whose own love for the Lord was revived as the result of His grace in the lives of her sons.

We rejoice in the marvelous grace of God. One can never tell what may be the outcome of a casual meeting in a waiting room of the outpatients' department in a local hospital. Nor should we underestimate the impact of a local church that seeks to reach out to its community with the truth of the gospel, expressing the love of God at every opportunity.

The Bearded Stranger
Ina Adams

I am seventy-four years old and I wish to tell of something wonderful that happened to me.

About four years ago I answered a knock on my door and standing there was a completely bearded stranger. He introduced himself as Pastor Colin Hussey of the Wesleyan Methodist Church. We proceeded to have a talk on the church and religion.

He asked me, "Do you go to church?" The answer was no, even though I believed in the Lord and considered myself a Christian. He asked me to come along to his church, which was within walking distance of my house. Out of curiosity I went along.

Well, I was surprised by the things I learned from going to church and attending Bible study classes. I learned what I had been missing all of those years. I have come to know the Lord and that He is my Savior. By confessing all my sins and opening up my heart to the Lord, what wonderful beautiful things have been happening to me. My prayers have been answered—not so much in the ways I have asked for them, but in the way the Lord knows that things should happen. I know that I love Him with all of my heart and I bless the day that the bearded stranger knocked on my door so that I could find out the things I have been searching for all my life.

From Darkness to Light
•••••••••••••••••••••••••
John Sweeney

I grew up in Cornwall, southwest England, as an only and very lonely child in a dysfunctional home. My parents finally separated when I was thirteen, a year after we migrated to Australia. From very early in childhood until about a year prior to my conversion, I existed in a "hermetically sealed" realm of self-imposed isolation from the real world and its people, for reasons unknown to me. I had invented and built around myself a realm of fantasy inhabited by creatures of a somewhat Dalinian surreality, which I animated at my own whim and will. To others outside my world, I was unreachable. I had a keen interest in science; so keen, I could have just about "sold my soul" for a telescope, a prism or a set of lenses. Forget about toy trains or wagons. I had no time for those.

At nineteen years of age I found myself sitting in a waiting room of a psychiatric clinic. I had referred myself to a psychiatrist after spending time in libraries, poring over psychology textbooks, trying to find out why I was "not like other children," as my mother had said many years before. There in the waiting room I picked up a secular magazine. I was struck by a front-page article about the conversion of a hardened criminal to Christ. As I read it, I felt the Holy Spirit saying within me, "This is for you." That night I prayed the same prayer this man had prayed, "God help me." Throughout the following year I personally experienced what I never knew had existed, love. In every breath of the wind I seemed to hear His gentle voice. In every cloud I saw His wonderful face and just as miraculously, I was actually wanting to love people for Him and because of Him.

After that twelve-month "honeymoon," I made a costly mistake. I took my eyes off the Lord and put them on man, placing faith in His followers instead of the One they were following. The result? A descent into ever increasing confusion and darkness. My cry turned from "I love you Lord" to "Where are you, Lord?" Now I was running to this minister and that counselor, reading every spiritual "how to" book I could get my hands on. More confusion, deeper darkness. His voice no longer was in the wind, His face was no longer in every cloud. He was gone. Had I done the unpardonable sin? Was I doomed? Engulfed with fear, I struggled on, mostly in my own strength, clinging to just a "photograph" of the Jesus who had been so wonderfully real and close to me. My life was a raging battlefield between faith and feeling, a veritable torture chamber of fear, bitterness, anguish and downright anger. My anger was against myself, against those I felt had misunderstood me, and yes, even against God. Yet something within me hung on through it all.

I had left behind me a trail of botched commitments and recommitments to the Lord, but my faith in Him, having been sorely tried, is strong. For it is not my faith, but His divine gift (Ephesians 2:8). My own human faith would have wilted and died long ago. You see, God is eternally faithful (2 Timothy 2:13), and His gifts are irrevocable (Romans 11:29). He did not leave me, I left Him. Does He place the solitary in families (Psalms 68:6)? You bet! I belong now to a wonderful, loving church family. Yes, even my dear mother—now in her healthy seventies—and I have been happily reunited after more than a twenty-year separation. I am now studying for a lay preacher's license and am successfully employed. In my spare time, I am working on a book entitled *A Divine Cosmology*, in which I aim to present a strong, theistic counter-argument to the predominantly evolutionist interpretation of the existence and origin of the cosmos.

> When Jesus is present, all is good, nothing is difficult,
> but when Jesus is absent, all is hard.
> How dry and hard art thou without Jesus,
> How foolish and vain if thou desire anything out of Jesus!
> To be without Jesus is a grievous hell,
> To be with Jesus, a sweet paradise.
> Love all for Jesus, but Jesus for Himself.
> From *The Imitation of Christ* by Thomas à Kempis

The Bookie's Son Gets a New Life

● ●

Peter Lyne

The home I grew up in was anything but godly. As a small boy I remember Dad as an illegal bookmaker and a greyhound trainer. Normal life was drunkenness, gambling, lying, cheating and so forth. I thank God for two godly Methodist grandparents who prayed for me. Pa never saw their prayers answered, but I was saved for several years before Ma died.

By the time I was fourteen, I had determined that drinking and smoking were stupid and that I would never do either. But three years later, I was doing both. At seventeen I left home and joined the Army, but home was still a part of me. My view of normal was quite destructive.

Shortly before my eighteenth birthday a Christian family, Ken and Mavis Perin, who lived near the Army base where I was stationed, began taking an interest in me. I remember one day I boasted to them that I had discovered how to use metal washers I took from the base in place of ten-cent pieces in vending machines. Poor Mavis was horrified. It was the first time that I remember someone whose motive for doing right was other than the fear of being caught. My dad had always said, "The only sin is getting caught."

Ken and another friend explained what it meant to be a Christian. I really was impressed by these people—they cared, they were honest, and they did not set out to impress anybody or use their friends. I thought I should be a Christian too, but when I realized the cost of following Jesus, I decided not to give my life to Him.

The next six years were possibly the worst in my life. My response was to drink harder, withdraw behind a cardboard cutout of what people expected and learn to hate for the sake of hating.

By the time I was twenty-three, I was a customs officer at Melbourne Airport. I did my job without mercy. Often I would get drunk and then drive home. It seemed to me that I deserved to be arrested and shown no mercy because I had shown no mercy. I was as bad as the people I arrested.

I broke up with my fiancée that year. (I think that is what you call undeserved grace. I am glad now that we did not go the distance, but it was rough at the time.) I remember one of our last times together. We were in my car driving to her home just out of Geelong in Victoria, where my family lived at that time. At the top of the hill near her home was a new church with a large lighted cross on it. It was a foggy night and just as we crested the hill, we broke out of the fog right in front of the cross. Helen said, "I don't want a church wedding. I don't believe in that rubbish."

In my heart I cringed. I thought, "How can we be married without God's blessing?" I realized then and there that God was real and His Son was Jesus.

In the following months I moved back to Melbourne and rented a flat in Sunshine, not far from where I grew up. I decided that I needed to get right with God. Whenever I was not too hung over on a Sunday morning, I would go to a church and try to make peace with God. I felt God was saying to me, "Go to the church where your sisters were married," and each time I would go somewhere else. Finally I obeyed. It was like coming home.

Somehow in that place, among those people, was the answer I had traveled over half the continent looking for—right where I started. Each week the highlight of my life was going to this old church and singing dreary hymns and listening to sermons I didn't quite understand. But I was with people who loved me. I no longer needed to drink. I didn't stop drinking, I just didn't drink any more. The need was gone.

After about ten weeks, on April 10, 1979, I went and spoke to Roy Taylor, who was one of the elders. I asked him about being "christened" and becoming a member. Roy explained that I didn't need christening, but what I needed was a personal relationship with Jesus Christ. I didn't understand that, and I backed away. I had images of having daisies painted on my jeans and told him that wasn't for me.

As I was leaving, I felt I was walking out on God, that I might never have another chance, and that I would have to face eternity without being at peace with God. I cannot ever remember feeling so scared. I prayed with Roy that night and I asked Jesus to be my Lord and Savior. I asked the Holy Spirit to fill my heart.

As I rose up, the fear in my heart was replaced with a tremendous sense of confidence and the words, "I shall fear no evil for Thou art with me."

The decision I made that night changed my whole life. It turned my life around and, from that day, God had His work cut out for Him, rebuilding my life in His image. I can honestly say that the twenty-four-year-old gambler's son no longer lives, but Christ has given him a new life which often falls short of God's glory, but is lived for Jesus Christ.

My bad temper is gone, my dirty mouth has been cleansed. I no longer consider my needs as being the only thing that is important. Above all, I have learned to love and no longer hate.

Indonesia

ndonesia is the largest Muslim nation in the world and the first mission field of The Wesleyan Church in the Philippines. The field opening was a miracle in itself, and the widespread growth of The Wesleyan Church in Indonesia is even more miraculous. Christians are continually under pressure from a Muslim-controlled government. A minister cannot move within the nation without registering with the police in each place he goes and then getting written permission for every meeting he is going to have, even though the meetings may be within our own buildings. The government can, and often does, modify both the times and who can attend meetings in the church. Many Christians must meet at dawn on Sunday because the government will require all people in a township to work on roads or other government projects on Sunday. A church cannot be built within one kilometer of a Muslim mosque, while mosques can be built anyplace. When the Bible school was built, three mosques were built immediately on three sides of the campus with huge amplifiers and speakers to blast the five daily Islamic prayers into the campus. A Muslim who becomes a Christian in Indonesia comes under immediate and intense pressure to return.

Serpent in the Book
•••••••••••••••••••••••
Benediktus Minonealdus

I was born to a devout Catholic family on the island of Flores. My father was a teacher and was a very religious man. However, we did not have a Bible because at that time lay people were not allowed to read the Bible. We just blindly followed the declarations of the Pope that were passed down to us through the cardinal, bishop, and the priest. I had never heard about the gospel of salvation or how someone could receive Jesus as their personal Lord and Savior.

After graduating from junior high school, I decided to leave my family and island and move to Yogyakarta on the island of Java. I began studying at a Technical Flight High School and got involved in seeking inner powers for the purpose of self-defense. I graduated from high school and then entered the heretical religious church called the Children of God. I read many of their books and advanced quickly in the organization. But God did not allow me to drown in this false teaching. One night I had a dream in which I saw many snakes coming out of the books that taught the religious beliefs of the Children of God. I knew that snakes symbolized Satan and that these teaching were from him.

In early 1987, I met Johny Simamora, a pastor from the Wesleyan Church who was studying for his master of divinity in Yogyakarta. He explained to me the gospel message of salvation. Eventually I became aware of my sin and need of a Savior. Finally I was ready to give my life to Christ. Pastor Simamora gathered with some friends to pray for me and to pray specifically for deliverance from the powers of darkness that had their grip on my life. This occurred in September of 1987. On December 25, I was baptized.

Since this time I have felt a wonderful freedom and, as a newborn baby craves milk, I have had a continual desire to read, memorize and comprehend the promises of God in the Gospels. I was born again! I began to go with Pastor Simamora and help him in his ministry. After a while I was no longer satisfied to serve God part-time. I finally decided to enter a Bible college to prepare myself for full-time service. I graduated with an master of divinity in 1993, writing a thesis on man's origin and comparing the biblical account in Genesis 1:26-31 with the theory of evolution. One of the requirements for graduating from this school was that I had to win fifteen people to the Lord. From this, I learned how to share my faith with others until the Lord helped me lead fifteen people to salvation in Christ.

Rev. Johny Simamora had become the director of the Wesleyan Bible College in Magelang and he called me to join the teaching staff there. I now teach Hebrew, Greek, apologetics and theology. In August of 1997, I was chosen to become the new director of the Bible college since Rev. Simamora is in the Philippines for further education. On weekends, I still serve in the small Wesleyan church in Yogyakarta where I was saved back in 1987. I am also sharpening my ability in the English language by taking courses at a local university. Please pray for me that God will use me to reach people who are lost and living in darkness like I was.

All for the Love of a Girl

Haris Suprayogi

My name is Haris Suprayogi and I am twenty-six years old. I am the first of six children. My family's religion is Islam. When I was twenty years old, I met a young Christian lady. We fell in love and began to go steady. At that time I did not think about our different religious backgrounds. I thought that everything could be worked out. But apparently she was not like other girls, because she was devout and was not willing to turn away from her faith. But I was different from my sweetheart because I did not know about worship and never worshiped according to my Islamic religion. Even so, I was unwilling to become a Christian because I knew that I would certainly be opposed by my family and neighbors.

The Lord had a different plan, however, and this was the beginning of a big change in my life. When I became aware of my growing love for my girlfriend, we agreed to marry. Our differing faiths were a big obstacle for us though. My fiancée said that she was unwilling to change her religion and was also unwilling for us to have two religions in our household. This started me thinking about the Christian faith. I wondered to myself why she was so bold to stand up for her faith. In other words, why was it not an easy matter for her to change to another faith? Finally, I began to wrestle with the decision. Should I not marry this girl, whom I loved, only because of religion? Or should I decide that it was better to just enter the Christian religion? The important thing was to marry the girl I loved.

Praise the Lord that His plan was different from my plan. When we decided to marry according to the Christian faith, it was not that simple. We had to go through lessons about Christianity and Christian marriage. Because of this I was challenged by the pastor with these words, "To become a Christian follower is not as easy as just following some theory. Haris Suprayogi, don't become a Christian just in order to get a girl. It must be a sincere, personal decision that is truly an expression of your faith in Jesus. You must believe on Him and receive Him as Lord and personal Savior."

This challenge opened my heart to begin to seek the Lord through the prayer that the pastor, Rev. Nurmala Simamora, taught me. The result was that I experienced a life change. Before, I was afraid to testify to my family and neighbors. Then I possessed the courage to witness by attending church with my fiancée and going through catechism classes with her. Finally, I was baptized and then married the girl I loved with the great blessing of the Lord.

I have been a Christian for about two years. My spiritual walk has been up and down. Sometimes I was faithful and obedient to the Lord's commands, but sometimes I was not as faithful to the Lord. But through the blessing of my pastor's counseling and guidance, I have finally been helped to live in obedience to the Lord. I am growing in the knowledge of my Lord and Savior. Praise the Lord, I have now experienced many changes in my life. Before, I did not know how to pray and never experienced the power of prayer. I have now seen how the Lord has heard our prayers for the needs of our church building project.

I have personally felt how the Lord has met the needs of my family because he has been so good to bless my family. I am now involved in the Mertoyudan Wesleyan Church's building project in raising funds to build our house of prayer.

Finally, may this testimony become a blessing to many people, especially to my brothers and sisters in the Lord. As a child of God, my life's purpose is that through my life the name of the Lord will be glorified and many people will be blessed.

Koran Leads to Jesus
● ●
Kusno

I am from a very strong Muslim background. From childhood I was taught to strictly follow the demands of the Islamic religion. Into adulthood my religion was the most important part of my life. My grandfather, a well-respected Islamic leader in our village, was my special teacher. Because of my earnestness in deeply studying Islam, my grandfather loved me very much. He intended to pass all his knowledge on to me so that I would continue in his footsteps.

As an adult I continued to study Islam at a more difficult level where I was required to master every part of the Koran. I studied much from all the Islamic leaders in my community so that my religious knowledge would become solid and I would be able to teach other Muslims. The people of my village, Bojong-Boyolali, considered me as one of the religious leaders because of all that I had studied and mastered.

My knowledge of Jesus, who is called the "Prophet Isa" in Islam, began when I studied the *Torekoh Sidikiyah* from the teacher Mohtar Mukti. The verse which was very interesting to me at that time was Yassin 36:58, which talked about Jesus, and also Imron 3:45, which clearly stated that Jesus is the foremost in this world and in the world to come. These two verses unsettled my thinking and I was anxious to find the truth.

First of all, I proved the power of Jesus' name to overcome each problem I faced by praying in His name. The results were incredible, as each of my problems were settled. My anxiety grew even stronger and became a question that had to be answered. Often I would think, "Why do I have to use the name of Jesus, when I already have the prophet Mohammed, who is highly exalted in my own religion? Why does the Koran itself say that Jesus, and not Mohammed, will be the foremost at the end of the age when, in fact, the Koran is Mohammed's book, the book of Islam?" Two great questions entered my thinking: who in reality is Mohammed, and who in reality is Jesus?

To find the answer to my questions, I decided to ask a Christian leader. This pastor's answer was incredible. He firmly stated that there was only one way of salvation and righteousness for sinners—that is by believing in Jesus. This also became a big question for me. How can this be? What about the religion I have trusted in all this time? My efforts to know more about Jesus did not end there. Besides asking lots of questions, I was given a Bible to read and study for myself. I spent a great amount of time searching for the truth and comparing the contents of the Koran to what was in the Bible, until I became very sure that what the pastor had spoken was true. I decided to place my faith in the Lord Jesus.

When I believed in Jesus, it was not that easy to confess my faith before my family or my community. They still considered me as their religious leader. Many fears rose up in my heart. If they knew that I believed in Jesus, they would ridicule and even excommunicate me. And what I feared did happen. Not only my community, but also my family strongly rejected what I believed at that time. They continually tried to persuade me to return to the Islamic faith.

But praise the Lord, my faith in Jesus at that time remained firm, and I was even strengthened through the opposition and rejection. The urge is growing in my heart to prove that my faith is true, because my eyes have been opened by the truth that I have come to know, although I do not understand it deeply. I give thanks now that not only have I believed in Jesus, but the Lord has also saved my family, even though my parents have not yet accepted or understood what I believe. Some neighbors have believed. The decision I made to believe in Jesus is a decision I will hold onto forever.

Even though the opposition is great for me right now, I believe that the Lord is working out a beautiful purpose in my life and ministry. I long to be used by God as His instrument to proclaim His workings in this world, so that my village may be won for His glory.

Spiritist Learns Meaning of Spiritual

Sri Nuryanto

My name is Sri Nuryanto and I was born into a fanatical Muslim family. According to our family genealogy, I am the thirteenth generation from Sunan Kalijogo, one of the nine holy men who spread the Islamic teaching throughout the island of Java. My own father was a fanatical Islamic leader.

But because of God's calling, my father repented and believed in Jesus in 1969. Our whole family became Christian. In 1974, we were baptized in the Java Christian Church. At that time I was in sixth grade, and my father always instructed me to be faithful to the Lord and attend church. Although I had become a "Christian," I did not know the Lord personally and was blind concerning the way of salvation. What I understood was that if I did good things, I would be saved.

Things began to change when I was in junior and senior high school. I became wild, was often drunk, and flunked out of school. I no longer went to church and fell into a dark valley. I ran around with gangs, became a robber, and was even called a cold-blooded murderer. People were afraid of me. In 1982, the police in Yogyakarta began an operation to hunt down known criminals. Many criminals were found "mysteriously" shot dead. I was able to escape and fled to the island of Borneo. I couldn't bring myself to return to my home in Yogyakarta. Since I had flunked out of high school, I decided to finish my studies, earning my diploma five years after leaving school.

In 1987, I joined a "spiritist" group and my main goal was to seek "knowledge." I was made the right-hand man by my teacher because I was very diligent in understanding his teaching. I often helped sick people and I had followers. People from various professions gathered at my house to study spiritism, young and old, men and women alike.

One day I woke up at 6 a.m., but had not yet gotten out of bed. Suddenly my stomach became very sick and painful, like it was being shaken up. I felt like I would die and my whole body was drenched in a cold sweat. I managed to sit up and face the white wall in front of me while I prayed. Suddenly I couldn't see anything. Everything became black, even though my eyes were open. Slowly the darkness vanished and on the wall appeared a star with many colors around the edge. The star became ever larger and suddenly in the center of it appeared a large throne with someone sitting upon it, but his face could not be seen. I thought that perhaps it was the Lord Jesus who sat on the throne. At that time I had not yet repented and, in fact, I had become increasingly known as a spiritist. And yet there was a change because I began to enjoy reading the Word of God, even though I did not understand its intent and meaning. I began to memorize verses such as John 3:16 and 1:12. I continued to memorize Scripture, but it was still difficult to understand because I was controlled by dark powers.

In 1992, I started a business which grew because the Lord blessed it, but strangely enough, I still did not want to go to church, and just threw my money away. My father and younger siblings all encouraged me to go to church, but I remained hardened. Finally, in 1997, my business went bankrupt and was repossessed by the bank. Because of my stress, I ran off to visit my sister (Sri Wuryaningsih) in Jakarta. She is the pastor of the Jakarta Wesleyan Church. She spent a lot of time counseling and evangelizing me from God's Word, but I did not pay any attention to her. When I got ready to return to Yogyakarta, she gave me a book entitled *Blessing and Curse*, written by Derek Prince. One month later, I returned to Jakarta and told her the changes that had occurred. At that time she had to attend district conference in Magelang for one week, and asked me to take care of her house while she was gone. She gave me another book entitled *Bread of Freedom for God's Children*, by Leo Z.

On Monday, March 2, 1997, my sister left for Magelang and I began to fast, read the Bible and the other book, and pray until Friday. Each day I only drank one glass of milk and ate two slices of white bread. Each time after I prayed, phlegm would come out of my mouth and I would cry. I was very confused and did not know what was happening with me. On Saturday, March 8, 1997, my sister Sri came home from Magelang. She had gone home to my place in Yogyakarta and retrieved seven antique ceremonial daggers which I kept as charms. Once I was offered $25,000 for one of those daggers, but I refused to sell it. On March 10, Sri invited some of her minister friends to come over. Among them was Rev. Peter Anakota, who had studied in the Wesleyan Bible College in Magelang.

They led me to receive Jesus as my Lord and Savior. First, I was led to confess my sins. My charms (the ceremonial daggers) were all burned together at 10 p.m. After that Rev. Peter, Rev. John Alexon Tamba, and my sister prayed for me specially to be freed from the evil spirits which had bound me. The Lord worked in an incredible way and His power accompanied His servants. I cried hysterically, coughed and vomited. That was the first ministry I experienced. They broke the curses which were brought about by the sins of my ancestors, my parents, and my own sins. For about two hours I was prayed over and my body felt very weak, but after that I felt very light and full of joy. My condition changed and I began to understand the Word of God. My days were spent praying and reading only the Bible and other theological books. The Holy Spirit worked in my heart and my life changed.

The ministers that I mentioned earlier faithfully ministered to me. I was prayed over seven times for deliverance. They discipled me so that now I can grow on my own and can minister to others. I praise the Lord because He saved me, chose me and delivered me from the dark powers. I, who was full of sin and contempt, the Lord loved and made His child. All of this was the grace of God to me, a sinner (Ephesians 2:8,9). I know now that salvation is not obtained through man's efforts, but because of God's grace. Praise the Lord because the Lord gave grace and faith, I believed, and was saved (Romans 10:9,10). And I am not afraid to face whatever happens because the Lord cares for my life and the Holy Spirit renews and seals me (Ephesians 1:13, 14; John 10:28; Romans 8:35-39).

I feel that the Lord is working in a very wonderful way in my life. On Good Friday, March 29, 1997, I was baptized and began being discipled so that I could serve others. Then on December 7, 1997, I was commissioned as an evangelist. I now assist in the ministry of the Jakarta Wesleyan Church along with my sister, Rev. Sri Wuryaningsih. We have formed a special ministry team to help those who are chained by dark powers such as magic arts, witchcraft, charms, idol worship, ancient customs, or who are under curses. The result has been incredible, as many people have come and have been helped by the Lord. I have decided to give my whole life to serve the Lord. I have been studying theology along with my ministry in order to enrich my knowledge of the Bible so that I will not be led astray or lead others astray. I hope and pray that this testimony brings glory to God and becomes a blessing to others. I ask for prayer from all my brothers and sisters, so that I may be used by the Lord to serve others until the end of my life.

Muslim Businessman Finds the Christ
●●●●●●●●●●●●●●●●●●●●●●●●●

Thomas Subadi

I was brought up on a farm. My parents were very devout Muslims and educated us children very strictly in our religion. When I graduated from high school in 1970, I immediately went to work for a furniture business. Because of my faithfulness and ability in carrying out my responsibilities, I was promoted to foreman in the factory. Then, in 1980, I was promoted to supervisor of the company.

Under my leadership the business operated smoothly with a total of 150 workers: 75 carpenters, 25 welders, 25 varnishers and 25 painters. Seeing the business prosper was very satisfying to me and I devoted all my thinking and time to my work. Things that should have been more important, such as saying my prayers, I neglected.

Finally, in 1985, the business went bankrupt because of the owner's personal problems. This was the beginning of the most difficult time in my life. I was out of a job and had to start all over from the bottom again. Everywhere I applied for work, the employers were hesitant to hire me as a common laborer because they knew I was the former supervisor of the well-known furniture company. As a last resort, I tried to open a small variety store in my home in order to provide for my family's needs. But that effort also failed to meet our financial needs and, little by little, all that we owned was sold off.

But praise the Lord, in the midst of those difficulties, the Lord touched my wife's heart. Before we married, she had been a member of the Catholic Church. But when she married me, she followed my religion and became a Muslim. One day she asked my permission to attend church and without thinking much about it I said yes. At that time I didn't know anything about worshiping at a church. After my wife had been going to church for several weeks, I noticed many changes in her. She was much more patient and did not complain about our financial difficulties. Not only that, she also displayed a joy I had never seen before. Sometimes she did not come home from church alone, but would bring other members home with her. Whether I wanted to or not, I always had to meet them. Finally, I realized that they were evangelizing me so that I would believe in Jesus. I did not want to open my heart to believe in Jesus because my Islamic faith was still strong. But from the start of their visits, I began to learn about the Christian life.

In 1987, The Wesleyan Church opened a preaching post in my city of Semarang. My wife was one of the members, which meant that the minister came to my home every week. He was a Bible college student on field training. As a result of this student's patience and persistence, I was finally willing to study about the Christian faith, even though it was against the principle of my heart to believe before I had any proof. But because of that principle, I felt increasingly compelled to study and find out who this Jesus really was. It so happened that this student was also from a strong Muslim background and was able to answer my questions, both from the Koran and the Bible. After three years of struggle, I came to understand who Jesus is and I gave my life to the Lord Jesus Christ

Papua New Guinea

P apua New Guinea is a field that was first entered by another mission field, Australia. PNG has approximately 2000 different language groups and the movement of people of one clan into another clan area has been a relatively recent phenomenon. This movement of people has caused problems in city areas where clan cousins often join together into gangs (often called *raskals*), surviving by criminal activities. One of the following stories takes place in Bougainville, where a civil war has been fought over mineral rights. During this war, the number of Wesleyan churches doubled, creating a shortage of ministers. Dr. Barry Ross's story comes out of efforts to give ongoing training to lay pastors in Bougainville.

"Raskal" Restored

••••••••••••••••••••••••

Betege Haro
(told by Don Floyd)

etege Haro was born sometime in the 1960s. His father Haro is a pastor. While Betege was still school age, Haro became a missionary to the Poloba people and went to the very remote outpost of Hala. Because there were no schools at Hala for his children, they were sent to board with various friends and relatives. Just like any European missionary, Haro faced the difficult dilemma of balancing his children's educational needs with their needs for a good family life.

Betege was reasonably bright in school. But further education and jobs are limited to the very elite. Betege did spend some time helping various church leaders who were from the same tribe as his father. But as a young man without any attainable goals, he eventually fell into sin. It began with liaisons with young women. Eventually Betege joined a *raskal* gang. *Raskals* are the criminals of Papua New Guinea. In time, Betege worked his way up through the levels of organized crime in PNG. Betege became widely known among criminals and the innocent people they attacked. Betege's gang carried out armed robberies and would stop at nothing to get what they wanted. Betege tells stories of stealing cars for getaway vehicles, and of shooting a white man in the leg during a payroll hold-up. He had gun battles with the police that put him in the hospital for months.

Betege became immersed in gang culture. The gang drank and smoked. Some members used marijuana to build their courage before committing crimes. Betege also remembers black magic rituals being carried out to ensure the *raskals* would be invisible to police during robberies.

Betege was put into several prisons and broke out of some of them. While in prison, he became even more hardened. His father Haro would follow his son around the country, trying to get him to settle down. Once the police burnt Haro's house to the ground because they thought he was harboring Betege.

In the last half of 1991, Betege finally served his time for the crimes the authorities knew about. He decided to leave the *raskal* life. However, he did not give up drinking, smoking, chewing betel nut or bad company. He had also developed a real arrogance, a bad temper and a fanatical love of rugby.

Within a couple of years Betege decided to marry. He had his moments of trying to be a good husband and father. But his love of rugby led him to neglect his family and his bad habits wasted their money. When Betege and his wife had disagreements, his violent temper often got the better of him. In the end, Betege's wife left him and took the children.

In late 1995, Betege became so disheartened by his situation that he decided to rejoin his old *raskal* gang. He headed for the coast to catch a ship to an outlying island of PNG. The night before he was to catch his ship, Betege and his friend used all their money on a wild drinking party. So the next day Betege had no money and couldn't board the ship.

At that time the lay Wesleyan pastor, Pendene Habagua, found Betege. He sat down and presented the gospel to Betege. Betege was a pastor's son and had heard it all before. But on this day Betege had come to the end of himself. He knew he needed a Savior and repented. That day Betege became a new creature. Betege soon found money for a bus fare and returned to the Highlands of PNG. He came to find us, Don and Cheri Floyd, who had long been his friends. Straight away he told us that he had become a Christian and was completely changed. We saw evidence that he had changed and began to disciple him.

We soon learned that while God forgives us completely, we still have to bear some consequences for our sins. Because of Betege's past, he faced many challenges. His wife and children were still estranged. People knew his past and didn't believe he'd changed. Betege also knew there were crimes he had never served time for, and he wondered if God wanted him to turn himself into the police.

We decided to use *Holiness for Ordinary People* in discipling Betege. Betege soon saw that the root cause of many of his problems was arrogance and a short temper. With that realization, he has begun to grow. Since then we've had the joy of watching some highlights. We were there the first Sunday he gave his testimony. In PNG culture, this is often the way you first let people know you have become a Christian. Betege was nervous, but managed to make his confession of faith. Later Betege was baptized. What a joyous occasion!

I also remember the first time his father saw Betege leading a church service. More than any other person, Haro has agonized over Betege. When he saw his son leading a worship service, it overwhelmed Haro. Racked with sobs, Haro had to go outside and cry with relief, joy and thankfulness. Today the church has recognized Betege's genuine change. Betege is now a student at the Wesleyan Bible College and believes God is calling him to preach.

Like any child, Betege has learned to walk slowly. Sometimes he falls down. But he is still walking with Jesus today. We have no idea what his future holds. Betege has terrific gifts and shows great promise. However, Betege still struggles with trying to restore his broken marriage and making amends for his past. His perseverance and devotion to Christ is a great encouragement to us. Please pray for him.

The Philippines

The Filipino society is community oriented, in contrast to North American society which is oriented toward the individual. You will see the effects of this aspect of Filipino society in different ways in the following stories of grace. First, it is very difficult for an individual to break out of a tight Roman Catholic community (more than 90% of the people in the Philippines are Roman Catholic) to become a Protestant Christian. Ostracism is probably as intense as in a Hindu or Muslim society.

Second, note how the church evangelizes through the pull of community. In fact, the Bible college becomes a part of the community aspect of discipleship. All young people are encouraged to go to Bible school. Those who are going to the university are encouraged to take a one-year Christian leadership course, and those who are going into ministry have four years of training at the Bible school. The Bible school becomes a community-bonding institution. Lay people bond with those who will be their pastors. This helps them to establish them in the faith before they enter the university and into secular business. It is also the place where individuals find their spouses. In most cases, pastors are actually a husband and wife team and are both ordained. Note how evangelism and discipleship are community projects in these stories. A revival meeting is a community-oriented style of evangelism and is especially effective in the Philippines.

The Filipino church expects it brightest and best to go into ministry. Church planting is a priority—for a six-year period from 1990 to 1996, an average of one new church was planted every three weeks. The church started the ministry in Indonesia and has sent missionaries to Sierra Leone, Zambia, and Cambodia. The Filipino church is rich in faith only, but it has been able to do these things as a community banded together in Christ.

Floundered at Sea

● ●

Agripino Marquinis (Dodong)
(told by Perlita Rabago)

Dodong works as a seaman on an international vessel. He was born a Catholic, lived as a devoted Catholic, and was determined to die as a Catholic. During one of his home leaves, he returned to find that his wife Edith had left the Catholic church and had begun serving the Lord in the Wesleyan church in Maasin, Leyte. Dodong was furious and offered his wife two options—either renounce her newfound faith or annul their marriage. Edith did not have difficulty giving her decision. Once and for all, she decided to serve the Lord under the church that had helped her establish a vital relationship with the Lord.

Dodong prepared all the necessary papers and documents and submitted them to his lawyer. After reading through the documents, the lawyer asked in surprise, "What? Are you filing for an annulment of your marriage just because of religious differences? No court will grant annulment on that basis alone."

Dismayed, Dodong left home and boarded the boat on which he worked. One day, he spotted the captain of the boat reading a black book. He thought, "That book he is reading looks like the book my wife reads every day." Mustering his courage, he approached the captain. "Sir, what is that book you are reading?" he asked. "Why, it's the Bible, Dodong. This is my guide every day since I accepted Jesus into my life. Without it, I would be lonely and lost," the captain happily responded.

That day marked a new interest in Dodong to read the Word of God through the help of the captain. The truth of God's Word sank deeper into Dodong's life. One day while on board his ship, he too accepted Jesus as his Savior.

He went home to his wife a changed man. He asked Edith to forgive him. In a men's convention in Cebu the last week of one September, Dodong said, "I will return to the boat next month but I will come home in October next year. I want you to schedule a men's convention in my place in Maasin, Leyte. Don't worry about your food. I will provide everything. Just come." He was so eager to share the Lord Jesus Christ with others.

Dead in the Cemetery
• •
Alberto Patacsil
District Superintendent, Central Plain, Luzon, Philippines

Our family lived at the back of the cemetery in Rosales, Pangasinan. I was ten years old when I heard clearly the story of Jesus through Miss Aurea Briones, a Bible school student. With her classmates, she came through the cemetery, wading through the knee-deep, muddy path to reach our house. Later on, they stopped coming because my grandfather, who was a caretaker of the Aglipayan Church cemetery, and my father, who was the caretaker of the Roman Catholic cemetery, were warned by their priests that they would lose their jobs if they entertained this new faith. However, the Bible school students' labor was not in vain, because my mother accepted the Lord Jesus as her Savior and Lord. Though the students were not coming to our house anymore, my mother went to Bible school every Sunday and regularly attended church services.

Years passed, with my relatives persecuting my mother and accusing her of being a traitor to the old faith, while the rest of the family stayed in the old religion. As a young boy, I often served as an altar boy. I was very close to the priests but had not experienced salvation. We just did the rituals inside the church, but never felt the love of God in them and through them. One night, March 10, 1969, my mother invited me to attend an evangelistic meeting in San Pedro, Rosales, Pangasinan. The house where this meeting was held was near the Bible school. I was amazed when the preacher spoke about sin. It was all about the things I was doing. It was true that I was a religious person, but I was the leader of my cousins in stealing guavas, mangoes, star apples and watermelons within the town of Rosales. I was also a gambler. I was quarrelsome and was in the process of choosing boxing as my profession.

Rev. Garcia's message penetrated my heart with conviction. He spoke of the love of God and His forgiveness, which drew me to kneel at an altar of prayer. Many concerned people surrounded me, helping me to pray. It was a lengthy time of weeping and confessing my sins and then accepting Christ into my heart. It was a joyous time which I'll never forget. That day my life was changed. Before my conversion, I had stopped going to school and wasted my time for four years.

I began attending the services faithfully in a house church. When the pastors appointed me to teach the junior high class, I felt inadequate. I was only an elementary school graduate while my students were mostly high school students. My *pastoras* (Miss Teresita Sabado and Miss Merly Subong) advised me to continue my high school, sensing that the Lord had a plan for my life. Even though some of my family members—especially my grandparents who were caring for me—opposed the idea, I went back to school. I continued with my responsibilities at home and at church. The busier I became, the faster time seemed to pass. I graduated from high school with honors, and my school principal selected me to represent the school in taking a scholarship examination at the University of the Philippines (UP). I passed all exams, but the calling of the Lord became clearer and clearer while I was at the UP campus. I had heard clear preaching about entire sanctification and holiness during camp meetings and conventions, but I had never experienced it because I had reservations and unsurrendered ambition in life. I wanted to be an engineer and dreamed of building bridges, roads, and tall buildings.

While I was in UP Biliman, Quezon City, pursuing my personal ambitions and basking in the pride of school, relatives and friends, I was yet in a time of crisis. It was midnight of June 10, 1975, in my room in the house of the secretary of the vice-president of UP, when I consecrated my life and surrendered my ambition to God. I confessed my stubbornness and asked to follow His will and plan for my life. I cried for help, asking Him to cleanse me of the root of sin and pride and to fill me with the Holy Spirit. That experience led me to testify about the love of God to the UP officials who interviewed me before releasing me to go to the Wesleyan Bible College to take up the ministerial course. I struggled with finances while in Bible school and my relatives and friends ridiculed me. There were times when my classmates were taking their examinations while I was sent out to find money for my school bill. I harvested *palay*, a farm crop, for one month, carrying sacks of palay on my back for a half mile, at one peso per sack. By God's help I was able to finish the five years of training and became a pastor to pioneer churches. Those hardships and pressures became my treasures in the ministry. To God be the glory!

God fulfills His promises when we obey Him (Matthew 6:33). He gave me a beautiful and consecrated Japanese wife and we have two children. He expanded the premises of our ministry (Psalm 111:1-6), not only building worship places but letting us see foreign lands. He confirmed in His Word the process to experiencing the life of holiness (2 Corinthians 7:1) and that is the core of our message. Thank God for His rich heritage.

The Making of a General

Alfonso G. Pablo

(told by Shinar Fe Lumahan and Filipina Pablo)

Very early in the morning Alfonso awoke to line up with other boys outside a factory, hoping to get a box of popsicles to sell. Sometimes all the boxes were distributed before his turn came and he had to go home empty-handed. This time, however, he got one box. Happily he walked around the community shouting, "Delicious Popsicles! Come and buy now!" Looking around he said to himself, "This is a fine day." The big boys were not there to tease and trick him. People were buying from him, too, unlike the other day when he had no choice but to eat all the melting Popsicles. In addition to selling Popsicles, he also pastured two male water buffaloes. He learned at the age of ten to enjoy watching the buffaloes fight, unaware of the danger then.

When he was six years old, his mother died, leaving behind ten children—five girls and five boys. Alfonso was the ninth child, but was equally loved and taken care of with the rest of his siblings. Alfonso earned his first few cents by selling Popsicles and shining shoes. With his earnings, he was able to buy some of his school needs. When he was older, he worked in their farm. He was a self-supporting child.

As a freshman in high school, he got very low grades because he loved sports more than school. Dismayed, his father let him quit school and do the farming instead. Alfonso learned his lesson and went back to school the following year. Despite his very shy personality, his teacher noticed his potential and appointed him as class treasurer during an election. The teacher's confidence in him struck a chord and he began to excel. From that time on, he was elected to various positions and ended up as president of the school's student body organization.

Poverty denied him the chance to go to college, so he worked on the farm for two years. He led the youth in his town to play sports and join dances. He led the tough guys too and had "gang fights." His father, who was one of the community leaders, often asked him before he went out at night, "Do you have your gun? I prefer to see you in jail rather than see you dead." This made Alfonso tougher.

At twenty-one, Alfonso got so sick that his family, thinking he was dying, summoned his relatives. He became stronger instead and while recuperating, searched for his younger sister's Bible and read through it. One day while standing by the window, he saw the ripened rice fields. He seemed to hear a small voice saying, "The harvest is truly plenteous, but the laborers are few." Was God calling him? He had not yet accepted Christ as his personal Savior. He tried joining two Protestant churches but was not serious about any religion. He realized God was calling him to be a pastor, but he reasoned himself out of it. To him, it was not a challenging job because pastors depended on love gifts from their people. He wanted to be a politician. Although he was not eligible to vote yet, he was already mingling with politicians. He dreamed of becoming the town mayor. After much thought he finally said, "Lord, if you will heal me, I will be a pastor."

One Sunday after getting well, he went downtown to gamble by playing volleyball. Suddenly he recalled his promise to God. A special urge to go to church overcame him. He thought of going to his older sister's church, which he occasionally attended, but when he dropped by his sister's house they had already gone to church. At last he decided to go to his father's church, which was just across the street. This was the church that he and his friends, when they were drunk, feared to enter during the night to sleep on its benches. They believed that the members' prayers were powerful and that they might be cursed. He entered the church and attended Sunday school. The teacher, who spoke in broken English, kept repeating the phrase, "Only clean hands and pure hearts can glorify God." The Holy Spirit applied the truth to his heart. He saw his hands with blood on them (as in the time he boxed an opponent and his head was cut as if by a sharp machete). He saw his dirty heart. When the teacher appealed for prayer he, along with others, knelt beside his chair and accepted Jesus as his personal Savior and Lord. He prayed, "Lord, make me your child," and wept bitterly. He thought that men were not supposed to cry, especially in public, but the tears kept coming. The change in his life was instantaneous. All appetite for worldly pleasures was gone. He stopped going to the dance hall. He did not touch wine or cigarettes anymore. He did not play volleyball or basketball to gamble anymore. His friends were amazed and asked his younger sister one day about the sudden change. His sister replied, "My brother is going straight now."

Six months after his dramatic conversion, he went to Bible college. He was twenty-two years old and still a babe in Christ. Offended one night by some students, he escaped into a nearby barrio where his relatives lived, about three and a half miles away. At dawn, he was out on the road waiting for a ride back to his hometown 56 miles away. He tried to stop an oncoming vehicle. Since it was still dark, he could not clearly see the car. As it stopped near him, he was surprised to see that it was the Bible college missionary's car. Rev. Robert Smith placed his arm around Alfonso's shoulder and Alfonso went back meekly with the missionary to Bible school. This time he became more serious and determined to follow the Lord.

However, the enemy did not stop trying to hinder Alfonso in following the Lord. He became sick and for a month could not stand for even five minutes. His right leg was so swollen that he could hardly put on his pants. His older sister, who was also a Bible school student, urged him to go home. His father wrote him to come home and be treated, but Alfonso did not like that idea. During a ministerial convention held at the Bible college in October 1962, God was near and worked wonderfully. Backsliders were prayed for and came back to the Lord. The missionaries and church workers surrounded Alfonso and began to pray for him. As they prayed, he was perspiring profusely. As he stood up, blood oozed from his nose. He gave a short testimony and was able to stand longer. God definitely touched him. He went back to his room strong and enjoying God's healing touch.

The next day he was examined by the local doctor and was advised to see the city doctor 81 miles away. Alfonso was able to withstand the eight-hour trip along rugged roads. When the city doctor saw him, he said he had osteomyelitis (an infection of the bone marrow). His bones had become brittle and his leg would have to be amputated to prevent the poison from spreading throughout his body. That night Alfonso felt the excruciating pain again. Satan whispered, "Why not jump out this two-story building and your pain will be over?" It was a real temptation. But Alfonso finally prayed, "Lord, please help me sleep for even just an hour." He went back to the doctor the following day. The doctor was so amazed that he exclaimed, "This is a miracle! God has healed you!" Alfonso went back to school and after a week or two was playing volleyball and basketball again. He took this healing experience as a sign that God had a plan for him. He felt that if he disobeyed God, his sickness would return.

About that same time, God was working in the life of a young lady He was calling into full-time ministry, but she was trying to evade it. Fely wanted to practice her vocation as a health worker for the government. She was then following up her final appointment. Her landlady, who had just arrived from the ministerial convention, related all the wonderful works the Lord was doing in the Bible college among the ministers, missionaries and students. The landlady mentioned the student who was miraculously healed. Since the Bible college was located in between the two cities Fely traveled to, she decided to drop by. The convention was still going on. Fely was met by some of her acquaintances, who asked her if she was coming to study in the Bible college. They said they were praying for her. She flatly answered, "No." She attended one service before traveling on. But the Lord was working in her heart. She struggled so much but finally gave in and obeyed. Missionary Florabelle Slater, affectionately called Mother Slater, prevailed in dealing with her. Fely decided to stay for the six-year Bible college training.

A month after graduation from Bible college, the divinely healed man and the obedient health worker were married. Alfonso and Fely have faithfully served the Lord in many different assignments, most notably as the general superintendent of The Wesleyan Church in the Philippines since 1989.

Building the Kingdom
•••••••••••••••••••••••••
Alfredo Lumahan (Engineer Lumahan)

On the rainy night of August 10, 1936, Alfredo was born to Florentina and Miguel Lumahan in the province of Pangasinan, 200 kilometers north of Manila. He was the fourth of six children. The family was poor and so, even as a young child, Alfredo learned early to cope with the pressures of life. He helped his father on their farm, and when they moved to Manila, he worked as a shoeshine boy and sold newspapers and ice cream bars on the streets of Manila. Through these jobs, he was able to put himself through school and help his sisters.

When he was twenty, he finished his course in marine engineering, but also contracted pulmonary tuberculosis. He was sent to the island of Mindanao, where his brother was living, to get rest while taking his medication. In Mindanao he was invited to attend a healing service at a certain Protestant church, where he believes he was healed. He felt relieved after the service and the symptoms of his sickness disappeared. Although he believed he received healing at that time, still he had not experienced a personal relationship with the God who healed him. He was in Mindanao for three months, during which he met Jovita, who would become his wife. She was studying to be a midwife.

He went back to Manila and entered courses for civil engineering. He was also working as a carpenter in a construction company where his uncle worked. He learned the "ins and outs" of construction and soon owned a company and had men working for him. Jovita came to Manila to take her board examination in midwifery. As soon as Alfredo learned that she was in Manila, he "pursued" her until they got married. Jovita did not go back to Mindanao for a long time.

Being a builder-contractor, Alfredo met and associated with people from different walks of life. Most of them were worldly and ungodly, and he went with them to places like nightclubs, bars, and movie houses that show indecent films. A great deal of his time was spent in his work or with work-related associations, and little time was left for his family. This lifestyle affected his family, especially his wife, who had been raised in a Wesleyan family. While she was patient and refrained from nagging, she never stopped praying for her husband.

In the late 1960s, missionary Virginia Wright was assigned to the La Loma Wesleyan Church, which was the only Wesleyan church in Manila at that time. Mrs. Wright and Magdalena Garcia went to visit Jovita and invited the family to come to church. Alfredo would drive the family to church every Sunday, but he would leave them and go check out his various building sites before returning to pick them up after service. He did not want to become a Christian because he thought he would become impoverished because of the many offerings he would be required to give to the church. He also felt he would lose a lot of his friends and business contacts if he became a Christian. In August of 1971, the La Loma Wesleyan Church had a week-long series of meetings, and Alfredo and his family were invited. Alfredo had no intention of attending, but during that week Rev. and Mrs. Daniel Pantangan, brother-in-law and sister of Jovita (and the first Wesleyan missionaries to Indonesia), stayed at their place while waiting for their flight to Indonesia. On the last day of the revival, they asked Jovita directions to the La Loma Church. Alfredo heard them talking and offered to drive them there. When they arrived, the speaker was already giving the message, so Alfredo sat in the last pew at the back of the church in order to "escape" easily. To his surprise, he was "nailed" to his seat and could not stand up. He could not understand what was preventing him from standing up to leave. He could not understand the message very well because the speaker, Rev. Chester Wilkins, an American, was speaking fast and using unfamiliar English phrases. But he understood enough. "Do you want joy? Do you want to enjoy life here on earth? Do you want to live forever with your Creator? If these are the desires of your heart today, then come and seek the Kingdom of God and His righteousness and all these things shall be added to you." The Lord spoke to Alfredo and soon he found himself at the altar. Crying, he asked God to forgive him of all his sins and then accepted Jesus Christ as his Lord and Savior.

"If any man be in Christ, he is a new creature: old things are passed away; behold, all things are become new" (2 Corinthians 5:17 KJV). Since his conversion that day, Alfredo has never been the same again. He opened his house for Bible studies under the leadership of Rev. Servillano Gomez, who was the pastor of the La Loma church at that time, and who later became a great influence on Alfredo's life. He invited his relatives, friends and neighbors to the Bible studies and converted his garage into a chapel. He never again went to the places he and his friends used to frequent; instead he invited them to church. He had more time with his family and never worked on Sundays again. Many people came to know the Lord in that small chapel through revival meetings, until this group of believers became an organized church. This was the beginning of more churches planted in Metro-Manila. Alfredo Lumahan and members of his family became deeply involved in God's work. Not only was he blessed spiritually, he was blessed materially. The more he gave to the Lord, the more the Lord blessed him. He also became a lay pastor and was later ordained. He has held several positions in the church. He was a member of the general board of administration of The Wesleyan Church of the Philippines for several years; he also was the national coordinator for the Wesleyan men's society, as well as a local church board member. Jovita is vice-president of the National Capital District women's society. Their children are all serving the Lord. Vilma was a missionary medical doctor in Sierra Leone; Richard was involved in a Christian Fellowship in Australia; Joel is active in the church in Florida in the U.S.A.; Jofre is working on a master of divinity at Asian Theological Seminary and is pastoring a church; and Alvin is the district youth president.

Alfredo Lumahan (Engineer Lumahan, as he is commonly called) gives God the praise and glory for what God has done for his family. He claims to be a sinner saved by grace!

A Little Woman with Big Shoulders

Auora L. Abelando (Auring)

M y family lived near a big Catholic church which also had a nun's convent. I was influenced by the religious practices I saw in the priests and nuns. The priests were good men and they sometimes played with the children of the village. I observed that the nuns were so faithful in their prayers. At the age of twelve, I dreamed of being a nun and a nurse, both signifying love and service to God. At the age of thirteen, my father brought me to Manila, where I was enrolled in a Catholic school run by an order of nuns. I enjoyed the religious life of prayer and daily mass. I would go faithfully to confession, which was required each Friday. But the more I confessed my sin, the more I felt the awfulness of that sin in my life. I felt tired of my sin, but still I committed the same ones week after week and confessed the same sins on Friday. I feared eternity.

Then one night my sister died unexpectedly of a hypertension stroke. The question came to me, "If I die unexpectedly, where will I spend eternity?" I feared death. I knew I was not going to go to heaven, for only God and holy people were there. I had some big doubts about purgatory, because I never heard of anyone who got a transfer from there to heaven. I was afraid of hell. There were times when I spent sleepless nights, afraid of death and the uncertainty of eternity. Every once in a while I would take my pulse to see if I was living or dying. From that time on, I began to try to find truth and assurance.

When I was seventeen years old I was an ordinary teenager, but I looked older than I was. My parents were both sick. I was the oldest, with four sisters and a brother. When the youngest sister was born, my mother was paralyzed and became a paraplegic. My mother and cousin began to go sometimes to services at the Wesleyan church. I was angry with my mother and cousin for going to this Protestant church.

I was also angry with the young man who persistently invited them and then came to get them for Sunday services and Wednesday evening prayer meetings. They sometimes came home late. One day when the young man came to the house, I told him my mother and cousin already belonged to the "true" religion and that I did not want him to convert them to Protestants. The young man told me that he was not interested in converting them to

Protestants. He wanted them to become citizens of heaven. The young man testified about how the Lord Jesus saved him from sin and of the wonderful change in his life since he had received Jesus Christ as his personal Savior. Jesus had given him peace, joy, and assurance of eternal life. This touched a soft spot and a great need in my life. Before he left, he invited me to attend the meetings and learn more about salvation. I did not want to go to a Protestant church, but my heart was hungry.

On Sunday I woke early and decided to wear the long-sleeved, white dress that I wore to my own church. In the Sunday school class, I heard the teacher teaching the Word of God; it was the first time I had heard the Bible being taught in this manner. I felt a deep conviction of sin. I saw the sinfulness and the awful condition of my heart before the Lord. In the worship service, the preacher spoke of the love of God that He sent through Jesus Christ, who came to die for our sins. The pastor invited those with hearts heavy and burdened with sin to come to Christ for forgiveness. As I prayed at the altar, I felt as if I was alone there with Jesus Christ. My heart melted with sorrow when I realized how my sins had grieved the Lord. It was as if I saw Christ suffering on the cross just because of my sins alone. I sincerely confessed my sin and asked the Lord for forgiveness. I was forgiven, the burden of sin rolled away and Christ came into my heart. My life was changed.

I was ambitious at that time and wanted to finish school and go into nursing. I almost had to quit high school in the fourth year because of finances. But by God's good providence, I received a scholarship reserved for students with high academic records whose parents where poor.

After high school I was employed by the provincial library. It is Filipino tradition that the oldest child is expected to support the family when he or she begins to work. The monthly pay is supposed to be given in full to the parents. I asked for money from my father, but he got angry when he realized I was giving it to the church. He would not give me any money after that. He even went to the church and told the pastor to convince me not to give money to the church because we were poor. My father also opposed my attending church. He wanted me to stay at home, care for my sick mother and the other children, and do household chores with my time.

When I was eighteen, my father died of a cerebral hemorrhage. The full responsibility of the family fell in my lap. My life was full of care and responsibility. My mother required constant attention and my brother and sisters, too young to help, needed care themselves. I was not prepared emotionally and psychologically to be both a parent and sole breadwinner. I did not understand enough about raising children. My brother and sisters had been brought up in deep poverty and the family could barely cope. They became very difficult to handle.

At that time my only hope was the strength and grace of God. I was determined to bring my brother and sisters to a saving knowledge of the Lord. My life and testimony were closely watched by the family. It was not long before they also accepted Christ as their Lord and Savior.

Relatives tried to help us by suggesting that we break up the family and farm all the children to relatives who could provide for them. I felt that if we were separated, my siblings would not serve Christ; so I decided to try to keep the family together.

A big trial came when my boss asked me to work Sundays. I stood on my conviction that Sunday was the Lord's day. My faith was tested when my boss told me that after the civil service exams, I would be replaced. The Lord proved himself and performed a miracle. First, the Philippine senate approved the forty-hour-week labor law and eliminated Sunday as a working day. Then, out of five employees in my office who took the civil service exam, I was the only one who passed and so became a permanent employee. My fellow employees saw the different kind of life I led, and gained appreciation for my faith. As a result, two of them received Christ as their Savior.

I loved the Lord so much. I had a heart to serve the Lord, just as many of my peers did in the church. Young people from my church were called to be pastors, missionary teachers, missionary nurses, and evangelistic singers. I was always left behind when the missionary challenge and call for full-time ministry was given. In a youth convention, three of my friends sang a song of submission. The chorus went something like this:

Not what I wish to be
Nor where I wish to go
For who am I that
I should choose my way
The Lord shall choose for me
'Tis better far I know
So let him bid me stay or go.

The Lord led me to surrender and commit my life completely to the will of God. The Lord revealed that my place of service was to be the church, and my mission field was in the home. He had called me to stay.

So I became the spiritual leader in my family. Family devotions were regularly held in the morning before everyone left for the day. I knew that the day's struggles and battles should be prepared for by the power of prayer. As "pastor" of the family, I tried to see to it that the spiritual needs of the family were met during devotion time. Spiritual problems, lack of victory, severe trials and temptations, struggles and battles were confronted and settled at morning devotions. My brother and sisters were established in the spiritual realm through family devotions, faithful attendance of church and all church programs and activities.

Even though my mother had been the first to attend this church, she had rejected it and still held strongly to her old religion. She opposed us and this "new religion." Despite being physically unable to carry through, she would threaten physical harm to us to try to get us to stop going to church. But the change she saw in our lives mellowed her. The village priest would sometimes come to minister to her, give her communion and take her confession. She would tell him about the change that had come to her children since they had joined this new religion. But then she would harden her heart again against us. I continued to pray for her. Three days before her death, she called me to pray with her and help her prepare to face eternity. My mother was so wonderfully saved that the doctors, nurses, and attendants at the hospital testified that a patient had passed away differently from others. She faced death with peace, and the glory of God was there in the room when she died.

I served in many different positions in the local church: Sunday school superintendent, Sunday school teacher for different classes, youth leader, youth advisor, and different positions on the local board of administration. I also took charge of the radio ministry of the church. This involved preparation of Bible studies, children and youth programs, and the "request and dedication" part of radio production.

When my sisters finished school and got married, I was able to go back to school and finished a B.A. in early childhood education and a M.A. in child care. In time I was freed from the family responsibilities and was able to resign from my job and go into full-time service for the church. I worked as a children's caseworker for the Wesleyan Christian Children's Fund. I was able to teach in the Wesleyan Bible College in Sinipsip, and also to work in the Bible school library.

Stewardship was one of the lessons I learned in the church—stewardship of time, talent, possessions, and money. I taught this to my sisters also. They were given weekly allowances, but they were responsible to give their tithes and offerings. I was not called to be a missionary but I have been faithful to pray and give to missions. I tell others that if they will give, they will never be in want; instead, they will be blessed spiritually and financially. I tell people, "The more you give, the more you receive and the more you receive, the more you give."

When one of my sisters was afflicted with cancer I visited her often and discovered that God had given me a gift for working with people who are on their deathbeds. This has led me to help a number of dying souls come to know the Lord.

Even with these blessings in ministry, I began to feel a deep need in my soul. I realized that something was lacking in my heart. I hungered for purity of heart, the holiness of life. The Lord revealed the awfulness of a self that is not under the control of the Holy Spirit. I saw myself as God sees—the awfulness of pride, jealousy, envy, anger, hatred, stubbornness, self-pity, and self-will. I asked God to burn out these awful sins in my heart and cleanse my life completely. I wanted the Holy Spirit to have complete control of my life. I made a complete surrender of life, ambitions, talents, and the future. It was a glorious experience when the Holy Spirit came to my heart in sweetness and glory. Since then, my life has become more rich and powerful, increasing in spiritual height every day to holiness of life.

Like others I have met many crises in my life. At the age of 46, when I was going through the physiological changes that time of life brings, I went through a deep depression. It seemed that all of the hardships and losses of early life came crashing down upon me at once. Others did not understand. I had to hold very tightly to the Lord to keep from falling into a pit. The light of the Lord was temporarily blocked. God in His faithfulness sent people who had access to that light, who walked through that darkness with me, to bring me from the pit of despair.

In all of these things God was faithful to teach new lessons for service. He gave me a new understanding of Himself, of myself and my human weaknesses, and of others and the emotional pain that they go through. He also helped me to understand how much we need to give loyalty, assurance, love and confidence to other people in need.

I am now 61 years old. I've been rewarded by seeing my brother and sisters loving and serving the Lord. I've helped to pioneer three churches and turned them over to full-time pastors. I feel God is calling me to pioneer a church in Bicol, so I will go.

I am single, but I know it is God's will. I feel that God has called me to "blessed singleness" in order to be a mother to many. I have always been deeply involved in children's ministry. My support is from my ministry; those who have come to know the Lord over the years are the ones supporting. It is to the Lord that we can be grateful and serve together.

A Widow's Vision
••••••••••••••••••••••••••
Aurora M. Cruz

In November of 1989 I became a widow with four children—three boys and one girl. I was engaged in the grain business, which is hard work. The business did well, but I found no satisfaction. Life became more complicated and there was no peace within. But for the sake of my children, I felt I had to push on. Eventually my health began to fail and it was discovered that I had a tumor which would require surgery. The operation was done on October 3, 1993, and my first visitor was Jesus Christ. It was then that I came to be certain of His reality. He talked to me! He touched me! He healed me physically and spiritually. I felt His wonderful presence in my heart, which made me hungry for the Word of God.

The Bible became a wonderful source of inspiration to me. I spent most of my time reading the Holy Scripture. The grace of the Lord opened my mind and gave me wisdom to understand His Word. Through God's Word I was born again in the Spirit, making me a part of the body of Christ and a child of God. As a child of God there was a wonderful overflow of blessing; beyond spiritual richness I found financial blessing as well. Life itself became satisfying.

I learned many truths from the gospel. One evening while in my room meditating, I became aware of the presence of my idols and images at their altars, which until that time I thought would be all right to keep as keepsakes. Considering what each of them cost, I thought they could just be kept as decorations. However, the Holy Spirit used my daughter Charisse to convict me. She said, "Anything you cherish other than God is idolatry." I was quite shocked at what she said, considering that she was a fourth-year student in the Dominican school and was herself Catholic in her religious belief.

As I grew in my relationship with God, my life became better. I began to have a great concern for unsaved people and learned to pray constantly for them. In the months that followed, I felt a stronger desire to know about Jesus. I invited my sister-in-law Rose to share more about the gospel with me. She regularly conducted a Bible study in our house on Fridays. I invited my children, friends, neighbors and relatives to join me, although not all came. A few months later, I desired to join a local congregation for worship on the Lord's day. The Lord inspired me to worship Him in the Wesleyan church in our town, Barangay Paul. I was hesitant at first, but the Holy Spirit cleared the way for me.

The first time I attended I went with my daughter Charisse, my daughters-in-law Glo and Marlyn, and my sister-in-law Rose. I immediately felt the warm enveloping presence of the Holy Spirit. The presence of the Holy Spirit in my heart gives me joy, making me able to praise and worship Him in spirit and in truth.

My life in Jesus has had many challenges. There are lots of trials and sufferings that go along with becoming a Christian. With all the travails in my Christian life, I have Jesus with me, who experienced all these things while He was on earth. His precious blood cleansed me and paid for my transgressions. I know that I am precious and special to Him and that He will never leave me or forsake me. He took things I couldn't bear and did things I couldn't do. Trials and sufferings make me closer to Him.

By God's abundant blessing I have been serving Him to the best of my ability. I have been given the opportunity to share my life and the gospel in three Bible studies. I thank God that He not only made me His child, but He also gave me power and fulfillment in the ministry He's entrusted to me. Serving the Lord is great and nothing else has ever been more exciting. The harvest is plentiful, but the workers are few (Luke 10:2). God needs all of us in the harvest field and everyone will be compensated according to his deed.

Better than Fish

Mrs. Awingan
(told by Rasmin Wag-e)

Mrs. Awingan was a pagan, worshiping the spirits. She and her husband were tribal people and had many customs and traditions related to their spirit worship. She became wonderfully saved, but her husband remained a drunkard and anti-Christian. He mistreated and abused his wife.

Mrs. Awingan invited her husband to go to church one Sunday. He replied, "Go to your church and I will go to my church in the river and catch fish for my lunch." The woman went to church and she was crying, testifying that her husband continued to reject her invitation to church. During lunch time, the husband said, "Wife, come on and eat. I have something to eat, but for you to be satisfied you will have to eat your fingers or lick salt." The wife replied, "It is better for me to lick salt and eat my fingers than to go to the river on Sunday—to go there without God and go to hell." After a few months, the man died without hope.

All the Way to the [Other] Bank

•••••••••••••••••••••••••
Benilda Lejano Cruz

enilda was a pious lady, a very devout Roman Catholic, but full of self-righteousness. She thought of herself as "holier than thou," being contemptuous of others' religious experiences in relation to her own. Happily married to Ernesto Cruz, they had two children, a son now in college and a daughter now in seventh grade. Mrs. Cruz was a graduate of the prestigious University of the Philippines. She finished the bachelor of science in business administration, majoring in economics. She pursued a master's degree in business administration in De La Salle University and became a bank executive.

Roberto Mortel worked for Benilda at the bank and invited her to a Bible study sometime in 1980, but she did not accept. After fifteen or twenty invitations, she finally consented to attend the Bible study. Mr. Mortel himself was conducting the Bible study. The first meeting revealed much to her. Several truths were introduced to her from John 3:16; John 3:3; Matthew 6:33; Ephesians 2:4-9; and 2 Corinthians 12:9. Her interest in Bible reading was aroused and later developed into hunger and thirst for the Word. Her first copy of the Bible came from Roberto.

Although she was a devout Catholic, she was never encouraged to read and own a Bible. All she had was a *missal*— the book used by the priest when saying a mass. Roberto encouraged her to look for a Christ-centered and Bible-centered church, where she and her family could worship and have fellowship with other Christian brothers and sisters on Sundays. In 1982, she found the Wesleyan church in Cainta which was very near her house, just about three blocks away. This was still a very new church building at that time. She read the sign in front of the church which said, "Christ-centered and Bible-centered Church." Then one Sunday, without anybody inviting her, she entered the church. Rev. Daniel Pantangan, the pastor and a former missionary to Indonesia, was preaching. Nobody noticed her entering the church; she sat in the last seat nearest the door. She intently listened to the preaching and found it inspiring, especially the illustrations given by Rev. Pantangan. After the service, she left immediately without anybody being able to talk to her. Later, however, she was told that Rev. Pantangan had noticed her coming in but did not have the opportunity to talk to her. Even the ushers were unable to catch her before she slipped out and was gone. They were unable to even get her name. So, not knowing who she was or where she'd gone, they prayed hard for her to come back. She did come back after three months.

Benilda was thirty-two years old when she received the Lord Jesus Christ on October 10, 1980. She soon gave up praying the rosary and reading the *Novenas*. She began to enrich her mind with the Word by reading the Holy Bible and other spiritual books and magazines. She gathered fortitude and boldness to throw away her religious household images, which Catholics call *santos* or *imahen*. After doing this she had a great peace of mind and heart. She learned to pray directly to God through the Lord Jesus, "the only way, the truth and the life," rather than through some other "mediator."

Benilda persistently shared the gospel with her mother, brothers and sisters, despite their persecution. She gave them tracts, Bibles and spiritual magazines. Her brothers and sisters are very closed Catholics—even up to this time. She, however, never loses hope because of the Lord's promise that His Word will not return to Him void, but will accomplish what He has purposed in Christ Jesus.

Benilda's lifestyle also changed. She gave up dance parties and watching vile movies, having lost interest in those things. The whole family, including their two children, are born-again Christians and are all going to Cainta Wesleyan Church. Her husband has given up smoking, drinking, gambling and the vices of the devil. There are now Christian songs flowing from their household and lips as they go about the business of the day. Family devotions and personal quiet time have become a part of their lives.

Benilda realized that her righteousness was a filthy rag in the eyes of God and that she was saved through the grace of God, not through her righteousness. Now she is projecting the righteousness of Jesus in her heart.

Benilda is now the vice-president of a commercial bank. In the church, (Cainta Wesleyan Church) she is the treasurer and has been a Sunday school teacher since 1982. Using the connections and trust she had in the banking community, she established and is the president of the Redeemer's Home Foundation, Inc., which is a center for abandoned babies. Benilda founded this project in 1997. This center now has eight babies ranging in age from one month to nine months. Rev. Robert Mortel, the man who first invited her to the Bible study, is the chairman. Three caregivers are taking care of the babies. A full-time social worker attends to administrative and management aspects of the orphanage. The Foundation gets its funding through donations from various individuals and a number of institutions. Benilda was called to this work through a near-death experience which is best told in Benilda's own words.

●●●●●●●●●●●●●●●●●●●●●●●●●●●

At 9:30 a.m., January 25, 1997, I took a simple pain reliever to relieve muscles pain below my chest caused by a prolonged cough. It was a self-medication which happened to be fatal to me. Around five minutes after swallowing the tablet, I felt difficulty in breathing because of an allergic reaction to the medicine. I instructed my driver, Jun, to take me to the hospital. My husband was in the church which was on the way to the hospital, so we picked him up. We traveled the distance from our house to the hospital, which is normally a thirty-minute trip, in fifteen minutes. This in itself is a miracle in Philippine traffic. While Jun skillfully negotiated the traffic, my husband became the traffic man, waving and signaling from the open window that we were in an emergency.

I was praying very hard and I tried to remember and claim some promises of the Lord such as Isaiah 53:6; Matthew 7:8; Jeremiah 29:11; and Hebrews 3:6. Finally we reached the hospital's emergency room. My vision was becoming blurred and my whole body becoming numb. I was gasping for air but it seemed no air was coming in, because the air passage has closed. I was convinced that my end was very near. And so I told the Lord, "My Lord, my Lord, please extend my life . . . my children still need me. I have not yet turned over my responsibilities in the office, church and at home. Moreover, I still owe my sister some amount of money. Please, Lord, I am begging you, please, please." When I inhaled and I could not breathe it out anymore, I knew than it was my last . . . the Lord had another plan for me.

I lost consciousness . . . I lost all my senses and I passed away. Why do I say this? I was told by Dr. Amiel de la Cruz that the heart monitor attached to my body started to register a flat line and my blood pressure registered zero. He says that I was flat-lined for ten to twelve minutes while they tried desperately to revive me. During the whole process I did not feel any pain.

There is one part of our being which never dies, the soul. I vividly saw my spirit separating from my body. This spirit was met by an angel who seemed to be a spirit in human form, taller than my spirit and brighter. In a moment I just saw myself with this angel in a very beautiful place. The place was beyond description. That beautiful place was enough to take away my fears and sorrows; in fact, I forgot about my family, my children and my concerns. There was excellent music. I do not know where it was coming from; it seemed to permeate the place from no particular source. The colors of the flowers of various shapes were pleasing. Maybe there were trees around . . . but the flowers were what caught my attention. Then I heard what seemed to be flowing water coming from a very far place and yet the sound seemed so near. The gushing water was actually a light . . . a powerful light. When we came into full view of the light, the angel bowed down and following the angel, I also bowed. Suddenly, I felt a special kind of joy and peace in my heart and I realized that the light that appeared before us was no less than our Lord. At the same time, I felt I was so dirty in the presence of a holy and pure God, and I also felt so ashamed because I had nothing to offer my Lord. I really had nothing to brag about. The things that I had done for Him while I was on earth, I thought, would be enough to make me feel great in the presence of our God. I was mistaken. So I said, "I am sorry Lord. I am sorry, my Lord."

Maybe the Lord saw that I was becoming uneasy, though sincere in what I was saying, so He asked me to recite Psalm 23, maybe to calm me down. So I recited like a little girl reciting a poem or singing a song before her parents. "The Lord is my shepherd, I shall not want. . . ." When I reached the last verse, "Surely goodness and love shall follow me all the days of my life and I will dwell in the house of the Lord forever," I wanted to give up my spirit . . . my whole being. So I said, "Lord I commit my—" I really wanted to say "my spirit" as Jesus had said on the cross. I attempted to complete the sentence three times but could not. Then the Lord spoke again and said in a very powerful voice, "My child, you will live, your mission is not yet over. Worship no one but Me. I am a jealous God. Serve no one but Me. I am the way, the truth and the life and no one comes to my Father's Kingdom except through Me. Share My Word. Share My love and go on with your plan." For each of God's commands I said, "I'm sorry Lord . . . Yes, Lord."

Now I want to tell you what this plan was before I go on with my heavenly experience. Sometime in October 1996, Rev. Paul Munshi related to us at the bank his testimony about orphanages/hospitals. I caught the vision. I told Mr. Robert Mortel about it and then I began to draft the idea. So I told the Lord, "Lord I have nothing. I am not rich. We only have a simple house, a company car and a few belongings." Of course, the Lord knows accurately who I am and what I have, so I didn't have to tell Him this. Yet the Lord told me in a loud voice like rolling thunder, "I own the heavens and the earth. Trust Me and obey Me." He only asked for my trust and obedience. I tried to find another excuse by saying, "Lord, I do not want to beg." I told Him this because by nature I am the type who would not bother anybody, especially for my needs—not because of pride, but maybe because I just don't want to be a burden to anybody. The Lord spoke again, this time even more powerfully and authoritatively, "Worry not. I will touch the hearts of people who will help you. Remember, the heavens and the earth are mine. Trust me and obey me." So what else would I say but "Yes, Lord." True enough, the Lord is faithful. Now we have eight babies in the Redeemer's Home Foundation.

After telling me to go on with my plan, the powerful light started to fade. I knew the Lord was leaving. So I spoke again, "Lord not yet, not yet," because I wanted to enjoy His presence longer. I noticed the Lord was determined to leave so I shouted, "Lord, I love you. I love you!" Then my angel brought me down to a place with two divisions—a lighted portion and a very dark portion. We alighted on the lighted portion. When I was three or four meters away from the dark portion, my angel pulled me back. But before he was able to do it, I heard the faint voices of many people coming from a deep place. The voices seemed to be weeping and moaning. The angel mentioned that this place was Hades, the place for unbelievers.

This is not the end of the journey. My angel showed me around the world. What caught my attention was not the interesting places of the countries we visited, but their people. I saw multitudes of people busy doing their own thing. Each of them appeared to be carrying a pail. Some of the pails were full of dirt. Some were half-full. Others were just dirty. The angel explained that the pails represent the hearts of people. The dirt represents our sins. He said that it took the blood of the Lamb to cleanse the heart. Each person must surrender his heart to the Lord Jesus Christ and allow Him to cleanse it by asking for His forgiveness and making Him the Master and Lord of his life. Only then could he be a child of God and, therefore, heir to the heavenly Kingdom. I began to have a full understanding of what it meant when He said, "Worship no one but me. I am a jealous God." I used to be very religious and full of piety. Now I realize it is Christ alone that I need for my salvation. My traditional religious beliefs cannot save me. I repented before Him. There is never any doubt in my mind that I have to worship Him alone.

I wish to end this testimony by quoting St. Paul's statement in Philippians 1:21: "For to me, to live is Christ and to die is gain." It is in death that I gained the glorious presence of our Lord, and now that the Lord has blessed me with this heavenly experience, I am committing my life to Him for His honor and glory.

Hidden Light

••••••••••••••••••••••••••

Charles Nagados Ampaguey (Chuck)

For my thoughts are not your thoughts, neither are your ways my ways,
saith the Lord. For as the heavens are higher than the earth, so are my
ways higher than your ways, and my thoughts than your thoughts.
Isaiah 55:8-9 KJV

I n 1965, I was born the fifth child of six in Baguio in the mountains of Benguet province. My father was an educated man from Ibaloi, but he was a pagan, believing firmly in the *Anitos* of the mountains until he died when I was seven. My mother was from the Bago tribe. The Bagos are considered the "Igorots of the lowlands" (Igorots are generally mountain people). Unlike my father, she was so religiously tolerant that she allowed us to join any religious activity in the community. We did not know she was a backslider from the Wesleyan church.

My father's death caused turmoil in our family. He was a disciplinarian who kept order and wanted us all to have an education. But my two older sisters had to quit college to work, while the rest of us went to high school and college with the help of various scholarships. These hardships made me question why God would allow my father to die so early. We were on the path to being a successful and prosperous family. Only later did I realize God's providence at work in our lives. The discipline impressed by my father and the hardships of our lives helped me to live free of *barkadas* (evil friends) and vice. I seemed to be a good boy to others. From my elementary to high school days I strove for the best. I joined academic clubs and extracurricular activities. I grabbed every opportunity to learn. I shunned social gatherings and had few friendships. I became a loner—introverted and self-centered.

It was also during those hard times that my mother was restored to her Christian faith. When some members of the Baguio Wesleyan Church heard about my mother, they started visiting the family and invited us to church. It was here that my mother was revived and my sisters got to know Jesus Christ as their Savior and Lord. Salvation was not yet clear enough to me, but I was impressed with the Bible stories that I heard during Sunday school. My favorite story was the story of Joseph, and I could hear or read that story again and again with appreciation. The first hymn I learned also became a favorite, "Higher Ground." But these things were purely aesthetic.

I heard the gospel message of salvation while attending church, but I did not apply it because "I was a good boy." I did not consider myself a sinner.

While I was in high school, I attended the Campus Crusade for Christ meetings. One of the staff members brought the message of salvation home to my heart. I realized that in spite of goodness, I was a sinner and needed a Savior. I had a feeling that is unexplainable, following my acceptance of Jesus Christ as *my* Savior and Lord through prayer. I went home from school with a joy I had never experienced before, but I didn't have the courage to share my experience with others, not even my mom. In church, God's Word and the messages of the songs took on new meaning. The story of Joseph and the song "Higher Ground" became significant, not just aesthetic. I stopped questioning God about my father and accepted it as His way. I understood this to be how the Lord led my mother back to Himself, and in turn the whole family. If my father had lived, we would never have had the opportunity to know Him and would have remained pagan. The hymn taught me that I could be the best possible only through Christ, and not by human knowledge or strength.

Since my conversion, the Lord has given me many challenges. Because my family was poor, when I wanted to go to college I had to pass the exams for scholarships. My ambition was to be a doctor. While waiting for the exam results, my mother convinced me to enroll in the Wesleyan Bible College at Rosales, Pangasinan. It was during a spiritual emphasis week where Dr. Saturnino Garcia was the speaker, that God called me to a ministry that was different than what I planned for myself, a ministry to souls not bodies. This decision became even more difficult when I learned from the newspaper that I was one of only two who had passed the government scholarship exams. After much prayer and turmoil, I decided to continue my Bible college studies. I finished my bachelor of theology in 1987.

After ten years of ministry, I married one of my former classmates from the Wesleyan Bible College, Roselily Bastawang. We are now pastoring the Wesleyan Fellowship in Hong Kong. This is a congregation of Filipino contract workers which is celebrating its fourth anniversary this year (1998).

As I look back, I can truly say, "Indeed God's ways and thoughts are higher than mine or anyone else's." To God be the glory!

Living God's Norm

•••••••••••••••••••••••

Cherry Tejero

I thank God for my godly family who had family devotions, took me to Sunday school, vacation Bible school, other local church activities and conventions. The Lord has let me experience these from my childhood. In all of these, I saw and felt myself dirty, sinful, hopeless and needing God's forgiveness. I prayed many times to be assured of this forgiveness. It was during one of the youth conventions after I graduated from high school that I gave my life totally to Jesus, promising Him that I would be what He wanted me to be. Then I had peace and joy!

It was also in these religious meetings and activities that I had a glimpse of missions. Missionary songs always made me cry for a reason I do not know. I'd always tried to hinder those tears, but I couldn't. One day, while I was reading my Bible to seek God's guidance, I was struck by the verse, ". . . I will give you the heathen as your inheritance. . . ." I entered Bible college and made myself available for the Christian ministry. After graduation, I was assigned to do various ministries and sent to different places where I had to learn other dialects. These were preparations for the call that God would give me to go to Cambodia.

Today in Cambodia, I can look at my past and say God has truly made all things work together for my good. He has preserved my life out of dark moments for a purpose. He has healed me from physical sickness. He has been very patient with me. While Cambodia is not a "safe place," I know that where God wants us to be is still the safest place to stay. Anxieties and fears come but, thanks to God, "He is faithful who called us." I am always calmed when I remember the fact that God is always in control.

Psalm 27:14 says, "Wait for the Lord; be strong and take heart and wait for the Lord." This verse is one I've learned and leaned upon during our ministry in the central Philippines. This has become our command as a family. I thank God for bringing us to Cambodia to know Him more and experience His love, grace and power in a way we've never known before. Our prayer and hope is to glorify the Lord Jesus while ministering to the Cambodians, as well as being ministered unto. God is truly good in our lives!

Farmed Out to Grow
● ●

Consuelo del Rosario
(told by Alejandrina Mondala del Rosario)

Consuelo came from a very poor family. His parents, Donato and Agripina, only wanted the best for their children. It seemed that the best way to care for the children was to farm them out to relatives who were better off financially.

At the age of five, Consuelo went to live with an uncle. He learned to work hard with boys who were older than he was. Work started early and eliminated boyish grins and the innocent frivolity of a growing child. At the end of a long day, he had no hug or loving word of mother or father, so he would often cry himself to a lonely, restless sleep. Sometimes in the night hours, he would wake himself up, calling for his mother or father in a dream that had more comfort than his life.

When he was twelve, he was able to return to his family but it was not a happy occasion. His mother had died giving birth to a seventh child. Consuelo dropped out of school in order to take up household duties for his family, and he stayed at home so other members of the family could go to school.

During a ten-day daily vacation Bible school (DVBS) near his house, he would sneak out and go to the classes whenever he could. The teacher told the children, "Jesus loves you. He really does. In fact, He died for you. But He lives again and now he is preparing a place for you." These words drove deep into the soul of this lonely little boy. There in that DVBS he found the Lord. To the best of his ability at that young age, He accepted Christ as his personal Savior and found relief, peace, and joy for his soul. One of his uncles lived near the oldest Wesleyan church in the Philippines. Most of the families in that area were members of that church. Whenever he could, he'd go there and found it to be an answer to his loneliness. The missionaries would often speak there. In one of those services the Lord stirred his heart and he surrendered his life to full-time service.

His lonely childhood was a part of the fabric that was to make him the man he became. In later life he would sometimes take on a difficult thing, sticking it out to the end for the sheer joy of seeing if he could accomplish it.

As an example, in the fifth year of his Bible college education, he had to leave because he couldn't pay his school bills. He packed his meager belongings and headed down the road. Others on the campus tearfully collected an offering and gave it to him for his trip, with a "Good luck and God bless." He had no place to go and no source of cash, but was bolstered by their concern. He smiled, squared his chin, and softly declared, "Don't you worry. I'll be back, you'll see."

He traveled the long road to Bukidnon alone. This was a mountainous jungle area with valleys good for farming. A good-hearted couple took him in and treated him like a son. He did all kinds of odd jobs, including logging. It was a test to his faith, but he was content with it. In later years he would look back at this difficult time as a balm to his soul. His hard months of labor won him back the opportunity to continue his original desire of service to God.

The quiet determination that others may have seen as stubborn self-will I saw as a quality of leadership. It is what won my heart to him. After 27 years of marriage, I've seen many of these paradoxes. There is pride coupled with humility, a strong core that is tolerant and patient, a quiet shyness that is friendly, a leader who is willing to follow. But above all, I have seen godliness.

Consuelo has now served in many types of ministry. He is presently the district superintendent of the Northwestern Mindanao District. While this is a new district for the church, he has served in the capacity of district superintendent for twenty years. In his last report to the district conference he stated, "I want to thank God for the trials. When obligations seem to press down with many cares, He's always there. And when we need physical as well as spiritual strength, we find His hands outstretched. I want to say I don't feel any regrets. My plans are in His plans, my ways, in His ways."

Disowned

Crispina Bayan Carbonel (Opin)

I was born in the small village of Labayug, Sison, Pangasinan in 1946, right after the second World War. My father was from the mountain tribes, but my mother was from the lowland Bago tribe. Because my parents were devout Roman Catholics, I was trained to attend mass every Sunday. There was daily family rosary prayer at six each evening. When I was nine years old my mother died, but my father was a strict disciplinarian and the training continued.

My father was a security guard at the harbor. When my mother died, he forsook all his former interests and even left his job. He focused his attention on his four children who were left behind. He began to farm and grow a big garden to support us. There was a famine in the country in the early 50s, but there was always food on our table. There was also a flat "board of

207

instruction" for wrongdoers. There was no room for argument or "sass" unless you wanted more of the same.

When I was twelve, some friends invited me to attend revival services in the Wesleyan church in our barrio. During that first night, I could not help but go to the altar to pray and ask for the Lord's forgiveness for the wrong I had done. I decided to serve the Lord with all my heart and from that time on, trials and persecution began. I was forbidden to go to any church but the Roman Catholic church. Because of my zeal, I began to sneak out through the window of my room to attend the prayer meetings and youth meetings at the Wesleyan church. I would sleep at my cousin's house and bring water early in the morning to my own house in order to get back in. When my father found that I was sneaking out, he beat me so hard with a bamboo stick that it broke in pieces. It was very painful, both physically and emotionally, but I cried out to the Lord and told Him that because I loved Him, I was willing to take the consequences. In spite of that experience, I did not stop but became more serious and continued serving Jesus and, at the same time, I continued sneaking out to services. One day I was caught the second time and my father beat me with a broom handle from head to foot, telling me that I was a most stubborn child. I was hurt so much that I decided to run away from home. I went to Ilocos Sur and stayed with my aunt for six months, without telling my father where I was.

My love for the Lord did not change and I continued to pray for my father. I thank God that He did not fail me. When I went home, my father was very sorry and regretted what he had done to me. He was glad I was back home and he asked for forgiveness. He permitted me to attend any church activities I wanted from that time on.

My pastor at that time was Rev. Elryn Lipaoen. He and his wife assigned me to be the assistant teacher in the primary department. I attended church seminars, youth conventions and camp meetings. One camp meeting during the missionary service, the Lord spoke to me that He was calling me to be a full-time minister. I obeyed and answered Him willingly. When I was sixteen in 1963, very much against my father's will, I went to the Wesleyan Bible College.

While I was in Bible college, the trials and persecutions did not stop. For four years my father did not send me even a single centavo for my tuition fees. I could never buy a new dress or a new pair of shoes. Sometimes I had to wash my clothes without soap. But I learned through the saying of the Apostle Paul, "In whatever state I am, I learned to be content." Praise God, He supplied all my needs and not my wants.

I finished my six years of studies and graduated in 1969, with no parent to pin my ribbons on or to hang a garland on my neck. But I was not discouraged nor dismayed. A week after that graduation, on April 8, 1969, the man who loved me escorted me to the altar in the Wesleyan Bible College tabernacle where we exchanged wedding vows.

My husband and I met as classmates at the Bible college. When he was two years old, he got a big boil on his neck that affected his whole body, so that he was very sick, thin, and malnourished. During the Japanese occupation, many lives were taken and people had to flee and hide in great fear.

My husband's family was fleeing to the mountains with this young sickly child who continually cried and whimpered. They feared the Japanese would find them on account of the boy, so they abandoned him beside the path. Because of the pain, hunger, and thirst the child cried and cried through the night and into the following day. The next day his grandparents were fleeing along the same path when his grandfather heard a child's cry. He stopped, put down his baggage and searched until he found the child. He was astonished to recognize his own grandson. He took the child in his arms and cried out to the Lord, "Lord, save and heal my grandson." The Lord saw and answered that prayer and the child was healed. The Lord performed a miracle and saved this little boy for a purpose. He was raised from that time by his grandparents until he went to Bible school at the age of nineteen.

After our wedding, we were ready for the battlefield. Our first assignment was in Bakun, Benguet, a place inaccessible by car. We had to hike the last sixteen kilometers, which included crossing a hanging bridge that was half a kilometer across. We worked with these tribal people for fourteen years. It took a lot of love and adjustment to work with people of a different culture, dialect and lifestyle. But we were sure of our commitment and dedication to the One who had called us there.

Because of God's grace, He has given us victory over trials that have come into our lives. God allowed another painful and severe tragedy to come to our family in 1995. Rachel, our youngest daughter (who was 22 and a second-year student in college), was stabbed to death inside the parsonage, and to this day no justice has been given. My husband and I were away at the time, in the mountains for an evangelistic service. Many souls found the Lord in that meeting, but one soul went forever to be with Him. I questioned the Lord, "Why did He allow this to happen? Where were the guardian angels?" It is hard to accept and to understand, but in the depth of my sorrow I also saw the goodness of God. "Thank you, Lord, for taking Rachel so that she did not linger and suffer. Thank you for preserving Arcely (her sister). They were sleeping in the same room, but Arcely was not injured." After uttering this prayer, comfort and peace began to reign in my heart.

Our family was in mental shock and confusion over this incident for more than a year, and I thought my world had come to an end. But praise the Lord forever and bless His name for the comfort and recovery He has given to our family day by day. Rachel was the joy of the house and a faithful volunteer at the church. Two weeks before she died, she told me that during her devotion time God had called her. It is true God called her, not to full-time ministry as we thought, but to Himself. It was a heavenly calling.

God has proven his faithfulness to those who serve and trust Him. There is no regret in answering His call and following Him and His will in our lives. The best kind of life is to live in the center of His will till the very end. Praise His Holy Name!

A footnote to Opin's story by Fely Pablo:

When Opin and Tony were married, there was no blessing from her father. Opin tried many times to be reconciled to her father, but to no avail. They thought perhaps the grandchildren would soften his heart, but he refused to be softened.

One day he got sick. He learned that somewhere in the mountains, where Tony and Opin lived, there was a tribal healer who could help him. He went to the mountain and stayed in an acquaintance's house. He would not go and stay with Tony and Opin in the parsonage, even though Opin pleaded with him to do so.

It was revival time in the little Wesleyan church. Opin had been praying for her father and invited her father to come to the services. He decided to go and, arriving early, with only a couple of people in the church, he sat down and began to smoke a cigarette. This, of course, shocked the people and one inquired, "Who is this man?" She was told it was Opin's father. Somebody said loud enough for Opin to hear, "Hey, the Pastora's father is smoking inside the church." This really embarrassed Opin. That night, however, when the altar call was given, Opin's father went forward and prayed. He received Jesus as his Savior and Lord. Praise the Lord!

The Wild Man
• •
Dionisio Sellem (Isio)
(told by Rasmin Wag-e)

Before he was converted, Isio was the tough and wicked boy in the village. He was a wild man. He and his *barkada* (or gang) stole chickens, goats and other animals to eat. They roamed around the village and terrorized the children and youth. They grabbed whatever they saw that could be eaten. I am five years younger than Isio and one day as I was bringing home food my grandmother had cooked, Isio struck the bowl from me spilling all the food on the ground. He did this on several occasions. He would ride his horse in the middle of the road and let it run as fast as it could, so that children and old men and women had to run for safety like scared rabbits.

His oldest brother got mad at him. One day he brought him to the town jail thinking this perhaps might scare him "straight" and reform Isio. After four days, the older brother visited him to see if Isio had gotten any better. To his surprise, there was no change, no remorse, no repentance. The brother brought Isio home and warned him not to do evil deeds again.

There was a week-long revival in the small Wesleyan church in their village. An old pastor who spoke another language (Visayan) preached stammeringly in Isio's language. Isio passed by the church and at the invitation of the other young people, went inside. The Holy Spirit spoke to him and when the preacher invited people to pray and accept Jesus Christ as their Savior, Isio went forward and prayed. He repented from all his sins. He was gloriously saved and testified of his conversion. Many had tears in their eyes because of the change they saw in the man they feared so much. Isio attended the youth convention and there he received his call to preach. After preaching for twenty years, he retired in 1995, but still continues to be involved in the work of the Lord in any capacity for which he is able. Many souls were saved and helped during his ministry as a pastor. He also preached in other local churches during revivals and evangelistic meetings. To God be the glory, for He changed a "wild" man to a meek servant.

Abused Wife Makes Good

Elvira P. Buzon

M y parents were Roman Catholics, but they did not know our Lord. They indoctrinated us in the typical Catholic religion and traditions. We prayed to many graven images which we were taught would help and protect our spiritual and physical well-being. I taught these same traditions to my family because I thought that was the way to be right in the eyes of God and people.

I got married when I was twenty years old. My marriage was an abusive relationship. I prayed to the idols which I was told represented our Lord, but the idols were deaf. My husband and I separated in June of 1980. Another trial came when my father died, leaving behind my very sick mother and youngest brother. Since I was the oldest of the seven children, I felt responsible to care for them. But being a single parent of two, as well as the sole support for my family, I could barely make ends meet. In December of 1985, my mother became critically ill and had to go to the hospital, where she died after a month. This brought us to total bankruptcy.

At the death of my mother, I requested the parish priest in our *barangay* (village) to officiate a mass in honor of my mother. There were two prices for such masses, and I had no choice but to take the cheapest. I was so disgusted with the parish priest that I decided "they're just after money, they're hypocrites." From that moment, I denounced my Catholic religion and stopped going to mass.

I began to search for a true religion. For a period of about three years I went to both mainline Protestant churches and various cults, searching for truth. I had many questions about religion which were not being answered. My life was a mess, I had no peace of mind and could not find the peace I sought. I have come to understand that the Holy Spirit was working in my life during those crucial times.

In September of 1986, I met a high school friend who gave her testimony of how her life was changed. I was amazed because I knew some of the vices this friend had while in high school, and I knew she too was separated from her husband. I was especially intrigued by her testimony about a "personal relationship with the Lord Jesus Christ." As I observed her, I could see that she was happy, contented and at peace in spite of her situation, which was much the same as mine. I started going with her to a home Bible study and then to church services where, in October of 1987, I received Jesus Christ as my Lord. From that point my life began to change, and I was at peace and blessed.

I reconciled with my husband, who also received Christ as Lord of his life. I got a good job and was promoted to supply officer for the Philippine army. This was a difficult position, full of pressure and temptation for a woman in a man's world. I became so preoccupied with my job and post-graduate courses that my relationship with the Lord became secondary. I drifted in a lukewarm condition for about five years. I thought that becoming a Christian was enough to free me from struggles and trials in life and that everything I did would be victorious. Then one day I woke up very ill and found myself continually in and out of the hospital. With this trial I realized my shortcomings with the Lord. I thank the Lord for waking me up. With the help of Rev. Franklin Pascua and one of the church's laymen, Leandro Vidad, I was reconciled to a full relationship with the Lord and healed from the illness in 1997.

I am presently an active member of the Fort Bonifacio Wesleyan Church and the president of the Wesleyan Women's society. My desire is to be a spiritual leader for Christ.

The Fruit Picker

•••••••••••••••••••••••

Estanislao Albano, Sr.

(told by Estanislao Albano, Jr.)

Estanislao Albano was one of the many young Filipino men who left for the United States early this century. Seeking the proverbial greener pasture, they got hooked on a new religion instead of the better life their families were hoping for. Estanislao found a better life, but it was not what the family expected. Estanislao sailed to the United States sometime in the 1920s. He spent a year or so in the cane fields of Hawaii to earn enough for the passage to the mainland. It was while he was in Hawaii that he first set eyes on and handled the Word. He had bought it, for no apparent reason, from a bookseller.

Born a Catholic, he read the book just like he would any other, and it was like any other book until he reached the description of heaven in Revelation. All of a sudden, he longed to see the place and he prayed to God that he would be allowed to. As he could not find anyone who could enlighten him on the subject, the experience soon receded to the back of his mind.

After a year or so, he moved on to California, where he found work on a lemon plantation. A fellow Filipino who had already received the Lord, Cornelio Bulayog, invited him to evangelistic services in a tent. Nothing happened the first night. But the second night, the Holy Spirit spoke to him about his sinful condition. He responded to the altar call, confessed his sins and received Christ as his Savior.

Estanislao was not really what could be called a bad person. He was not addicted to any vice and did not remember doing any wrong to his fellowmen, but that night he saw that his goodness was not enough.

Not long after that night, while atop a tree picking lemons, he heard the clear call of the Lord for him to return to his country to preach the gospel. He said yes, but asked how he could preach the gospel effectively when he had only finished grade five. He haggled with the Lord for the opportunity to go to school before returning to the Philippines. The Lord responded positively to his request, and by working and saving, he was able to study by either attending school full-time or by working and studying at the same time. During his last year in school, he pastored a church with Filipino members. By 1947, he felt he was ready to come home. By then he already had a master of arts and, more importantly, a bachelor of divinity degree.

When he came home in 1947, the preparation for opening the Wesleyan Bible School at Cabanatuan, Nueva Ecija, was in full swing. In 1948 when the school opened, he became a teacher. He was married to Eufrosina

Cosmiano five years later in Mindanao. She had been one of the students and was assigned to Mindanao as pastor after graduation in 1951. They were back in Bible school after the wedding.

In 1955, the new work in Tabuk, in Northern Luzon, was about to be left without a pastor, as the field trainee assigned there was going back to school. Church authorities felt that someone should go. When they heard about the need, the Albanos gladly packed their bags and thus began their service to the people of Kalinga. This lasted until Estanislao's death 35 years later. (There was a break of four years when the couple was assigned to Bakun, Benguet and Saytan, Pugo, La Union, from 1962 to 1966.)

The early years in Kalinga were spent with the Guilayon people, who remember the family walking back and forth, through hills and streams, across the ten kilometers between the churches in Magnao and in Nansibakan, with their youngest child on Estanislao's back and the two older children in tow. Their labors have borne fruit as there are now third-generation believers among the Guilayons.

The Albanos retired in 1970. They continued to work in God's vineyard as lay ministers until early 1990, when Estanislao was immobilized by illness. Estanislao passed into his heavenly reward at 9 a.m. on Sunday, July 1, 1990, at age 84. An hour before his departure, he used his last earthly vision to read Romans 5, one of his favorite chapters.

His funeral wake did not have the usual atmosphere. Tears flowed, but on the whole it was a remarkable celebration of the blessed hope of every new creation in Christ Jesus. Estanislao believed this hope was worth renouncing the opportunities of America and risking the disappointment of family. He and a handful of other Filipinos of his generation brought this hope back to the Philippines with them so that other countrymen would benefit. It was a glorious gathering of representatives from three generations of the Philippine Wesleyan Church. His coffin served as the impromptu pulpit.

Balancing the Books
●●●●●●●●●●●●●●●●●●●●●●●●
Fedencia Arconado

I married into a Wesleyan family and moved to the remote place of Midsayap, Catabato, on the island of Mindanao, where my brother-in-law was a pastor. It was through my husband's family that I came to know the Lord. Their life was different from the lifestyle I had known. Every day the family came together for Bible reading, devotions and prayers for everyone. There were prayers before mealtime; conversations during the day were words that were pleasant to hear, with no obscenities. There was love and camaraderie, no harsh words or fighting. I kept saying, "What is there about them that I don't have?" Hearing the Word of God explained by my brother-in-law, I came to realize that a Christian lifestyle is Christ living His life through you.

I was brought up by Roman Catholic parents. We went to church every Sunday and memorized the "Hail Mary," as well as other prayers, but they were just formalities. During high school I studied in a Catholic school. After my graduation, I planned to be a nun in Baguio City at the St. Louis College. I had my confessor, but due to the outbreak of the second World War, my ambition was not fulfilled. After the war I returned to Manila, stayed with my relatives and enrolled at the University of Santo Tomas taking subjects in law. It was during my first year in college that I met my husband and got married. I was then twenty-three years old.

We did not stay long with my brother-in-law's family in the parsonage, but soon went to Catabato City and stayed with my husband's other brother who was a soldier. I found a job as a secretary in a business firm and my husband found a job as passenger solicitor for a shipping line, enabling us to rent our own house. God had a plan for our lives and supplied our needs. Since my brother-in-law was a well-known pastor in The Wesleyan Church, our house became a stopping place for students coming and going to the Bible school, which was sixty miles away. We also opened our house for services on Sunday. Students from the Bible school came during weekends and sometimes church leaders would come to visit.

While we lived in Cotabato City, the Lord spoke to my heart. I went to the Bible school and attended the ministerial convention in October of 1962, staying for two days. I went to the altar during the altar call and asked the Lord to forgive and wash away all my sins by His precious blood. Right there I fully received the Lord as my personal Savior and Redeemer. Everything was changed, and I became a new creation. The things I used to do, I didn't do anymore. There was a deep yearning in my heart. Joy, peace, and deep contentment were mine. I enjoyed the fellowship. I wanted to stay for the rest of the convention, but I had to return to my family. We were already well-established in Cotabato City, but when I talked to the Lord I said, "If you have plans for me, Lord, do it; not my will but Yours be done." That's what He did.

When I returned to Cotabato City after my two days at the ministerial convention, a Wesleyan lady dropped by my house. She was on her way to Davao City (about 300 miles away) to follow up on her application for a national appointment as a health worker. I shared with her about the ministerial convention at the Bible school. I told her that many people prayed and were saved. Backslidden students and even pastors flocked to the altar and came back to the Lord. I told her of my newfound joy and peace. I told her of the longings of my heart, how I wanted peace, and how the Lord gave it to me in that convention. I told her about one of the Bible school students who had been divinely healed. Perhaps I was too enthusiastic, because Fely Arciaga decided to make a side trip through the Bible school before going on to Davao City. Later I learned that she never went to Davao City on that trip but, instead, enrolled in the six-year ministerial course at the Bible school. Eventually she married that student who was divinely healed, and is now our general superintendent's wife, Mrs. Alfonso Pablo.

My husband was surprised at my changed attitude. Even the people in the office where I worked were surprised. One of the biggest changes was the way I dressed. I had always used heavy makeup and was very fashion-conscious, but those things lost importance in my life. I talked to my husband about moving to Kabacan, where the Bible school was located. We prayed about it, and when I went to visit my friends at the Bible school, I asked them to pray about it as well.

There was a parcel of land for sale right at the gate of the school, and this was what I wanted. We sold our house in Cotabato City and with the proceeds we bought the lot and built our home. I resigned from my job, but my husband continued to commute to Cotabato City. I enrolled in the two-year Christian Leadership Training course. Many of my classmates from those days are now the leaders in The Wesleyan Church. I worked in the Bible school as treasurer under missionary Darlene Meeks, and also taught a bookkeeping course in the school. I began to work with Magdalena Garcia, who was the national superintendent's wife at that time, in the Child Care Fund. We visited different churches and helped the most needy families.

Mrs. Garcia asked me to teach the Sunday school class on Sundays in the tabernacle. I was petrified and wanted to refuse because there were well-trained people and church leaders in that class. I cried to the Lord and asked Him to help me and put the right words in my mouth. As I stood before the class, my fear disappeared. The Lord answered my prayer as we explored the lesson.

I cannot forget the missionaries who were at the Bible school in those days. Among them were dear friends such as Mother Slater, Rev. and Mrs. Robert Smith, Rev. and Mrs. Paul Meeks, and Rev. and Mrs. Paul Walborn. They were a blessing to me and my family and were often in our home. Our sixth child, the only girl among five boys, was born at the Bible school. She grew up at the Bible school and was often in the care of the students, since I worked on the campus.

In 1981, my sister called me to go to Manila because my mother was sick. The Lord had other plans for our family at that time. Four of my grown children were already in Manila, and eventually we were all in Manila. All of them are now married.

I applied for a position at Asian Theological Seminary, the largest evangelical seminary in Asia, and was supported and recommended by one of my friends from the Bible school in Kabacan who now taught in the seminary. I became the cashier in 1981, retiring in 1991. After my retirement, I accompanied my mother to Calgary, Canada, where she had citizenship through some of the family that lived there. I returned and visited Manila and the ATS business office where I had worked as cashier. I jokingly told them I was ready to reapply. The new business manager took my joke seriously, went to the board with the proposal, and rehired me. So, at age 72, I am again working for the Lord. My secret with the Lord is 1 Peter 5:7, "Cast all your anxiety on him because He cares for you." When you trust in God's Son, darkness gives way to light.

Righteous Judge Needed

• •

Fermin Bal-e
(told by Rasmin Wag-e)

In the early 1950s, Fermin was converted to Christianity from paganism through the ministry of Rev. Bonifacio Urbano, the pastor in Bakun, Buguias, Benguet. He was a changed man. One day a crime was committed and he was falsely accused. He tried to defend himself, but to no avail. He was imprisoned in Muntinglupa, Metro Manila, at the national penitentiary, where he stayed for four years. He maintained his Christian life inside the prison cell and never questioned why the Lord had let him go there. He read his Bible, prayed, and witnessed to other prisoners. He kept his faith, believing that someday he would be released and knowing he had not done any crime.

One afternoon while working in his garden in the prison compound, he heard a voice, "Fermin, pack your things and go home! The authorities of the prison office learned that you have not committed any criminal act and so they will let you go." He hardly knew what to do and he could not believe it, but he joyfully packed his things and bade good-bye to his friends in prison. The people and his family were surprised when they saw him at home, but they were full of joy because righteousness had prevailed. This experience made Fermin more committed to the Lord. He continued to testify to the goodness and greatness of God. He is now dead but He is with the Lord, the just Judge.

A Simple Story of Faith

Hilario Saldaen
(told by Rasmin Wag-e)

Sometime in the early 1950s, a pagan man named Hilario, who lived in the mountains of Buguias, in Benguet province, went to cut trees for firewood. Rev. Bonifacio Urbano, (the pioneer pastor in that area), handed him a gospel of John. He took the booklet and proceeded on his journey, but later got tired. He sat down under a tree and brought out the booklet from his pocket. He opened it and came across the passage where Jesus was ridiculed, tortured and nailed on the cross. He was so touched he cried, "If that is true that Jesus died for my sins, I will accept that Jesus and ask Him to forgive my sins. I am sorry Jesus, I am a sinner. I need to be saved. I am now ready to give up worshiping my gods and spirits, so You can forgive me so that I can go to heaven." After thinking and thanking the Lord for forgiving him, he continued on his journey to cut trees for firewood. He put the booklet back in his pocket and joyfully did his job. In simple faith he received, and with that simple faith he returned home with a new attitude. He began to attend the church with his family. Hilario lived a simple life by his simple faith. When he found truth, he acknowledged it as truth and lived by it. He is dead now, but surely he is in heaven, for he remained faithful to the Lord till his death.

Doing Well Is Relative
●●●●●●●●●●●●●●●●●●●●●●●
Joe P. Mangubat

I was raised in a close-knit Roman Catholic family. I became an engineer by profession. I was very zealous in everything I did—academics, sports, community service and leadership in various aspects of life. I had a desire to acquire wealth, have prestige, position and fame. Those are the common desires of men.

In 1980 I married a Christian wife, who struggled in our relationship. We had four children by 1989. I thought of myself as fulfilling everything a man could have wanted in life. Still I kept on searching for something that would fill an emptiness in my life that was not satisfied. I feared the unknown. I feared death. I didn't realize that the joy and happiness I was seeking was spirituality and godliness on the inside, not wealth, prestige and fame.

In a pretense at compromise with my wife, sometimes I would go with her to the Wesleyan church. I had even read through the Bible twice prior to my encounter with God. Pastor Pantangan from the Cainta Wesleyan Church used to visit our family from time to time in 1987-1988. Then Pastor Cagungao organized a Wesleyan men's society. Because I saw myself as a community leader, I gathered seven men for a community meeting. After this meeting we started a Bible study, and I began to read the Bible, searching and meditating on God's Word. It seemed that every time I opened the Word now, there was an emotional, brokenhearted repentance that welled up within me. Finally I opened my heart to the warm embrace of the Lord and found peace for my soul. He pardoned me, accepted me, gave me His assurance, and in His way, began to use my unworthiness. God saved me. I accepted Christ at age 37. Not only me, but my wife and children came to the Lord.

As I began to walk and commune with Him, my daily desire was to be like Christ. I hungered for His word and my heart was broken for the salvation of His creation. He gave me a new compassion for lost souls. I began to especially pray for Japan, India, China and Korea (Jesus Christ is King for these countries too). But for me the Christian life was not simple and easy. I struggled against the devil's schemes until the Lord, in an abundance of grace, purified my heart, filling me with His Holy Spirit and giving me victory over the world and the flesh. It is difficult for me to explain the meaning of "holiness in life." But to me, it is the constant daily presence and direction of the Holy Spirit. He makes my heart pump "love, love, and love." No more and no less.

Everything in my life was changed. By God's grace I went from a self-serving, self-contained person to an openhearted, loving person. If I were to take a new name, I would be proud if it were "LOVE." My one and only loving God paid a high price for me; now His love is mine. Yet it is not mine only, but it is for all His holy children. God's love, which He has given, is being expanded daily within me.

I have endeavored to be a spiritual leader for my family. Regular family devotions became a main part of our lives. My oldest children each went to Bible school for a year before going to university. They have promised that if God calls them to full-time ministry, even if they are in the university, they will follow God's leading. Even my third child, who is nine years old, has made a commitment to enter Bible school before going to the university. I want my family to fully follow God's leadership, and I would be honored if the Lord should call any of my children into full-time service.

I have worked overseas and have always made myself available for His service in Bible studies, choirs, Sunday school teaching, preaching, visitation, song-leading—anything the Lord wants me to do. I pray that the Lord will make use of this hungry, thirsty soul for total service.

There are two things in which the Lord has especially blessed us. First, we had four girls. My wife did not want anymore children, but in 1990, she got pregnant again and we prayed desperately that the Lord would give us a boy this time. I earnestly bent my knees, beseeching the Lord to give us a boy. On March 3, 1991, a healthy boy was born to our household. Thanks be to my Almighty God.

Second, the Bible study in my home began to grow and Pastor Melvin Aquino assigned two couples to help us expand to a Sunday fellowship time as well. This went so well that the pastor encouraged us to use our garage and start a Sunday School. These are things we prayed diligently about. On the first Sunday, there were five adults and thirty children. In time, this has become a church, and is no longer my garage!

Like other children of God who are saved by grace, there are many things I could share about His goodness and His greatness in my life. My only boast is in Christ, because of His goodness. I thank Him that in everything He is refining and using us. In His timing we are willing to be used anywhere for God's glory, honor and praise in His Kingdom. To God be the honor, glory, and praise. Amen!

A footnote by Fely Pablo:

Their garage—in fact, their whole house—was used as a place of worship from 1991 to 1996. Their new church is located in a strategic place. It is a beautiful building. The people of this church have raised the funds for its construction. They (even the children) have sacrificed things like vacations and "wants" in order to give to the building project. They also prayed and fasted. They have not completed the whole project, but they are worshiping in it now.

The Danger of Slow Learning

•••••••••••••••••••••••••
Jun Albano

Slow learning in spiritual matters invites misery, pain, disaster and a host of other negative realities. It can also lead to hell. I know all this because I started to habitually resist spiritual learning.

For eleven straight years after I finished Bible school in 1976, I didn't take the knowledge that heaven is for the saved and hell for sinners—a basic spiritual truth—seriously enough to realign my life with God's will. Had He chosen to take my life at any time during those years, I would be in hell for all eternity now. What a sad fate that would be for someone who grew up in a parsonage and went to Bible school for two years.

Misery was a constant companion during those years. One morning in 1981, I woke up on a bench outside a Manila police precinct. I was picked up dead drunk the night before. Sometime the following year, I actually went to jail for a day because of an incident that would not have happened had I stopped drinking after the earlier experience. I was losing all my money in gambling and worked for years without advancing, just because I was not conducting myself on the job as an honest-to-goodness Christian would.

But even after years of the sad side effects of vice and pleasure seeking, I still wouldn't take seriously a lesson I had learned earlier—that the most peaceful and joyful life men can ever know is found in living in the center of God's will. I realize now that my sense of values then was so muddled and my self-control so loosened up, that I was deaf to the voices of my own conscience and the old spiritual lessons.

It would not be accurate to say I had forgotten the spiritual truths I had learned. They were still in my mind. In fact, there were many nights when, remembering the terrors, He would come during my sleep. There were also times when, finding myself in situations I could not handle, I would seek His forgiveness and even make vows to serve Him henceforth. But all of these would be forgotten as soon as situations eased up. The lessons were really not lost but they didn't affect the conduct of my life.

During those years God, was an entity I went to when I was in grave need. But the Lord is patient and loves slow learners, although sometimes not in a gentle manner. In 1987, He allowed me to get myself in an unprecedented mess. I recognized right away that nobody except God could help me out and I gave up to Him this time for good. It is possible that terrible experiences could have been avoided had I, instead of backsliding, grown in my spiritual life during those years.

After two years, I have reintegrated the spiritual lessons I had learned earlier into my life. But I still have to fight old battles, especially in the area of humility. I realize that pride is one of my worst enemies—it often spoils my best intentions, shoos people away and gives me bouts with guilt. I am still having a hard time countering it, but I know God has the remedy for it.

I am doing much better trusting in the Lord. I fully accept the fact that relying on the Lord is a primary requirement for a triumphant life, both in the spiritual and nonspiritual realms. All my days are now lived through strength derived from His promises. I am in a place where I can fully appreciate what David said in Psalm 27:13, "I had fainted, unless I had believed to see the goodness of the Lord in the land of the living" (KJV).

I still may not be learning spiritual lessons fast enough, but there are two differences: I am now a slow learner bound for heaven, and it is no longer fear of hell that is motivating me but a desire to please the Lord.

The Making of a Missionary
Reynaldo M. Rafael, Jr. (Jun)

I grew up as a confused, spoiled son. My father was a military man who was very strict, while my mother tolerated and defended even the bad behavior of her children. My father's discipline had made me proud and boastful, fearing no one. I became a street  fighter in our area. If I was in trouble, my mother was there to rescue and defend me, whether it was my fault or not. She always covered for me so that my father would not really know my bad doings. I indulged in doing bad things not only in our neighborhood but at school too. I engaged in many fights, which put many of my friends in the hospital. I was so notorious that my father told me not to use his family name anymore. I had been caught by policemen many times and he never attempted to get me out of prison. But my mother, along with my uncle who was also a police officer, was always there to bail me out and arrange my cases. I became involved in a group selling drugs and marijuana without the knowledge even of my mother.

I was in the worst of conditions when I was hospitalized because of too much drinking. Diagnosed as having heart and lung problems, I was bedridden for three months, physically and emotionally deteriorating. One day, three young men from the Wesleyan church in our city visited me at the hospital. I recognized one of the men as the one who taught me to start taking drugs when I was only eight years old. I clenched my fist, wanting to box him, but when he approached me, took and held my hand and told me they wanted to pray for me, I was not able to punch him. After their prayer, questions came into my mind. "What happened to these young people? Why are they praying for me?" I felt the love and compassion in his prayer.

These young people visited me again and invited me to attend the church. I had no intention of attending church that particular Sunday. But I was so restless that I hesitantly decided to visit their church and was touched by how the members lovingly welcomed me. That Sunday morning, April 24, 1983, I gave and surrendered my life to God. I accepted Jesus as my Lord and Savior.

The Lord completely changed me that day. Everyone in my family and our neighborhood, as well as my former classmates and friends, could not believe that I was really changed—no more fights, no more alcohol and drugs, no more women, no more gambling. It was really a radical and instantaneous change! Most of them predicted my new way of life would only last for a month or two. But I was changed by my great God and this change is complete and lasting. That year I also received God's call to be in full-time ministry. I went to the Bible college and finished my bachelor's degree in theology.

I was a local church pastor for nine years before going to Cambodia as a missionary, where I am now serving. Truly, our God is a merciful and forgiving God, saving even the worst sinner—a powerful God who can change the lives of men. Praise Him!

A New Sacrifice

Liganay Salvador

(told by Rasmin Wag-e)

In 1960, Mrs. Salvador was a strong animist. She had several images in her house and amulets hanging from the ceiling. A person who entered her house for the first time might be afraid of all of these fetishes. She offered chickens and pigs to the spirits whenever she worshiped them or did a memorial for her dead parents or relatives. She wore beads around her neck, earrings and other spiritist's charms.

At first, she was indifferent to the pastor visiting her house. But after three months of constant visitation, the pastor was able to befriend her. She was invited to go to church. She went to church and was very observant. She saw that many of her neighbors were in the church that Sunday. Her interest was captured, so she kept going to church Sunday after Sunday. One Sunday morning, the message was so strong that the Lord worked in her heart. She was convicted that she was under condemnation. She began to shiver and perspire. It became so noticeable that several church people began to pray for her until she knelt at the altar of prayer. The Christians who were around her emphasized that she must repent from her sins and renounce all her pagan practices. She prayed with all her heart and stood up with joy. Jesus changed her. She invited the pastor and the elders of the church into her house one day and asked them to gather all the images and amulets and throw them out of the window. They then burned them all. Her husband rejoiced with her and together as a family they continued to serve the Lord.

"Born Agains" Not Welcome
●●●●●●●●●●●●●●●●●●●●●●●●
Lita Manarang
(told by Fely Pablo)

L ita is a sweet woman, now in her late forties. I met Lita in 1987 when we had just arrived in Valenzuela, Metro Manila, to work in the general headquarters. We usually pass by her house along the road as we go to work. One day while we were walking together for a Sunday afternoon activity, she told me, "It is very good to serve the Lord! I didn't know it was like this. Vergie did not tell me about it."

Vergie, her older sister, had already been a member of the Valenzuela Wesleyan Church for two years. Vergie tried inviting Lita to church some years before but Lita did not accept, so she stopped inviting her. Lita was a very devoted Roman Catholic, had many images in her home and took good care of them. She religiously went with her companions from house to house, parading their images during the evening. She walked a long road just to go to church. At the door of her house was a sign written, "BAWAL PUMASOK ANG BORN AGAIN" (No Born Again Is Allowed to Enter).

One evening Lita and Rudy, her husband, were watching a healing program on TV. Rudy was very sick at that time. They listened to the preacher intently and when the preacher prayed for the sick and led them in prayer, Rudy followed the prayer. He got healed at that moment. This experience struck a chord in their hearts and Lita and Rudy began to search for a church. Lita remembered the church her sister attended. One Sunday Rudy and Lita came to the Wesleyan church. Rev. and Mrs. Solomon Cagungao were then the resident pastors and they faithfully followed them up with Bible studies in the home. In one of these Bible studies, Rudy and Lita received Jesus as their Savior and Lord.

Lita has grown very fast in the Lord. She seldom misses any church activities—Sunday school, worship service, prayer meetings or women's activities. She usually gives her testimony when given a chance. She always gives glory to the Lord even in little things. Not long ago, I asked her how long she had been serving the Lord and she replied, "Oh, it is already ten years. It is not taxing to serve the Lord. I am enjoying." During the testimonial time in church prayer meeting she added this, "Before I accepted the Lord as my Savior, I was very sickly. But since I accepted Him as my Lord, I am very healthy." Lita was asthmatic before.

Rudy has not grown as fast as Lita. He comes to church once in a while, but if there is a Bible study in their home, he is there. Lita is very persistent in reading the Bible with him and praying with him. Lita is very happy that Rudy is a very generous man. He is a carpenter, specializing in roofing, and he shares his resources and volunteers labor for church buildings. Lita has three sons, all married, and five grandchildren. Lita usually appeals for prayer for her family. Her children, daughters-in-law and grandchildren come once in a while to church, but she knows that they need more of the help of the Lord.

Devout Pagan Becomes Devout Christian

●●●●●●●●●●●●●●●●●●●●●●●

Lorenzo Gunaban

I was born June 6, 1926, at Guilayon, Tabuk, Kalinga, in the mountain province. My father is Gunaban and my mother is Agunas. I have four brothers and two sisters. We are natives of Kalinga of the sub-tribe of Guilayon. We have our own tribal customs and traditions.

During the Commonwealth government, education was compulsory, and so I obtained a little education despite my parents' opposition. We believed in a god which we called *Kabuniyan*, who supplied all the needs of life. As a boy I was taught that there is a good spirit and a bad spirit. When someone got sick, we prayed to the bad spirit, *Kanyaw*, to restore the health of that person. At harvest time, we believed that the good spirit of *Kabuniyan* gave the good harvest, and a thanksgiving feast called *imonaw* was offered.

The Kalinga tribe's beliefs about their god were altered when the government established a school in our place. Politics and teachings of Christianity also affected our beliefs.

It was true that I had a sense of the power of the real God, but I was full of confusion and distress. I wondered if there was really a true God, for there was violence, sufferings, famine and wars. I was wondering what matters to men—pagans and Christians alike—if this is the situation. So I remained unsettled in life and I was content with my own righteousness in obeying the government laws.

In 1956, Rev. Estanislao Albano, one of the pioneer workers who came from the United States, held evangelistic services in our area. After the services were completed, Rev. Albano and his family came to stay in our place, Nansibakan. There was already a Pilgrim Holiness Church in Tabuk Poblacion, pastored by Rev. Honesto Valdez.

In Tabuk, my brother Rafael had a boarder in his house who was a member of the Pilgrim Holiness Church. He invited my brother to church and, not long after that time, he got saved. The pastor, Rev. Valdez, and my brother came to our barrio and shared the gospel. I tried to attend the services, but I clung to my Kalinga god and my customs and traditions. The enemy worked and the church in town was closed. My brother Rafael brought Rev. Albano to our barrio. I accepted Rev. Albano with his family as my visitors, but they told me that they wanted to stay longer with us. We worked together so that we could have food. During the nighttime we had services, and my family and my brother's family would attend.

Because of our constant fellowship, I began to love the pastor. We went hunting for deer. I had three dogs that ran after the deer and we followed them. The pastor was amused as we carried home a very big, very heavy deer.

I became a barangay lieutenant and usually the meetings were held in my house. I introduced my pastor friend to my co-community leaders. The pastor then visited each one of them in their homes. I was observing the life of the pastor and discovered that he really was a man of God. His life convinced me to learn more about God and His creation. I became more interested, so I did not miss any Sunday services.

Rev. Policarpio Labadan, from the Pilgrim Holiness Church district office, visited us. During his visit I accepted Christ as my Savior and Lord. I was so aggressive for the Lord then. As the head of the community, I enforced the hearing of the gospel on my people. So the gospel was widely spread among the Guilayon people.

One day I heard that we should support God's work. Rev. Albano and a new pastor, Rev. Bonifacio Urbano, who was also a pioneer worker in another mountain work in Benguet, was with me as we were strolling on my farm. I saw my cows grazing and I told the pastors that one of the female cows would be my offering to the Lord. They were surprised.

I now fully understand that the transforming power of the gospel is the only answer to all the problems of men and society, in whatever level of society and whatever kind of person you are.

My family and I helped the pastor build the first church in Nansibacan. This became the mother church in the Kalinga area of the whole Northern Luzon District. In the Guilayon tribe, we now have five churches.

As the people of the Guilayon tribe migrated to the capital town, churches were planted there and the church at Dagupan, Tabuk, was re-established.

Tiny Person, Large Ambition
Mamel Rafael

My father left to work in another country when I was nine years old and was not able to visit us until eleven years later. I grew up with a grudging bitterness towards him, in spite of his good intentions in working abroad. He faithfully provided our basic physical needs but I just felt I needed more than what money could give. We needed his presence, guidance and love. I always envied other kids when I saw them with their fathers by their side.

I grew up with responsibilities I would not have had if my father had been home. I am the oldest of three children, so I stood side by side with my mother in deciding family issues. I somehow assumed a part of my father's responsibility in decision-making, listening to family problems as my mother would open them up to me, and helping in sorting out solutions for those problems. Life for me had not been so normal and enjoyable (at least for my age during those times). I had to think, act and decide like an adult would while I was still young. This added more bitterness in my heart. I also wore a "masculine" mask, though I was so fragile inside. I always pretended to be strong and tough like I thought I should be. I studied hard and excelled at school. I aimed to succeed in any endeavor so that I could be rich and famous, thinking this would satisfy the emptiness I was feeling during those times. I also thought that if I could have lots of money, it would cover the longing and loneliness I had in my heart.

I received a scholarship and went to a university in Manila to continue my education. My home city is around 120 kilometers from this university, so I had to stay in a boarding house with my cousin. My cousin happened to be a Christian, as were some of the boarders living with us in that house. All the Christians in that house decided to have a Bible study every Friday in our place, and my cousin invited me to attend their Bible studies. I was very hesitant at first, but I yielded after several invitations. After attending several sessions, I surrendered my life to Christ. That was July 1982, when I was seventeen years old. The Bible study leader talked about the love of God as our Father and as our Savior, His compassionate heart, and His offer of forgiveness. I just suddenly understood what he was reading and realized how wonderful God's love for me was. His love as Father and Savior was the kind of love I had been longing for the past years of my life! It was so wonderful to know that I have a Father in heaven who loves me, who cares for me, who will always protect and provide, and will always be with me! I also realized I was a sinner and needed to be forgiven. I always thought before that I was a righteous person, but then the Lord reminded me of my disobedience, the bitterness I had in my heart, the anger, the lying I usually did, the bad words, those wrong priorities and motives, my neglect of God and other sins. I then repented from my sins, received His forgiveness, and accepted Jesus Christ as my Lord and Savior. I had been crying a long time when I felt God's love and forgiveness enveloping my whole being. I used to attend a Protestant church, but this was the first time God's Word became so clear and true to me. I remembered we had a Bible in our house but I had never read that Book even once. That was also the first time I realized that it was the Word of God.

My life was never the same again! The Lord powerfully changed me and is continually molding me. The anger, bitterness and bad words were gone. I learned to forgive my father and myself. My attitude toward my responsibilities was corrected. My priorities radically changed! God, who had usually been the last, became the first. The Lord took off the mask and taught me to be honest with myself and with others. I find satisfaction and fulfillment in the Lord. He also helped me focus my eyes on treasures above and not on earthly wealth.

After I received Him, I faithfully attended and involved myself in the campus ministry that regularly conducted the Bible study in our boarding house. Then summer came, and I had to spend my vacation at our home town. When I arrived home, I asked my friend if she knew of any Christian church I could attend when I was home. She happened to be a member of Cabanatuan Wesleyan Church, and she invited me to attend that church. As I attended the church, I felt I had always been a part of that church family. I felt the love of God manifested in the lives of the brethren. I also saw the great need for ministry through The Wesleyan Church.

The Lord started calling me to be in full-time ministry in 1983, as He continually showed me the need for workers. I struggled so much in the midst of opposition from family members and in surrendering my ambitions to Him before finally answering His call after almost a year. I then entered the Wesleyan Bible College in Rosales, Pangasinan in 1984 and graduated in 1989. I got married in July 1989, and worked in a local church as a pastor together with my husband until 1996. We were assigned to two pioneer areas and one organized church within this period. In 1996, God called us to minister here in Cambodia as Wesleyan missionaries. We have been experiencing several trials and difficulties, but the Lord is always faithful in carrying us through. These trials can never equal the joy we have in our hearts as we see Cambodians being led to Christ, being nurtured and then see them serve our true living God.

I am so thankful to the Lord for taking me as one of His children and enabling me to be one of His servants. I would never exchange this new life He has given with me with anything in this whole world. When people ask me why I suddenly gave up my high ambitions and chose to be in the ministry, I often tell them, "I never gave up my ambitions; I only chose the highest and noblest one—the one that will remain through eternity."

The Devil's Gang

Mamerto P. Acosta

(District Superintendent, Northern Mindanao District)

E very individual has opportunities to make choices which will determine success or failure. But God in His love has prepared a secure life for us if we live in His will. I praise the Lord for the privileges He has given me since the time I accepted Him as Savior and Lord.

I am third in a large family of eight children. We were very poor, and even now I look back on those days of hardship and struggle with internal emotion. I was born and grew up in Lucia, Ilocos Sur, and after high school I was sent to Mindanao, where it was thought my relatives could help me. I enrolled in the University of Southern Mindanao, taking the bachelor of science in agriculture courses with the help of both my parents and my relatives. I did well for two years and received a partial academic scholarship that encouraged my parents to support my studies.

Being released from the strictures of my parents, I began to run with the wrong crowds. I joined a fraternity and got involved in liquor, drugs, and physical rivalries between the fraternities. I became a member of the El Diablo gang. We often got into trouble because of our nighttime escapades, and were called before the barangay officials for explanation or disciplinary action. In my last year of school, when I should have been attending to my thesis and the major portion of my studies in soil science, I neglected everything. I married hastily and finally dropped out of college.

Our parents blamed us both, but we loved each other. I was not a responsible husband and instead of making a living for my family, I continued to act like an unmarried person. My wife, Marissa, would often cry uncontrollably, so we decided to move to another place and start again. But I just took my vices with me and we were nearly destroyed. I didn't want to hear any advice from Christians. Oh, what a depraved lost sinner I was.

Our Christian neighbors made friends with us and through that contact, my wife received the Lord Jesus as her personal Savior. As a wife she changed from a nag to a loving, understanding person who prayed continually for me. In understanding love she pointed out my negligence. We had two children, and in order to please her, I would sometimes go to church with them.

My wife carried her burden for me for a year. Then in January of 1984, at the age of 25, I found the Lord in a revival being held by Rev. Benjamin Ganibe. At the altar of prayer I poured out my heart, asking forgiveness from all my sins. My wife and the church members surrounded me with their prayer and rejoiced at my conversion. I resigned as a member of the Citizen Armed Forces Geographical Unit (national guard) for I felt it would hinder my growth as a newly born Christian. I went to many people to make restitution. I endured a lot of ridicule from my old friends, but the Lord is so faithful and encouraged me in my new faith. My pastor, my wife, and the church members became my support group. I finally came to the place where I surrendered my whole life to him. He sanctified me wholly for His purpose. My wife and children were happy because our home became a truly Christian home. Our fiery, hot-tempered quarrels disappeared. I was trusted as a Sunday school superintendent and a delegate to district conference. I put my whole life into cooperating with the church, but I still felt something was not fulfilled. I was feeling uneasy, that perhaps the Lord was asking more of me. I had many excuses. I was already a family man, but perhaps it would not be possible to support my family. Was there no other person better than myself who could do this? I thought if I was going to go back to college, wouldn't it be better to go back and finish my last year of college? If I did anything else, my parents wouldn't understand. These were my mind games.

In one of the Wesleyan men's conventions held in Santo Tomas, Davao del Norte, the Bible college speaker was Dr. Alfonso Pablo. He spoke on "The Calling for the Harvest." I knew for sure that God was calling me to full-time ministry. My family and I decided to go to the Bible college for formal training. I sold all our belongings because I knew they would hinder me in following Him. We enrolled in the Wesleyan Bible College in Kabacan, Cotabato, in the second semester of 1988. We struggled because our little savings were soon drained. But we found support in God's people at the school. I often thought of backing out, but God was always there providing our needs. I will always remember those days when we learned to trust in

God. There were many days when we only ate the fruit we could gather and learned to bend the knees in all situations. We continually received the blessing of the Lord through the many friends God touched on our behalf. We found support for our needs through the last year of college.

During our stay in the Bible college, I served as president of the student body and as student pastor in a provisional church until it was organized. Our first assignment scared us to distraction. It was a place called "Canaan," and it seemed to be occupied by giants. It was a big, old church. There were many who felt, and let us know in no uncertain terms, that this was not a church for a first-assignment pastor. We went with trepidation and a lot of prayer to this challenge entrusted to us by the leadership of the church. By God's grace we saw growth and reopened a daughter church which had been damaged and had lost members to another denomination, but who then returned to the fold. We also helped open another church which has grown enough to be organized. The district board of administration gave us the Pastor of the Year award in 1991, for which I give God all glory.

There have been failures along the way, but God has helped me to see them as learning experiences on which victorious ministry might be built. I was on the district board of administration from 1992-1996 and directed the district Sunday school, as well as the Theological Education by Extension course. In our seven years of ministry, whether in big or small churches, I have never questioned God's call and direction in my life.

God has given me a supportive wife and healthy children. MayAnn, the oldest (now in her third year of college), feels that God has called her to be a missionary teacher. Both our children (Mark is a high school senior) are blessed by the vocation into which God has called us. I did not expect to be the district superintendent and feel that this is a big challenge and honored responsibility that I know cannot be done without God's guidance.

Victories have come because God's people have stood behind us to give moral support. To God be the glory for His people and His plan!

Child of the Gambling Den

●●●●●●●●●●●●●●●●●●●●●●●●●
Mansueto Bustamante (Mansing)

I was born in November of 1930, the youngest of ten children. Being the youngest, I was spoiled and loved by all the other family members. Even as a young child I learned to gamble and drink *tuba* (coconut wine), just as my parents did. My parents used their house as a gambling den to make a living. They were not Christians, but belonged to the Aglipayan Church, a split from the Roman Catholic Church founded by a Filipino priest named Aglipay. The family was not religious and only attended the fiestas and celebrations. The Word of God was not taught in our home.

I grew up with a deep sense of the spiritual, always imagining about heaven. Sometimes God spoke to me through dreams. In one of these dreams God came to earth to get His children, and I was the only one left. My parents woke me up when they heard me crying in my sleep.

When I was twelve, there was an open air evangelistic service sponsored by a Baptist group. My friends invited me to go and I heard a message from Matthew 3:10: "The axe is laid unto the root of the trees . . ." (KJV). I was convicted by God's Word. Isaiah 55:11, which says, "My word . . . shall not return unto me void," became a truth in my life. I could not get away from that message. This brought fear to my heart and I knew that if I should die, I was not ready to meet God. Sometimes I could not sleep thinking about my spiritual condition.

In 1945, when I was fifteen, my parents moved to Capiz, Iloilo, where they ran a fish farm. In my first year of high school, I enrolled in the Baptist Home School. Every morning there was a chapel hour, and I had a hunger for spiritual things. In one of the chapel hours the pastor asked if anyone wanted to be baptized. I volunteered and was baptized. However, after baptism I couldn't see that it made any difference in my life. I continued to sin and live like that through high school.

In 1950, after graduation, I asked permission from my parents to go to Mindanao for the adventure. I was twenty years old. In Mindanao, God brought me to Lupon, Davao Oriental, where I worked on a fish farm. I continued with the sinful life, often drinking late into the night with my friends.

In 1951, I stayed in the home of an Ilacano couple who, even though they were not Christians, allowed some Wesleyans to conduct a Bible study in their home. I attended the Bible studies and God spoke to me about my spiritual needs. I was invited to the Lupon Wesleyan Church. The language was Ilocano, which I didn't understand, but somehow the message lodged deep in my spirit. My hunger for the spiritual life deepened. The Wesleyan Bible School was started in Kiamba, South Cotabato. Young people were challenged to go study there, so I went, even though I was not a Christian. At the Bible school, during the chapel times, other students told how God had saved them and changed their lives. I was blessed by these testimonies. But I was questioning, "Why are these things not happening in my life?" Sometimes I prayed that God would save me, but there was no answer. I had no peace for six or seven months. I was struggling in my heart until one day in chapel, God worked mightily. I was so convicted that I went to the altar to pray. God forgave my sins. That very hour my life was changed, and joy and peace poured in. After this, I began to have a burden for lost souls. I had a desire to go back to my home in Iloilo to testify as to what God had done for me. I knew I was called to preach the gospel. I was the only Visayan student in the Bible school, as the school had been originally started among Ilocanos.

Bible school life was hard and I had no financial help, so in 1953 I had to go back to work. I went to Malalag, Davao del Sur, to work on my cousin's fish farm. At first I was strong in the Lord but then, after some time, I began to go with my friends and was soon back where I had been before.

In 1954 I married a simple, humble Christian woman. Even though I was a backslider, I wanted to have a Christian family. My wife was patient and had a calming effect on my life. She continued to encourage me to go back to the Lord. Then in 1960, I had a misunderstanding with my Muslim neighbor, who threatened my family. I decided to leave that area. Remembering God, we decided to look for a place to live that was close to a Wesleyan church. I determined at that time that I needed to go back and serve the Lord. I had been backslidden for seven years and in that time, I had no idea what had been happening at the Bible school. The Bible school had been transferred to Kabacan, Cotaban, and was only fifteen kilometers from the place where we had relocated. The Bible school students had a preaching point in the town where I lived, and one of the students was a friend of my sister-in-law. This Bible school student, Mamaclay, told the missionary, Mother Slater, that I was in the town. Mother Slater knew me and sent the student to invite us to a special meeting at the school. Before they came, they had a special prayer for my family. We attended the convention and my family and I were reclaimed.

I decided that I needed to resume my schooling and calling. It was more difficult this time, because I now had four children and a wife. Laura, my wife, also enrolled in the Bible school. In my last year of schooling, I began to have a kidney problem. The operation took all our money. An eye operation bankrupted us. I decided to drop out of school, even though the faculty advised against it.

Everywhere we went we started a new house church. In 1974, we started the church which has been organized now in Sampao, Kapalong, Davao del Norte. I had nine children by that time and the oldest was already studying in Bible school. Although I was working as a lay pastor, deep down the call was still in my heart.

In 1979, I was riding on a public bus when it collided with a dump truck. Many passengers were wounded and two died. My son and I were safe, but God spoke to me. "Son, if I didn't have a plan for your life, you would be dead." Right away I was reminded of God's call. I went immediately and told my family, and my wife urged me to return to Bible school or there might never be another chance. I was worried about the needs of my large family, but Laura assured me that we could manage and that it was better to do what God wanted than what seemed a safe path. Because of her conviction, I returned to school to finish the one semester left for my bachelor of theology. We sold our residential lot to pay for the schooling. Laura and the eight children stayed behind and she continued to pastor the church while I finished school. My daughter, Minda, and I graduated together in 1980. She is now married to Rev. Samuel Basmillo, who is the district superintendent of Eastern Mindanao District.

We have been assigned to a number of churches since that time. God has supplied all our needs. We were lay pastors for ten years and have been full-time pastors for eighteen years. We have four children who are working as full-time pastors (three girls and one son). One daughter is a lay pastor and has planted two churches in three years by God's help. The other four (one girl and three boys) are faithfully serving the Lord as lay people in God's Kingdom. Laura and I have now retired, but we haven't quit.

The Inheritance
• •
Rasmin Wag-e
(General Director of World Missions of The Wesleyan Church of the Philippines)

My parents were both members of The Wesleyan Church, so they directed us to attend church Sunday after Sunday. I was a sinner but thought that since my parents were both Christians, I was a Christian too. In my early teens, I was good morally. I did not go with gangs and do naughty deeds. Because

I attended church, I presumed I was okay and need not repent of my sins. I was the youth president at the age of fifteen, the youngest to serve in that capacity.

During a revival, the Spirit of the Lord showed me what kind of life I really had, although I was the president of the youth and attending Sunday school and church services. He showed me that I was a hypocrite, unsaved and undone. The message that night struck me and I surrendered my life to the Lord. A pastor accompanied me to the altar of prayer. Different pastors were stationed in our church, and each one of them helped me grow in my Christian life. I was fifteen years old when I got saved. In 1952, I was baptized in the Bued River by Rev. Wayne Wright, our missionary.

As I walked with the Lord day by day, I began to sense something lacking in my life. I had heard the life of holiness preached many times before the Lord opened my heart, and I saw the condition of my heart. During the youth convention in December 1955, I surrendered everything to God and let Him clean my heart of the root of sin. At the same time, the call to preach became clear to me. In October 1956, after graduation from high school, I went to Bible school in Cabanatuan City, graduating in 1962.

I and my family have pastored several churches. I served in different capacities, such as zone leader and district secretary. I was the first one to be elected as general secretary of youth. I served as district superintendent for eleven years. I taught in the Bible college and I became the president of the Bible college for four years. At present, I am serving as the general director of missions of The Wesleyan Church of the Philippines.

During those times that I worked with the Lord in different positions, there were problems, needs and struggles. But I entrusted them all to the Lord, who brought the victories. The greatest lesson we learned was "to lean on Jesus." We learned, too, to be humble when we were in those different positions. We did our best with what we knew and in prayer we asked for directions and decisions during those times.

God supplied all our needs. God protected us from all dangers. God made us victors over our struggles, needs and problems. Today, I am happy to be in the work of the Lord, working even at the age of 61. It is a joy working with the Lord.

Salvation of an Assassin

Reynaldo V. Rafael, Sr.

I was born into a devout Catholic family. Although I was baptized as an infant and believed and understood that I was already a Christian, my life then was always a turbulent maze of confusion and remorse.

During my childhood and school days, I assisted our parochial local priest in our place as sacristan and received a few centavos to satisfy my desire for a good time with my friends.

As I grew older, sin also grew with me. I joined other boys in our neighborhood in their sinful habits, including smoking, drinking, gambling and going to cabarets. My life then was no different from other boys of my age who did not know God at all. Although I went to church and partook of the Holy Communion, sin still ruled in my life.

It was in 1946 that I experienced the most horrible, humiliating and tragic event in my whole life. I was arrested and put into jail for an offense I had not committed. Adding insult to injury, I was not only whipped and boxed, but also tortured with water, the same punishment perpetrated by the Japanese soldiers to those persons who defied their rules during their reign of power.

The irony of it was that my cousin, who was then the immediate commanding officer, was the one who ordered my beating and torture. While I was on the brink of death, I promised to take vengeance if I had the chance to live. For me, what they did would be their haunting ghost every night of their lives.

I was very lucky that after many months of incarceration, I managed to escape from my guards during their merriment. I went to Santiago, Isabela, and joined my brother-in-law, a member of the armed forces of the Philippines stationed in Cordon, Isabela. As I had all the requirements for immediate enlistment, I was drafted as a private and sent to Camp Ord, Tarlac, for a six-month refresher course. I was stationed in different towns, barrios, cities and other neighboring provinces. During my incumbency as a sergeant, I wrought widespread havoc in the places where I was stationed or assigned. Still the hate and anger was imbedded in my heart and mind. I couldn't forget the past days where I was beaten and whipped for no apparent reason. Their mockery of me was still ringing in my ears, so much so that I had to go on with my promised revenge, come what may. My alias name, Kamlon, was a byword in every sector of the community. Whenever the name was heard, people would scamper for safety for fear that they would be victims of my

237

vindictive passion. The time came that my comrades-in-arms, as well as my commanding officer, feared me. I was treated like and compared to a fierce, devouring lion, a savage and wild being. They had no other choice but to take me in as their comrade-in-arms, although in their hearts and minds they wanted me finished. Because of my disgraceful conduct, I was dishonorably discharged from the service. However, after some months, I was fortunate to work with a powerful politician in our place. Once more, my name and wanton cruelty were displayed.

During that time I lived in misery and always experienced sleepless nights—not because I was bothered by my conscience, but for the simple reason that I had not yet succeeded in carrying out my promise of revenge. In agony and discontentment, I was somewhere between failure and success, and it seemed to me that I was all alone living in the dungeon of darkness.

On the order of this powerful politician, I began to put wayward persons out of circulation. Those who had no nerve and strength to execute these unscrupulous and incurable persons always sought my help.

While I was living in sin, without anybody—not even God, it seemed—interfering in my affairs, I began to doubt His existence. This destroyed my faith in Him until one night when I was ready to retire, I was ordered on my two-way radio to report to this politician at his residence. I reported as ordered. When I arrived, he tossed me a rolled-up paper and ordered me to annihilate the persons listed. I was later informed that those persons were his political adversaries. As a good soldier, I had no other recourse but to just nod my head.

Before I left the house, I unrolled the paper and hurriedly scanned the names listed. To my dismay I found the name of my brother-in-law, who was then the incumbent barangay captain in one of the neighboring barangays. I was really tongue-tied. I was not able to say a word, but just begged to leave. When I was inside my service car, I asked my personal driver, a *kumpadre*, whether he was satisfied to be a member of the liquidation squad headed up by me. He confided that he could no longer take the injustices perpetrated by our squad. He further reminded me that the persons we liquidated in the past had nothing against us nor had committed any wrongful acts against us, but were put down upon the order of our boss. My *kumpadre* continued that if we did not stop the nonsense killings, we might suffer the consequences, sooner rather than later. We parted ways and promised not to return to work.

The one-week deadline given us passed, and I did not report to our boss. Later on I was informed that my boss, together with his men, were after me for liquidation. An order had been circulated that they had to get me, dead or alive. I was listed as their number-one enemy.

While I was in the midst of sin and had nowhere to go, my dear wife, who was always beside me during the clear as well as the dark days and moments of my life, reminded me that now was the time for me, a very long time sinner, to come to Jesus Christ for aid. She told me to be sorry for my sins and ask Jesus to forgive me and accept Him as my personal Savior and Lord. When my wife asked me to go with her to church one Sunday morning, I didn't say a word. I just went with her. There I witnessed for myself how the young and old testified to the saving grace of God, and how they could live above sin. It seemed to me that these people had been hypnotized by a very powerful being, but when I witnessed how they lived, I understood that they proved their testimonies. They had clean, humble and sinless lives. I decided then that if those young and old people were drawn to Christ, then I would be glad to be hypnotized also, if only to remove the sin from my life.

Heavy conviction grasped me and I lost my interest and longing for everything except to have what my wife called *salvation*. But I thought then that I could not be saved. I would be forced to go to hell praying on my knees. Really, I was very, very tired of my sinful life and I desired never to return to it.

Finally, God saw my heart's intention and desire. He opened heaven and joy and gladness entered the inmost core of my heart and all my burdens and heavy loads were gone. God really portrayed His undying love to me and I had great relief. From that very moment, my life was completely changed. I had new aspirations. I had a great hunger and thirst for God's Word. A desire for service to Him flooded my heart. This strong desire and determination caused me to struggle and work very hard to be a humble worker in His vineyard.

To tell the truth, there was nothing special about me, yet God made himself real in such a way I have not forgotten. I thought about how, as the years in my life passed, God continued to talk to me while I was still with the world, living in misery and sin. The Spirit of God called after me on numerous occasions. I remember well the time when I was left alone and half dead by the New People's Army who had ambushed us. My commanding officer and two companions were felled by bullets from our ambushers. I had fought many battles but I did not suffer even a scratch, which only shows how the Lord really loves me. The Lord has done a great thing for me and my family. He not only saved me, but also filled me with power, strength, knowledge and his Holy Spirit. Since then it has been such a pleasure and joy to serve the Lord. December 25, 1982, is my date of new birth when the Lord saved me, but for me it seems only just yesterday. He has been so good to me. His words are still ringing in my ears. He said, "Son, forgive those who have wronged you. I have an important mission for you."

It was only then that I fully realized that God really had a plan for my life. He had done so many other miracles for me and my family. My son Junior and his wife are missionaries in Cambodia. I really enjoy and still enjoy the victory He gives by His grace. I am always prepared and ready to be with Him at the end of my life here below.

At present I am a pastor at Obrero Wesleyan Church, Cabanatuan City, Luzon. To God be the glory. My favorite verse is Philippians 1:21, "For to me, to live is Christ and to die is gain."

Saved in Arabia
• •
Rodolfo F. Fabregas

I grew up in a strong Roman Catholic family. As a child I was required to attend catechism classes where we memorized prayers. My mother would lead us in prayers every night before our family icon.

When I finished school, I went to Manila to seek employment and pursue my dream to go to college. I got a job as a laborer and began to associate with the construction laborers. We drank heavily and often spent the night in a drunken stupor. One night we robbed a *jeepney* (public taxi), taking from the passengers pens, eyeglasses, watches, rings, necklaces and money.

About a year after this, I found a job as an elevator boy in a hotel. The pay was good, the work was pleasant and I worked the night shift so I could go to college. I took an examination that qualified me for a partial scholarship. I earned a degree in civil engineering and immediately began working on a government irrigation project. In November of 1974 I married. I continued to live my life with reckless abandon, drinking liquor and going to night clubs, especially when I was working projects away from home. When our second child was born, I realized that my income was insufficient for the needs of my family, even with the extra money from moonlighting with contractors I knew from my work.

I applied for a job in Saudi Arabia and was hired. I arrived in Saudi Arabia in September of 1980, just five days before my 32nd birthday. I was so lonely that I developed insomnia. My homesickness was aggravated by the fact that there was no liquor or night spots in the whole kingdom. Sometimes I would remember the prayers of my childhood and would try to seek God, but I didn't find any relief.

One afternoon in the hallway of our building, I met a rather short man who introduced himself as an engineer in the company where I worked. His name was Lito Valena (he was from the La Loma Wesleyan Church in Manila). He invited me to a Bible study in his room and I replied, "Yes, I will try," which meant I had no intention of going. At 8 p.m. there was a knock at my door and I recognized Lito calling my name. I pretended to be asleep but he was persistent. Finally I went to the door and then went with him to the Bible study. During that first meeting my mind was elsewhere and I don't remember anything about it. At the second meeting I tried to evade Lito, but he would not be evaded and blocked every escape. I was afraid because I knew these meetings were illegal in Saudi Arabia and the punishment was prison time and deportation. At the third meeting I was sneaking out of the building when Lito caught me. Again I was "forced" to attend. In that meeting there were about six men and Lito discussed the need of repentance and the love of Jesus Christ for sinners. This message came to me with tremendous force. I saw myself as a very sinful man who needed to be set free and forgiven by God. And so that very night, January 21, 1981, I repented and prayed for forgiveness of my sins and accepted Jesus Christ as my Lord and Savior. I returned to my room full of joy in my heart. For the first time in many weeks, I was able to sleep without drinking cough syrup, which I was becoming addicted to.

From that time on, I became very interested in the Word of God. I got a Xerox copy of the book of John and read it every night. Later on I was very active in Bible study and I started gathering and copying Bible study materials and song sheets. When Lito was transferred to a remote area, I was left in charge of the group.

When I returned to the Philippines on my first repatriation, I showed my wife what I had been sharing with her in my letters. She was amazed at my new language and behavior. My former drinking mates in the barrio, upon hearing of my arrival, trooped to my house hoping for a big drinking party. They went home full of food, but disappointed by the lack of liquor. At the advice of Lito, I reported to the pastor of the Wesleyan church in Cabanatuan City, and began to attend that church with my family. My wife also accepted the Lord and got involved in the music ministry of the church.

I worked in Saudi Arabia for another four years, taking a repatriation every year. We continued and expanded our Bible studies, braving the danger of detection and punishment. Then when I returned to the Philippines for good, I accepted an assignment as lay pastor in a newly organized Wesleyan church. It was my joy to serve the Lord in this way. I studied through a Theological Education by Extension program and attended enrichment seminars.

As is common to every Christian, I had my share of testing and it was painful. We were harassed by rebels and intimidated to contribute to a cause that was against God. It was evident that to ignore their "requests" would have severe consequences. We had to flee the area, resulting in the loss of our house and business. We settled in a city where the rebels did not operate. There were other fiery trials but the Lord was there to support and give victory. Praise His Name!

I continued to serve the Lord as a lay pastor and as a member of the district board of administration. At this time I am pastoring another newly organized church on the outskirts of Cabanatuan City. We are in the process of erecting a beautiful church building which the Lord has enabled us to do.

I praise God for this wonderful opportunity to serve Him in my capacity as an engineer and lay pastor. All glory and honor to Him! Amen.

The Cultic Priest's Son

●●●●●●●●●●●●●●●●●●●●●●●●

Rufino Wesley Doay Kimao

I was born April 8, 1935, before the gospel came to my place in Bakun, Central Benguet, in the mountain province. My family was very poor and my parents were uneducated, knowing nothing about God. We were of the Kancana-ey tribe. My father was appointed as a priest to the pagan god Kabonian, which all the people worshiped. This influenced me in my early life to be a strong pagan in my beliefs, while living under the bondage of sin and committing many kinds of sins in my life. This pagan way of living filled my life with fear, a lack of peace, absence of joy and no hope. This way of life brought me to a place of deep longing in my spirit to change my life and be happy. It is this desire which led me to seek the Lord for peace and joy.

A pioneer pastor came to the school I was attending and gave me a tract about salvation. I read this tract sincerely and it created a deep longing and hunger in my heart to know God and to seek salvation. One of my schoolmates and I went to a night gospel sing in a tiny chapel to hear the Bible teaching by the pioneer pastor who had handed out the tracts. Then I began to regularly attend Sunday school and morning services at this tiny chapel. The singing and the gospel message were sweet to my ears and went down to my heart. The gospel reminded me of the honey my father got in a cave in the forest. It helped me to be faithful in attending the services at the church, until the Holy Spirit helped me to see my spiritual need to seek salvation.

I was saved when I was eighteen years old during the morning service on October 15, 1953, under the ministry of Pastor Bonifacio Urbano. The church was a small *cogon* grass chapel built in my village. That was the Sunday I really found salvation. The Holy Spirit worked through the anointed message to draw my heart and break my rebellious spirit. I ran to the altar when the invitation song was given. I was trembling and crying while confessing with deep sorrow the sins that I had done in my life.

After praying, I stood up and looked at the mountains surrounding Bakun Central. It seemed that all the mountains were dancing with the joy and salvation I felt in my soul. Oh, how joyful and happy I was for the real salvation of my soul from the darkness of sin! By the wonderful grace of God, He brought me out of the miry clay of sins that I had committed. I was full of joy and gladness for the inexpressible love of God poured out into my heart. I knew I was blind but I thanked God I could see. This was due to the forgiveness of all my sins, which were covered by the precious blood of the Lamb that was shed on Calvary to pay for the sins of the whole world.

After my conversion, the Holy Spirit helped me to live faithfully in the center of God's will. I began to grow in grace by living the life of righteousness both inwardly and outwardly. I separated myself from my worldly friends and worldly ambitions and from all kinds of pagan traditions. I gave up all worldly pleasure and vision that would contradict my faith in Christ. I determined to live a godly life in the community by lovingly serving the Lord with all my heart and life.

As a young Christian I was not expecting the persecution that came. My parents came to hate me for denouncing pagan practices, traditions and beliefs. They disowned me as a son. Even my extended family rejected me because of my Christian faith. This was such a great trial to me, I thought I could not overcome it. I cried out to God in my distress and He helped me by His grace and gave me victory.

One time one of my hot-blooded relatives who hated my God very much came to attack me with a sharpened machete. This was during a pagan ritual in my parents' house in which I refused to participate, even though I was at home. The people shouted and the evil spirit of this relative subsided so that he did not kill me. I believe the Lord protected me that day for my stance of faith.

This particular ritual, *caniao*, is a pagan celebration feast that is done inside a house where sickness has come. The whole family performs *caniao* by sacrificing many animals in the yard surrounding the house. These sacrificed animals are offered to idols and the spirits of persons who have died. This is done so that sickness will leave the premises and give longevity and prosperity.

After the *caniao* for my mother was over, my mother's sickness got worse because it was tuberculosis. Tuberculosis cannot be healed by offering the bile of animals killed in the yard. Because this pagan belief could not cure her, my mother was brought to a turning point in her life and she decided to go to church with me and serve the Lord. I was happy to take my mother to church with me. Sunday after Sunday, I carried her on my back because she was too thin and weak to walk.

On the third Sunday I took her to church to worship God, she told me to let her sit in front near the altar so she could easily hear and understand the message. As the message was being given about what sin is, the Holy Spirit told her that she needed to give her heart to God and confess her sins from her youth to her adulthood. After praying, she stood and testified that God had forgiven her sins. She said she would serve the Lord no matter what might happen, until death took her. I thank the Lord that this was true.

I was so glad and thankful to the Lord for how He wonderfully saved my mother from sins in her old age. My mother was the first woman converted in our village. Even though my mother lived for the Lord only a short time, she was the first old woman to die with great assurance and a clear testimony. When she died, we tried our best to follow the Christian way of burial. We covered her body with a white blanket, put it in a wooden coffin, and buried her in the cemetery. Christian music was played by musical instruments, and no pagan traditions of burial were permitted. My mother's Christian burial became the standard for Christian funerals, because it was the first. In the year following this incident, many old folks came to believe the teaching and preaching of the gospel and came to join the church to worship the true living God of heaven. This is how the church in Bakun was established by God's help.

Almost all of my relatives came to hate me, especially when I refused to compromise with the pagan way of burial. They hated me and coveted my father's fields. So when my mother and father died, they took the lands which I should have inherited. This was a great blow to me, for by custom and law, the land should have come to me. These things made me deepen my resolve to obey God rather than men. I prayed for God to help me. There had been a ringing down in my heart for a long time, like a telephone that would not stop until answered. That was God calling me to go to Bible school. The ringing stopped when I responded to that call.

About a year after my conversion, God had begun to speak to my heart about going to Bible school to prepare my life for the ministry. I should have gone in 1955, but my parents were still living and nearing death. Since I was the only child who could help them, I was not able to go, even though I felt the call urgently down in my heart. When my parents died in 1956 about one month apart, I was able to go to Cabanatuan City to answer the call of God. I felt it was an answer to prayer that I was able to go to school. I found that Ilocano brothers who lived in the lowlands were praying and fasting for me. This was a strong influence on my Christian life. Every time I was able to attend conventions and camp meetings in the lowlands, I found much concern for me. I was known as "the Igorot young man." The missionaries also showed great concern and came to visit us in Bakun.

I went to the Bible school in answer to God's call by the Holy Spirit. Many times I tried my best to find an excuse to escape the call of God because I did not feel worthy. But I could not escape the call of God. The word I heard was as sharp as a sword cutting through the excuses of my heart, so I could not run. When I obeyed, God helped me in every way, from my studies to my financial needs. God supplied my needs until I graduated in January of 1962, especially through some of His people in Mindanao who paid my school debt.

After graduation, the Holy Spirit spoke to the heart of our district council not to give me an assignment in the established districts. They just prayed and waited for the leading of the Holy Spirit. The Holy Spirit began to lay it on my heart to survey a new place in the Benguet area to begin a work for the Lord. The Holy Spirit led me to the town of Kabayan, a place I had never stepped in before.

The Lord challenged my heart to work among the I-balloy tribes to win them to Christ and to build a nice big church in which the people could worship God. I moved there with my wife (who is from Mindanao) in May of 1965. The Lord helped us to establish that church. Then the Lord transferred us to another new place to establish a church in the city of Baguio in 1968. Since that time God has led us to pioneer churches in three other places as well.

I am very thankful for the faithfulness of the Holy Spirit who called me and led me over these many years. I have been honored to be the first Igorot convert and the first called to the ministry. God has directed me in the calling of pioneer ministry. By His grace, my life has been an example to other Igorot people in the churches in Benguet, for they have seen what God has done wonderfully in my life. Many young people have been challenged to give their lives to God by going to the Bible college in answer to God's call. Thank the Lord!

This is how the work in Benguet grew and was established by God's help. It became a separate district in the church in 1989 and is called the Skyline District of Northern Luzon. Thank the Lord! It is true as the Bible says, that "the effectual fervent prayer of the righteous man availeth much" (James 5:16 KJV). And the motto "prayer changes things" is also true and brings the development of good for God's glory.

The Mistake

• •

Saturnino Compal
(told by Estanislao Albano, Jr.)

I n the eyes of many fellow members of the Wesleyan church in Pinamulaan, Carmen Cotabato, in Mindanao, the marriage of Julita Urtizuela to Saturnino Compal in 1962 was a grave mistake on her part. She was a faithful Christian young woman, while it was apparent to all that he only went to church to please her. Furthermore, he already showed evidence that he had a weakness for the bottle. But it was a mistake that set to motion a chain of events in the control of the Almighty.

Due to the hard life in Pinamulaan, the young couple—both of whom were immigrants from Labayog, Sison, Pangasinan—returned to Luzon. It was a time of new settlement in Tabuk, Kalinga, Mt. Province in 1965. He worked as a farm tenant and a carpenter on the side, while she took care of the home front. Sometime after their second child came, he started drinking in earnest. He picked up drinking buddies in the neighborhood and before long, people began to avoid their street, especially after nightfall.

Saturnino remembers a lot from those years. Of lying to Julita about his real share from the farm produce so he could pay for the drinks he got on credit. Of getting fined for hurling a *bolo* (a large knife) at a drinking buddy which fortunately missed. Of the time he slept on the roadside because he was too drunk to carry his body home. Of stealing dogs in the neighborhood to sell for eating in order to continue the drinking sprees.

When he got into difficult situations because of his drinking and his bad company, he would try to quit the bottle. But his resolve would melt as soon as his friends invited him to the next drinking session. The bottle's hold over him was almost complete. He never neglected his work, however, and he also never got in the way of his wife's religion. In fact, he always urged his children to go to church with their mother. As for himself, he never went to church and when he saw the pastor or other members of the church approaching the house, he would slip out, sometimes through a window.

It was his open attitude towards his family's churchgoing which set his appointment with the Lord. Bound to the last service of a revival in the church in 1975, Marciano Paroy, an old drinking buddy who was converted earlier, and his wife Felisa passed the house to pick up Julita. Because all five children wanted to go with their mother, Saturnino volunteered to go along so he could carry the youngest. That was his only intention. He now recalls that the proceedings had no effect on him until the altar call came and Rev.

Domingo Catalon and his wife sang the Ilocano translation of "Have You Counted the Cost." The lines of the song made him ask what would happen to him if the Lord's mercy ran out before he could do something about it. It was then that a force he could not resist led him to the altar. Not knowing how to pray, he just cried until someone assisted him. But that was how his worldly life ended.

Before his baptism into the church, his former drinking buddies, who after learning that he was converted took to calling him "Pastor," gave him a baptism of sorts. After failing to make him take a drink, they poured the liquor on his head. He walked away and from that time they never bothered him again.

Saturnino never looked back to his old world and instead has steadily grown in Christian stature. The Tabuk Wesleyan Church congregation respected him and has made him, in the last two decades, either assistant Sunday school superintendent or Sunday school superintendent without break. He is third in line to the pulpit. On occasions when the pastor-in-charge and his wife, Eufrosina Albano, are absent, he preaches the sermon. He says that he feels nervous every time the occasion arises, but somehow he always manages to fulfill the task. Not a bad ending for a story that started as a mistake.

Leading the Little Children
• •
Shinar Lumahan and Jun Pablo
(told by Fely Pablo)

Mother Slater once said "children have many conversions." She was talking about children praying to the Lord at an early age, sometimes many times, until they are mature enough to be established in their faith. Shinar went to the altar as early as five years of age in a children's church meeting. She prayed earnestly a number of times in daily vacation Bible school, church services and when we dealt with her naughtiness at home. When she was seven years old, she took a pencil case from a classmate and then lied to her mother about it. One night after family devotions, she couldn't sleep. She was sobbing deeply. Her father heard her and went to the room to see what the problem was. There she confessed her sin and prayed for God's forgiveness.

Jun had many trips to the altar as a child. One memorable trip was in children's church where he headed for the altar with such conviction that he

247

did not open his eyes. One of the adults had to catch him and guide him. In a revival service at the local church, some of the pastor's children were retrieved by their parents and ushered to the altar for prayer. Jun waited in vain for his dad (Dr. Alfonso Pablo) to come. When they were home, he asked his dad with some degree of disgust, "Why did you not come and usher me to the altar? Roy's father prayed with him." Alfonso replied, "I want you to go voluntarily to the altar."

When Jun was nine years old, there was a heavy thunderstorm. We learned the next day that a short distance away, two men were killed by lightning. Jun was so fearful that he ran to his father. His dad inquired, "Jun, if you were struck with the lightning, would you go to heaven if you died?" Jun did not answer but he disappeared. After a few minutes he came back with a beaming face. His father was surprised when Jun said, "Yes, Dad, I am ready to go to heaven." "How come?" his dad asked. "I went to pray," Jun replied.

Shinar in now married to Rev. Jofre Lumahan and they have a daughter, Shekinah Renei. Shinar has finished her bachelor's in religious education and an undergraduate degree in English. Both Jofre and Shinar are on study leave from church duties and are working on master's degrees (Jofre in ministry and Shinar in Christian education) at this writing.

Jun went to the one year Christian leadership course at the Bible college but did not feel a call to full-time Christian ministry. He told his father that he was willing but not called. Today Jun is serving the Lord in a secular business. He has a bachelor's in political science and a master's in management and administration. Besides working in a business firm, he teaches classes in two universities.

Rebel to Reverend

Silveriano Gomez
(told by Fely Pablo)

Silveriano comes from Pampanga in the central part of the Island of Luzon. He was given a scholarship by the Philippine government to study in the United States. He was returned to his homeland after only two years because of antisocial actions. After getting back to the Philippines, he went to Mindanao and then to the remote barrio of North Cotabato, where he befriended a Muslim *datus* (a rich and influential leader among the Muslims). He was known as "Marcing" among the Muslims and Christians of the area.

He became a disgusting person in life and was himself disgusted with life. He let his hair grow and grew a long beard. He sought out fights as if he had a chip on his shoulder. When drunk, he would stand in a crossroad and cause traffic jams by holding up traffic and challenging anyone to fight with machete or pistol.

In a small barrio called Pinamulaan stood a little Wesleyan church. The pastor was Samuel Palionay, a Visayan, who got a burden for Marcing. He prayed for him and wanted to meet him, but found no chance. God gave Samuel an idea for a way to reach Marcing. He got several scripture tracts and *Timec Ti Kinasanto* (*Voice of Holiness*, the church's magazine) and rolled them together, tied it with a string and a stone, and threw it up to the tree house where Marcing lived (apparently he was afraid to live at ground level). The pastor delivered his papers in this manner several times.

One day there was a revival meeting at the little Wesleyan church with Rev. Antonio Hidalgo, who was one of the first graduates of Luzon Bible School, as the evangelist. Marcing went to the church one night and sat in the back. When the altar call was given, he went forward and prayed. People were amazed to see him and equally amazed at the night-to-day change that came in his life. After some time, Pastor Samuel Palionay brought him and Nenita, the woman he had been living with, (she had also prayed for God's forgiveness), to the Bible school. It was a twelve-hour hike just to get to a road. They had to cross a treacherous river on a swinging cable bridge spanning a breach of 45 meters. It was more than fifteen meters to the water's surface and appropriately named "River of No Return."

Mother Slater was the missionary and the president of the Bible school. She counseled Marcing and let him have a hair cut. With his beard shaved, he was a tall, handsome young man with a fair complexion. Mother Slater would not allow him to be at the Bible school with Nenita until they were actually married. After they were married, they came to the Bible School in 1963. They had no means of support but the Lord carried them through.

Marcing had a difficult time complying with the school's rules and regulations. It was very hard for him to be under the authority of others, but he learned to be humble in God's grace. One day he became hungry for God's holiness in his heart. In a service he fell to the floor prostrate, "plowing" his face into the cement floor before the altar in desperation, seeking God's help. Whenever Marcing testifies to this experience, his face glows and tears stream down his cheeks.

He graduated from the Bible school in 1969, and after a few years pastoring in the south, was moved to Metro Manila. He pastored the only Wesleyan church in the city at that time, La Loma in the suburb of Quezon

City. In 1976, a man who was to become an influential layman in the church, Alfredo Lumahan, was saved in a revival meeting in the La Loma church. Mr. Lumahan (who is commonly called Engineer Lumahan) owned a construction firm and with Pastor Marcing, pioneered four new urban church plants in the Metro-Manila area.

In the early 80s, Marcing became an interdenominational evangelist and had a great effect in many evangelical churches in the Philippines. Two years before he turned sixty, he retired and returned to pastor one of the Wesleyan churches that he and Engineer Lumahan had planted in Fort Bonifacio. He said at that time, "After I have been to many churches, I found out that there is no one like The Wesleyan Church. You cannot see the value of your church until you get out from her."

Rev. Silveriano went to be with the Lord on April 25, 1998, because of a heart attack. He had three sons, one of whom is a pastor, and a daughter by his wife Nenita.

Recruited in a New Army
• •
Monico Tejero (Nick)

I was born in a family who claimed to be Christian, and when I was an infant I was baptized. From childhood until I was twenty years old I thought I was already a Christian, because my parents believed and taught me that I was a Christian. I tried to live a good life through my religion, but I failed. Through works I thought I could get near to God. But still I couldn't feel God's presence, nor did I have a personal knowledge of Him. On the other hand, I found myself living in the world of sin.

As a young man I had many ambitions in life, but due to poverty, I joined the army. There, I found out how sinful my life was. In 1976, I was assigned in the coastal area of Southern Mindanao, in the town of Palembang, Province Sultan Kudarat. There was a newly opened church there called the Wesleyan church, pastored by Rev. Cecileo Baltazar. Some young people from that new church invited me to join their fellowship. Out of respect, I consented to their invitation. Later they invited me to their Sunday worship services, and many times I joined them.

As I listened to the Word of God, little by little God began to open my eyes. He created a thirst in my life which is something that I can't explain.

Even though I was hindered because I did not understand the language, I continued coming to church. But still my life was not changed. One day, the pastor asked me a question, "Which do you prefer, Nick, to serve God or to serve the government?" That question made me restless and sleepless for many days and nights.

On May 23, 1977, I joined a young people's convention at Kiamba, Cotabato. There I saw the happy faces of the young people—church members and Bible school students alike. Still my life was empty and I had a longing for something satisfying. One evening, in my room during my devotions, the Lord spoke to me. God was dealing with my life and my sins. I couldn't hold back my emotions but cried out aloud, not minding the presence of my roommates. As I was groaning and grieving for my sins, my pastor came near to help me. I left the room and he followed me outside. There I poured out my sins to God. I confessed to Him that I was a sinner and asked Him to forgive me. By His power and grace, He forgave me. I accepted Him as my Lord and Savior. I knew from the depths of my heart that I was born again.

I was awakened at dawn the following day by some Bible school students singing some heart-searching and consecration songs. As I carefully listened and followed the words of the songs, God spoke to me. Again I cried aloud, first for joy because I believed I was born again, and secondly, because I felt God calling me to the ministry. Another pastor (Rev. Willie Millarie) helped me as we went outside the room. At that time, I promised to serve God, whatever the cost, and consecrated my life to Him. After the convention, I went home with joy and peace. I thanked God, for He had answered my longings.

I was trying to live my new found experience and I kept myself busy in church activities. But that did not last long. I found it very difficult to live a Christian life and at the same time work with my comrades in the army who were not Christians. My Christian life became inconsistent. After a year of preparation, finally I decided to leave the military without finishing my term.

I entered Bible school, even though nobody promised to help supply my needs. My parents couldn't afford to help because they were too poor to support two college students. God assured through His Word that He would supply all my needs, if I put His will first (Philippians 4:19; Matthew 6:33). For five years in the school, God proved true to His promises. I remember while in school, that whenever there was preaching about being called for service and missions, my heart was challenged.

In 1985, God gave me a life partner, Cherry Laiz. I thank God for giving me a partner who truly loves Him and the ministry. Her dedication was proven when we were assigned to a pioneering work where the dialect was strange to her. By God's help, after two and a half years of toil, a church and a congregation existed. Later they called us to teach in the Bible college where my wife formerly taught for five years. While there, our son Mark was born. After two years in the Bible school, we were transferred to a new work on the island of Cebu. We served as full-time pastor for just one year. The following year, the leadership of the church appointed me to be a district superintendent of that pioneering district and at the same time to serve as pastor in the church.

In 1996, the Philippine General Conference accepted a partnership mission work in Cambodia with the North American General Conference. I tried to be a part of the mission work as a prayer partner and financial supporter. Later, when the work needed another Filipino missionary, I did not hesitate to accept the challenge, for I believed it was God's mandate.

Now we are in the land of His choice. As of now, we are preparing for the task the Lord asks us to fulfill. We are studying language and at the same time we are involved in teaching and church ministry. God willing, we can start our Bible Institute next year.

As I recall my life in the past, I can't help but thank God. If not for His love and grace, I would not be what I am today. I know that I am resting in the center of His will. To Him be the glory!

Epilogue

Amazing Grace

God is amazing. His grace is at work in every culture, in every people. The creativity of God in bringing people to Himself has no equal. Annie Kamara of Liberia was broken by a terrible civil war and a church that brought her a message of deliverance, forgiveness and hope. Amelia Matavele, sick and demon-possessed, was confronted like Paul with a great light while walking the streets of Maputo, the capital of Mozambique. She immediately had a desire for God's Word that led her to humbly seek forgiveness and find deliverance from evil spirits.

Chin Ho, raised a Buddhist in communist Cambodia, came to Christ through a gospel booklet and a radio broadcast. Kaki, a smuggler, gambler and drunkard in Western India, was pronounced terminally ill, but through the intercession of his wife, God spoke to him in a vision and miraculously healed him.

Tanya, a Ping-Pong champion in Russia, became curious about Christianity when a missionary showed interest in her sport. Trading Ping-Pong lessons for lessons about God eventually led to her conversion and enrollment in Bible college. A Costa Rican prostitute came to Christ when the Christian mother of the man who fathered her child befriended her. The creativity of God in loving people to Himself is unlimited. It is our joy to serve and worship such a God.

Grace for Me

These portraits of grace have become a mirror for me. As I read what God is doing around the world, I recognize afresh what He is doing in me. I see my need and my hands reach out to receive His love. Although my father and mother were wonderful believers and ministers in the church, my sin separated me from God and I needed to be forgiven and redeemed by the blood of Christ. I needed His grace and He gave it. In January 1961, God came to me and made me a new person. I have been richly blessed over these many years as He has continued to give grace during personal crisis, family need and financial difficulty. And every day the Holy Spirit comes with new grace, more hope and greater help.

Grace for You

Perhaps as you have read these stories your life has been encouraged by "the God of all grace . . . who will himself restore you and make you strong" (1 Peter 5:10). Or perhaps you have begun to see what might happen in your life if you were to truly experience the grace of God in its fullness. What God has done for the people in this book, He can do for you. His power, creativity and love are available to all who will receive Him. No issue is too difficult, no sin too great, no pain too deep that God's grace cannot heal and bring hope. If you need prayer or counsel, please contact us. We want to help you discover the fullness of grace in your life, so that your own "portrait" might be drawn by God.

Grace/Wesleyan World Missions
P.O. Box 50434
Indianapolis, IN 46250
Email: wwm@wesleyan.org
(317)-570-5160

Grace for Others

Wesleyan World Missions' deepest passion is to help others know God's saving, sanctifying and renewing grace. The challenge is immense. Four billion people still live outside of God's saving grace; half of them have yet to even hear the message of salvation. As you read these stories, God may have spoken to you about being part of our "grace team." Literally hundreds of men and women each year travel across the globe investing their lives in others. They go for a couple of weeks, a couple of years, or for the rest of their lives. They are people of all ages and professions—teens and retirees, pastors and plumbers, health care professionals and counselors, work teams and teachers. But they are all using their gifts to be people of God's grace in very needy places. Open your heart to what the Lord is saying to you and contact:

The Mobilization Team/Wesleyan World Missions
P.O. Box 50434
Indianapolis, IN 46250
Email: wwmgonet@wesleyan.org
(317)-570-5170

The mystery of the new millennium reinforces the reality that every man, woman and child in the world faces eternity and has only one lifetime to get ready. The vision of taking the message of God's love and grace to these people requires that God raise up those who would participate in this vision by sharing their financial resources. We are praying that God will raise up a "grace team," people who will give significantly so that the life transformation seen in these pages might be multiplied across the world. We invite you to write or call the Director of Development at Wesleyan World Missions. Thank you for opening your heart to God's voice.

Don Bray
General Director of Wesleyan World Missions